June Manning Thomas

PLANNING PROGRESS

LESSONS FROM SHOGHI EFFENDI

Foreword to this edition by Todd Smith

Foreword to first edition by Anna C. Vakil

Planning Progress: Lessons from Shoghi Effendi/ June Manning Thomas, author

© 1999 June Manning Thomas
c/o Association for Bahá'í Studies
34 Copernicus Street
Ottawa, ON
K1N 7K4 Canada
https://www.bahaistudies.ca

First edition, first printing 1999
This printing July 2024

Manning Thomas, June 1950–
Planning Progress: Lessons from Shoghi Effendi/ June Manning Thomas
Includes bibliographical references and index
Softcover: ISBN 978-0-920904-31-2
Ebook: ISBN 978-0-920904-40-4

Every effort has been made to acquire permission for copyright material used in this text, and to acknowledge all such indebtedness accurately. Any errors and omissions called to the publisher's attention will be corrected in future printings.

All rights reserved. No part of this publication may be reproduced, stored in a retrieval system, or transmitted, in any form or by any means, without the prior written consent of the publisher.

Cover image: *Progress Bahá'í World Crusade 1953–1958*, supplement included with *The Bahá'í Faith: 1844–1952: Information Statistical and Comparative. Including Supplement: "Ten Year International Bahá'í Teaching and Consolidation Plan 1953–1963"* (Wilmette, IL: Bahá'í Publishing Committee, 1953).
Cover and book design: Nilufar Gordon

To my friends in Africa
───────────────
greatly beloved continent of Shoghi Effendi

Contents

TABLES	vi
FOREWORD - TODD SMITH	vii
FOREWORD - ANNA C. VAKIL	xxi
PREFACE	xxv
ACKNOWLEDGMENTS	xxxi
CHAPTER 1: Planning for Human Progress	1
CHAPTER 2: Spiritual Principles of Planned Progress	11
CHAPTER 3: Envisioning Change	33
CHAPTER 4: From Goals to Action	59
CHAPTER 5: Monitoring Implementation	93
CHAPTER 6: Leadership and Social Change	121
CHAPTER 7: Planning Progress	149
APPENDIX	165
BIBLIOGRAPHY	179
NOTES	185
INDEX	203

Tables

2.1	A few spiritual principles for planning human progress	30
3.1	Three key global plans led by Shoghi Effendi	46
3.2	Shoghi Effendi's use of the concept of vision	53
4.1	Moving from goals to action: objectives and strategies	74
4.2	Moving from goals to action: responsibility and encouragement	83
5.1	Types of evaluation: policy research	98
5.2	Monitoring action: feedback	103
5.3	Monitoring action: stages of the plans	116
6.1	Ten Year Crusade: national pioneer goal areas assigned by Shoghi Effendi (1953)	140
Chart A-1	A process for a very simple plan	170
Chart A-2	A process for a simple plan	172
Chart A-3	Sample worksheet of a simple plan for a steering committee of a community center	177
Chart A-4	Blank sample worksheet of a simple plan	178

Foreword
to 2024 edition

It has been a quarter of a century since this book was first published. When I read it some twenty-five years ago, I remember being immediately struck by its many insights, and so took it upon myself to study it assiduously, knowing that the lessons it contained applied directly to the work of the institutions I was serving on at the time. I had already developed an abiding appreciation and love for the writings of Shoghi Effendi, but this book further deepened and broadened my understanding of the scale of his achievements and his unparalleled capacity to systematically articulate a vision of growth, encourage unity of purpose, appeal to both heart and mind, and thereby strengthen the resolve and canalize the efforts of an ever-growing worldwide community of consecrated souls eager to serve their beloved Faith and promote the betterment of humankind.

Now, twenty-five years later, it seems especially timely to revisit the lessons articulated in this book for at least two reasons. The first is that they underscore the significance of, and shed further light on, what the Bahá'í community has achieved over the last few decades, particularly with respect to the way it operates in seeking to transform the material and spiritual dimensions of life at both the individual and social levels. In this regard, the Universal House of Justice affirms that the community is today "distinguished by a mode of operation characterized by study, consultation, action, and reflection,"[1] which has profound implications for the vibrant culture it is developing; the latent potential it is releasing among individuals, communities, and institutions—"the three protagonists of a new way of life";[2] and the impact it is having on the society-building process overall. As the House of Justice observes, the Bahá'í community is steadily increasing its capacity to apply the Teachings in a variety of social spaces and to collaborate with those in the wider society who share a yearning to revitalize the material and spiritual foundations of the social order. In the transformative alembic of these spaces, to the extent possible, individuals and communities become protagonists of their own development, an embrace of the oneness of humanity banishes prejudice and otherness, the spiritual dimension of human life is fostered through adherence to principle and strengthening of the community's devotional character, and the capacity for learning is developed and directed towards personal and social transformation. The effort to understand the implications of what Bahá'u'lláh has revealed and to apply His healing remedy has now become more explicit, more deliberate, and an indelible part of Bahá'í culture.[3]

The House of Justice, moreover, emphasizes the magnitude of this development and its implications for the future, stating that "[t]he conscious grasp of the process of learning and its extension worldwide, from the grassroots to the international arena, are among the finest fruits of the first century of the Formative Age," and that "[t]his process will increasingly inform the work of every institution, community, and individual in the years ahead, as the Bahá'í world takes on ever-greater challenges and releases in ever-greater measures the Faith's society-building power."[4] It also stresses the singular role that Shoghi Effendi played in setting the community on its path of learning, recounting that while he consolidated the understanding of the believers regarding their mission, he "also guided the believers, step by step, to learn how to effectively establish the structural basis of the Administrative Order and systematically share Bahá'u'lláh's teachings with others," and that he did so in the following interactive manner:

> The Guardian patiently directed their efforts by gradually clarifying the nature, principles, and procedures which characterize that Order, while raising their capacity for teaching the Faith, individually and collectively. On each vital matter, he would provide direction and the believers would consult and strive to apply his guidance, sharing their experiences with him and raising questions when they faced perplexing problems and difficulties. Then, taking into consideration the accumulating experience, the Guardian

would offer additional guidance and elaborate the concepts and principles that would enable the friends to adjust their action as needed, until their efforts proved effective and could be applied more broadly.[5]

In this book, Professor June Manning Thomas provides the reader with an in-depth study of how Shoghi Effendi shepherded this process of capacity building as the endeavors of the community gained in strength and complexity during his ministry. By examining his approach to planning, monitoring, and guiding the efforts of the believers, Thomas clearly illustrates Shoghi Effendi's mastery at cultivating their capacity to act systematically and apply their learning ever more widely. For this reason alone, her book is worth a close reading.

A second reason it is timely to revisit the lessons in Thomas' book is that they help us to better understand, by contrast, the degraded state into which leadership and citizenship have fallen today. This matter is especially urgent considering the "plethora of destructive forces and events" now facing humanity, which, as the House of Justice explains, include "environmental degradation, climate change, pandemics, the decline of religion and morals, the loss of meaning and identity, the erosion of the concepts of truth and reason, unbridled technology, the exacerbation of prejudices and ideological contention, pervasive corruption, political and economic upheaval, war and genocide"—all of which "have left their traces in blood and anguish on the pages of history and the lives of billions."[6]

Owing to such forces of disintegration, many across the globe find themselves dismayed by the state of the world and beleaguered by the estrangement they feel towards one another: "But with every passing day, we see too the condition of the world grow more desperate, its divisions more severe. The escalating tensions within societies and between nations affect peoples and places in a myriad ways."[7] People are, for example, distressed because there is a seeming dearth of the collective will and capacity needed to address the growing threats to humanity; because their ways of life are being eroded by rampant turmoil, conflict, and intemperate technological developments; and because rank disparities and persistent discrimination impede many from flourishing as individuals, citizens, and members of communities. There is also the escalating fear that democracy itself is collapsing as the forces of illiberalism swell in country after country.[8]

It is important to remember that, alongside the destructive forces, "hopeful constructive trends can also be discerned which are contributing to that 'universal fermentation' which Shoghi Effendi said is 'purging and reshaping humanity in anticipation of the Day when the wholeness of the human race will have been recognized and its unity established'." These trends include "[t]he diffusion of the spirit of world solidarity, a greater consciousness of global interdependence, the embrace of collaborative action among individuals and institutions, and a heightened longing for justice and peace," all of which "are profoundly transforming human relationships."[9] Yet, humanity continues to be "gripped by a crisis of identity,"[10] a state of being that is aggravated by prejudice at the individual, cultural, and structural levels, as well as by other exacerbators of polarization, such as hyper-partisanship, radicalization, and various kinds of fundamentalism.[11] The result is the normalization of division and discord in pursuit of the preeminent goal of factional vindication. In this respect, the House of Justice observes:

> Without a vision of shared identity and common purpose, [peoples and groups] fall into competing ideologies and power struggles. Seemingly countless permutations of "us" and "them" define group identities ever more narrowly and in contrast to one another. Over time, this splintering into divergent interest groups has weakened the cohesion of society itself. Rival conceptions about the primacy of a particular people are peddled to the exclusion of the truth that humanity is on a common journey in which all are protagonists.[12]

From a Bahá'í perspective, these deleterious conceptions and struggles are all symptoms of humanity's disregard for its inherent oneness. As the House of Justice continues:

> Consider how radically different such a fragmented conception of human identity is from the one that follows from a recognition of the oneness of humanity. In this perspective, the diversity that characterizes the human family, far from contradicting its oneness, endows it with richness. Unity, in its Bahá'í expression, contains the essential concept of diversity, distinguishing it from uniformity. It is through love for all people, and by subordinating lesser loyalties to the best interests of humankind, that the unity of the world

can be realized and the infinite expressions of human diversity find their highest fulfilment.[13]

In view of such observations as well as the mode of learning evolving within the Bahá'í community, I have found Thomas' book to be especially helpful in understanding the following three overlapping themes—among many others—as they pertain to the present condition of society: vision and historical consciousness; power and authority; and modes of communication. Taking into account recent guidance of the Universal House of Justice, these themes are discussed below with the aim of foregrounding the enduring relevance of Thomas' examination of Shoghi Effendi's approach to planning, administration, and communication. Likewise, much can be gleaned from the book's examination of the Guardian's leadership style that bears on the question of how those serving in positions of authority can suitably play their essential part in addressing the challenges of immediate global concern.

Vision and historical consciousness.[14] There is presently a lot of emphasis on the importance of thinking and being in the moment, of training oneself not to become wrapped up in the past or overly concerned about the future. Many would agree that there is merit to this perspective, which is a central feature of Stoicism, Buddhism, and other philosophical and religious traditions. For example, it is doubtlessly important to make the best of every moment—to live every moment to the fullest—which implies not being weighed down by circumstances over which one has no control. In addition, when conversing with someone on spiritual themes, it is most befitting to be entirely present, treating the exchange as a "conversation between two souls—a conversation distinguished by the depth of understanding achieved and the nature of the relationship established."[15] The same is certainly true when meditating on the Sacred Word and when communing with God. Prayer, the House of Justice explains, "is the essential spiritual conversation of the soul with its Maker, direct and without intermediation. It is the spiritual food that sustains the life of the spirit. Like the morning's dew, it brings freshness to the heart and cleanses it, purifying it from attachments of the insistent self. It is a fire that burns away the veils and a light that leads to the ocean of reunion with the Almighty."[16]

Today, however, living in the moment has become conflated with what Kierkegaard identifies as an aesthetic mode of living, that is, a way of being that is tangled up with the pursuit of diversion in an effort to avoid boredom, to escape the discomfort of tribulation, or to fend off feelings of despair that accompany the state of anomie and mediocrity pervading more and more of society. This hollow mode of being is reinforced and propagated by our consumer culture, in which many of us are captivated by the idea of (if not consciously committed to) amassing transitory indulgences that are relentlessly promoted by advertising, influencers and politicians, and social media algorithms and posts. As a result of this consumerism—this "opium to the human soul"[17]—and the associated inundation of frivolous images and (often) reductionist opinions from all directions, many of us lose sight of our purpose as citizens and so end up living empty lives, incessantly looking for that next moment that will proffer some modicum of pleasure if not some semblance of meaning.

Again, this is not to deny the importance of living every moment to the fullest. But in order to do so well, we learn from Shoghi Effendi's writings that it is vital to develop a historical consciousness, which provides context—and thus significance—to everything we do. This perspective of history, moreover, must be global in scope and consider all human beings as protagonists on a collective journey toward the inevitable realization of the oneness of humankind—a journey that is concurrently propelled by the forces of disintegration and integration, both of which "serve to carry humanity, each in its own way, along the path leading towards its full maturity."[18] "Such is the view of history," the House of Justice states, "that underlies every endeavour pursued by the Bahá'í community."[19] It, moreover, "endows every instance of social action with a particular purpose: to foster true prosperity, with its spiritual and material dimensions, among the diverse inhabitants of the planet."[20] In short, the meaning of any moment is immensely enriched when infused with this embracing conception of social evolution.

This is a key theme in Thomas' book. For example, Thomas effectively demonstrates how Shoghi Effendi continuously drew the believers' attention to this vision of the unfolding of history and employed it to effectively contextualize and guide their efforts. She highlights the extensive statements of this vision in his writings, which he framed in relation to world events as well as to the epochs and ages of Bahá'u'lláh's Dispensation. She also explains that the Guardian regularly referred to the vision in shorter messages and cables to the believers, linking it to their special missions and their specific plans of action. He thus methodically situated their smaller visions, or their shorter-term plans, within this "bigger vision." Put another way, he fostered an evolving unity in diversity of narrative consciousness around a common core of beliefs concerning the inherent nobility, oneness, and purpose of humankind.

Building on Thomas' analysis, and in view of subsequent guidance of the Universal House of Justice, it might be added that in taking this approach, Shoghi Effendi helped the community to think coherently and to transcend certain habits of mind, such as those of compartmentalizing areas of action, "of reducing an entire theme into one or two appealing phrases," and of perceiving "dichotomies, where, in fact, there are none."[21] This is not to say that there are, for example, no such things as dichotomies. Indeed, not every either/or is a fallacy: sometimes reality really is either this way or that (a certain event did happen, or it didn't; a certain person told the truth, or didn't; this fact is the case, or it isn't, etc.). Similarly, the capacity to focus is vital: it is important to be able to concentrate on a specific issue, element, or endeavor in order to effectively address, understand, and/or carry it forward. But without moderation, the tendencies to distinguish and focus can become overly reductive, leading to dogmatic, superficial thinking that shirks the intricacies of certain realities and so neglects their underlying interrelations. These tendencies can, for example, lead to unduly favoring some facts over others, the selective interpretation of those facts, and even the conjuring up of facts in support of conspiracy theories. Currently people are assailed by such reductionisms in the form of simplistic social media posts, obsessive partisan bickering, and other forms of speech focused on reducing individuals and groups to labels and on otherwise stigmatizing, "othering," denigrating, or even demonizing them. As such, this fragmented mindset feeds various pernicious bigotries, including racism, sexism, national jingoism, and other instantiations of gratuitous intransigence that rationalize disparities, conflict, persecution, and war.[22]

Conversely, thinking coherently involves being able to focus on different endeavors (or elements) in their own right while also considering how they relate to other endeavors and, further, how a given constellation of endeavors is, or can be, mutually reinforcing and animating. Thomas provides an expansive window into how Shoghi Effendi regularly attended to these dynamics in his own guidance to the believers. We are assisted to conceptualize what is involved in thinking in terms of complexity and interconnectedness and in placing different lines of action into an evolving, narrative context that frames how they are working together.[23] Her analysis of Shoghi Effendi's approach in this regard seems directly applicable to what the Bahá'í community is learning about today. In its 30 December 2021 message, the House of Justice underlines the significance of this growing capacity in the following terms:

> Over the last series of Plans, the community's capacity to maintain focus on the Faith's most pressing needs emerged as one of its most important strengths. However, this sense of focus has to accommodate many lines of action, all of which must advance without being in competition. This calls for an expanded vision, a nuanced understanding of coexisting imperatives, added flexibility, and heightened institutional collaboration.[24]

Power and authority. Another major issue facing society concerns how power is conceived of and abused. Power is commonly viewed as control over others or equated with the capacity to secure what one wants in the face of resistance. It has certainly been used to oppress people, to keep them in their place, and—through propaganda, fear, backbiting, manipulation, the construction and propagation of disinformation, as well as various physical means—to deceive, condition, and force groups and individuals into submission or acquiescence in accordance with the wishes and ideologies of those in authority. Of equal concern are the micro workings of power, including those identified by thinkers such as Foucault, who explains how biopower and disciplinary practices normalize populations; and those highlighted by feminist thinkers, who analyze the many ways in which women have been, and still are, oppressed by men. Yet, it can also be argued that such conceptions are actually distortions of the true nature of power that blind us to its arguably more genuine expressions, particularly those that are mutualistic, participatory, and inclusive, and that consequently encourage both individual and collective flourishing.[25] On this theme, the House of Justice states:

> Clearly the concept of power as a means of domination, with the accompanying notions of contest, contention, division and superiority, must be left behind. This is not to deny the operation of power; after all, even in cases where institutions of society have received their mandates through the consent of the people, power is involved in the exercise of authority. But political processes, like

other processes of life, should not remain unaffected by the powers of the human spirit that the Bahá'í Faith—for that matter, every great religious tradition that has appeared throughout the ages—hopes to tap: the power of unity, of love, of humble service, of pure deeds. Associated with power in this sense are words such as "release", "encourage", "channel", "guide" and "enable". Power is not a finite entity which is to be "seized" and "jealously guarded"; it constitutes a limitless capacity to transform that resides in the human race as a body.[26]

When power is conceived of in this way, those in positions of authority seek to elicit latent potential, to foster collective volition, and to cultivate an evolving unity in diversity of vision-building and exploration. In so doing, they actively help to deflate the "power over" dynamic that has driven the historical struggle for dominance and recognition.

Thomas enables us to appreciate how Shoghi Effendi encouraged this elevated understanding of the dynamics of power and authority. In addition to invoking the power of vision and stressing the importance of looking to the end of any endeavor, the Guardian showed that effective leadership involves combining exhortations to action with affirmations of love and encouragement. It also requires the daily cultivation of spiritual attributes. These attributes, or virtues, according to Thomas, include "devotion, courtesy, purity of motive, and radiance of spirit"[27] all of which must be fostered in an effort to govern in accordance with the standards of equity and justice. In this connection, Thomas quotes the following admonition of 'Abdu'l-Bahá: "The spiritually learned must be characterized by both inward and outward perfections; they must possess a good character, an enlightened nature, a pure intent, as well as intellectual power, brilliance and discernment, intuition, discretion and foresight, temperance, reverence, and a heartfelt fear of God."[28]

Thomas goes on to explain that "[i]n this view, the leader is a person of influence in the community, of learning and high character, spiritually mature, and in control of his or her own baser temptations and inclinations."[29] Such leaders, including those elected to membership on institutions, strive to approach their task with modesty, humility, and with a heartfelt yearning to consult with, to learn from, and to release the potential of those they are called upon to serve. Their foremost conviction, in the words of 'Abdu'l-Bahá, is that "[m]an's greatness lieth in humility, and his abiding glory is found in lowliness, self-effacement, and servitude to the servants of the Lord. This, verily, is the greatest attainment in this resplendent Day."[30] They, moreover, understand, according to the House of Justice, that "[w]ithin the environment thus created, institutions invested with authority see themselves as instruments for nurturing human potential, ensuring its unfoldment along avenues productive and meritorious."[31] As Thomas summarizes the lesson from Shoghi Effendi, effective institutions offer love, support, and encouragement, imbuing the efforts associated with plans of action with a sense of nobility and purpose so that each person feels inspired to contribute as much as he or she is able.

In this same spirit, those in positions of leadership also see themselves as active participants among the three protagonists—the individual, the community, and the institutions—working for the betterment of the world,[32] each of which "has capacities and qualities that must be developed" but which "is incapable of manifesting its full potential on its own."[33] That is, these leaders take to heart that it is only when the three protagonists strengthen

> their dynamic relationships with one another that their powers are combined and multiplied. 'Abdu'l-Bahá explains that the more the qualities of cooperation and mutual assistance are manifested by a people, "the more will human society advance in progress and prosperity"; in the Faith, this principle distinguishes and shapes the interactions of individuals, institutions, and communities, and it endows the body of the Cause with moral vigour and spiritual health.[34]

In short, it could be concluded that the three protagonists only truly progress when each is nourishing the other two and all three are congruently oriented toward serving the common weal. They all benefit to the extent possible when they are in dynamic interplay with one another. With this concept in mind, it is decidedly beneficial to read Thomas' book for key insights into how Shoghi Effendi attended to the development of the individual, the community, and the institutions, and how he consequently laid the groundwork for their evolving dynamic relationship.[35]

Modes of communication. The subject of communication, alluded to earlier, warrants further attention given the prevalent manner in which people and their leaders express themselves. We have, generally speaking, learned in society to embrace competition as a natural mode of relating to one another, based on commonly held assumptions that correspond more closely to Hobbes' conception of human nature than to Rousseau's, who assumes humans to be naturally compassionate.[36] We are in many ways conditioned to believe that we can only prosper at the expense of others.[37] This belief, moreover, is often tied to the additional belief that we are naturally adversarial and self-interested creatures, driven to satiate our material desires and rationalize our yearnings for status. Taken together, this "distortion of the human spirit"[38] infects various realms, including politics, which tends to become ever more partisan given that opposition, debate, and confrontation are considered basic to the way things operate; the legal realm, which is obviously adversarial; business, where getting ahead often means defeating the competition; the media, which is growingly complicit in the fragmentation and polarization that contaminates much of society; and academia, which tends to function through the contest of ideas to the point where many scholars (some certainly more than others) derive purpose from demolishing the ideas of their peers.

While the competitive mindset has arguably produced beneficial results, it is proving insufficient for solving the crises that now confront the peoples of the world and for counteracting the rising despair at the apparent inability to solve them. In studying Thomas' book as well as guidance of the House of Justice, it seems clear that what is urgently required at this stage in the development of humanity is the capacity to think and act collaboratively, which in turn requires the internalization of a revised set of assumptions about human nature and purpose. These include the conviction that we are fundamentally good and noble, but that, without proper education, we are prone to succumbing to materialistic impulses. With this conviction and the vision outlined by Shoghi Effendi as part of our worldview, the aim becomes one of mutual upliftment and of creating environments in which souls "advance their understanding together, humbly sharing the insights each possesses at a given moment and eagerly seeking to learn from fellow wayfarers on the path of service."[39] Indeed, the watchword becomes one of humble service conjoined with a mode of learning focused on capacity building, fostering universal participation, and developing a consultative will aimed at effectively tackling problems of pressing social concern.

Such an approach to expression differs greatly from the way speech is currently practiced, which stifles progress in a number of ways. In its present combative mode, freedom of speech leads to entrenchment, factionalism, radicalization, and conspiracy theories that are perpetuated by the spread of propaganda, disinformation, filter bubbles, and ideological echo chambers. The culture of contest[40] permeates how we interact with one another such that discourse often consists of reductionist, dogmatic, and antagonistic speech that betrays flimsy (or deliberately distorted) links to reality. It thus creates an environment in which constructive dialogue becomes all but impossible to pursue while the voice of demagoguery—and the fantastical realities, delusions of grandeur, and cult of personality that both emerge from and feed it—becomes increasingly brazen. In the name of "telling it like it is," such speech "employs a style of expression which robs language of its decorum." Moreover, "in a time when stridency is commonly presumed to be a quality of leadership, candor is crass, and authority speaks in a loud and vulgar voice."[41] As the House of Justice more recently summarizes the present situation:

> One conspicuous symptom of society's deepening malaise is the steady descent of public discourse into greater rancour and enmity, reflecting entrenched partisan points of view. A prevalent feature of such contemporary discourse is how political disagreements rapidly degenerate into invective and ridicule. However, what particularly differentiates the present age from those that preceded it is how so much of this discourse occurs in full view of the world. Social media and related communication tools tend to give the greatest exposure to all that is controversial. . . .[42]

There are, of course, elements of the current pattern that should be retained in some form. These include being candid and attending to facts. As Thomas makes clear, Shoghi Effendi's approach to communication explicitly highlights the importance of both. Yet, she also makes clear that to facilitate mutual development, speech must also convey genuine praise and spiritual intimacy. It needs to appeal concurrently to both mind and heart. In this regard, Thomas explains that Shoghi Effendi exemplified the value of understanding the population he was addressing and with whom he was working—of being attuned to their circumstances, values, and motivations; of establishing clear, yet inspiring objectives in accordance with the capacity of the population, suitable strategies to achieve these objectives, and built-in measures to readily assess progress; of ensuring that all objectives and strategies reflect noble values and praiseworthy principles, and are additionally consistent with the inclusive view of history that should contextualize every noble endeavor; and of regularly reminding the population of its accomplishments, evolving capacities, and the ever-expanding horizons of possibility opening up before it in view of its evolving vision of the more distant future.

Finally, we are reminded by the guidance that the most productive speech entails speaking with a kindly tongue; with moderation; with a commitment to finding points of unity, harmonizing perspectives, and building a common framework of understanding; and with divine love. Speech infused with such characteristics is essential for opening up minds, breaking down seemingly intransigent barriers, and facilitating the search for truth. Indeed, such characteristics give speech its true power and so conduce to both individual and social transformation. In the words of the House of Justice:

> Ultimately, the power to transform the world is effected by love, love originating from the relationship with the divine, love ablaze among members of a community, love extended without restriction to every human being. This divine love, ignited by the Word of God, is disseminated by enkindled souls through intimate conversations that create new susceptibilities in human hearts, open minds to moral persuasion, and loosen the hold of biased norms and social systems so that they can gradually take on a new form in keeping with the requirements of humanity's age of maturity.[43]

When reading Thomas's book, it becomes evident that Shoghi Effendi continuously demonstrated to the Bahá'í community the vital importance of radiating this divine love.

TODD SMITH, PHD

Oshawa, Ontario, Canada
July 5, 2024

Foreword

IN ITS BROADEST SENSE AS THE LINK between knowledge and action, planning represents the quintessence of what it is to be human. While other species primarily respond to their environment, humans have the unique capacity to act upon, imagine, and create new alternative environments. Despite this capacity and all it has allowed us to accomplish throughout the ages, as we enter the twenty-first century, there exists much cynicism about our collective ability to plan a better world.

Most of us are familiar with the adage that the best laid plans "of mice and men" often go astray, and we can call to mind many examples, either in our personal and work lives or in public policy, of elaborate plans that never came to fruition. Some of us may also have had the experience of finding out about plans made in our localities or at our workplaces only after the fact, accompanied by the sense of exclusion we inevitably feel as a result of these kinds of closed-door proceedings. We can also probably recall examples of "effective" planning that has created unimaginable suffering or hardship—some in the name of a twisted morality, such as the Final Solution toward the end of World War II, others in the name of development, such as the campaign of involuntary sterilization of impoverished women in India a few decades ago.

What has gone wrong? The answer may lie in the reality that planning sits at the intersection of our scientific and spiritual capacities and therefore draws on capabilities we are only just beginning to develop. It is on this theme that Professor Thomas has much to offer in this remarkable book on the lessons that can be learned about planning from Shoghi Effendi, a spiritual leader of the Bahá'í world community whose life spanned the first half of the twentieth century.

In many ways, failure to recognize the inherent interdependence of reason and spirit is at the root of our apparent failure to plan. At the formulation or plan-making stage of the planning process, the disjuncture between scientifically based action and spiritually based ethics creates a number of problems. First, it leads us to misplace our priorities, resulting in the pursuit of goals that do not match our real needs or collective aims. For example, consider the long-held view, now being questioned, that economic growth alone can resolve problems of underdevelopment. A second consequence of the lack of spiritual principles to guide decision-making processes is contention and dispute in the community. This is illustrated in the sometimes intense debates that have arisen from decisions made in many North American cities to promote casinos as a means to achieve local economic development. A third result of the severed connection between reason and spirit at the formulation stage of planning is the persistent conflict that exists between labor and management in many large and small organizations. The importance of the spiritual principle of consultation, where people enter the process with humility and a willingness to compromise, would contribute greatly to breaking this deadlock.

At the implementation stage when plans are actually carried out, the chasm between reason and spirit affects us just as profoundly. Very often, particularly in the realm of policy, those who did not originally support a given plan because of partisan politics or factionalism do everything in their power to prevent it from being implemented. As a result, the faults or defects in the plan remain forever unknown because its implementation was thwarted. Understanding and practice of the spiritual principle of unity in decision making, where even dissenters support the implementation process, would prevent this from happening. A further deterrent to effective implementation of plans is lack of commitment, even among supporters. Most of us can probably recall examples in our personal lives of decisions we made but never implemented. Staying the course of a plan may require, in addition to simple determination, a level of commitment that comes from submission to a higher reality than the human will. Remaining committed to a plan on a collective level, especially when doing so involves struggle and sacrifice, requires a constant stream of encouragement and praise, inputs which are at the very least psychological if not spiritual.

Finally, after implementation begins, plans need to be flexible. Certain actions may have impacts that were unforeseen, or, alternatively, factors previously considered neutral or unimportant may turn out to have a significant influence on our actions. Switching or modification of plans, which usually results from monitoring and evaluation, requires humility toward the process as a whole and may at times call for a willingness to acknowledge having made mistakes. An attitude such as this can be facilitated by a spiritual process of continuous action and reflection.

This book is essential reading for at least four reasons: first, because it clearly identifies and describes the spiritual principles that help make planning effective and shows how Shoghi Effendi put them into practice. Drawing on the sacred writings of the Bahá'í Faith, Professor Thomas outlines the mechanisms for developing vision, goals, and lines of action, as well as the important roles that consultation, inspiration, and encouragement can play in the planning process. These principles are of use to teachers and practitioners of planning or management, since spiritual standards are not yet an integral component of education or practice in either of these areas. Consequently, this book represents a first attempt at making a direct connection between reason and spirit in the field of planning. Particularly useful to overburdened practitioners with little time for outside reading are the bulleted summaries at the ends of four of the seven chapters.

The second reason this book is important is that by dissecting the style and actions of Shoghi Effendi as planner, through meticulous analysis of his written works and letters, Professor Thomas argues convincingly for the need for planning in any and all human endeavors. Shoghi Effendi, perhaps more than any other figure in the twentieth century, did not rely on "crisis management" for response to the day-to-day requirements of the Bahá'í world in his masterful leadership of the global community from 1921 to 1957. Rather, all of his actions fit within a systematic approach to the management of change, an approach that he was willing to modify as circumstances demanded. The lessons learned from Shoghi Effendi as planner are applicable to individuals as well as local and national communities. Individuals in the Bahá'í community have been encouraged for many years by the Universal House of Justice (the elected institution which now provides spiritual leadership to the Bahá'í world community) to develop and carry out their own plans for personal development and the promotion of the spiritual principles outlined in the nineteenth century by Bahá'u'lláh, the prophet-founder of the religion. Local and National Spiritual Assemblies—annually elected administrative bodies responsible for guiding local and national communities respectively—have been instructed in like fashion to formulate and implement plans. The guidelines contained in this book, including the primer on planning in the appendix, therefore provide an essential reference and resource for individual Bahá'ís and institutions at all levels.

The third reason this book is essential reading is that it takes a subject which has for some time been considered the exclusive domain of people with expertise, and translates it into nontechnical language that is accessible to everyone. Shoghi Effendi's planning record and Professor Thomas's description of this record provide clear evidence that mastery of planning skills is achievable even for those without formal training in planning. If planning is an essential human attribute, then we can all learn to develop that capability. In this way, the book contributes to a growing literature in the planning field on "citizen-planners."

The fourth and final contribution this book makes is to ordinary people everywhere who may consider themselves agents of change. Within the descriptions and analysis of Shoghi Effendi's planning style lie many gems and suggestions of how to provide real leadership. Leaders are not only those who hold official positions of prominence but also those people who occupy the backstage, informally assuming responsibility for helping a group, organization, or community to develop, progress, or advance. Some refer to these individuals as "sparkplugs." Just as mastery of planning principles is attainable by everyone, so too is the capacity for leadership. That the world is sadly lacking in genuine leadership is apparent to most of us, either from direct experiences at our workplaces or from even a cursory examination of events reported in the news media. More examples of enlightened leadership of the sort demonstrated by Shoghi Effendi would go a long way in contributing to a dignified and better life for all people.

ANNA C. VAKIL, PHD, MCIP RPP

Planning Program, Department of Sociology and Anthropology
University of Windsor, Windsor, Ontario, Canada
January 10, 1999

Preface

IN 1995, I WAS INVITED TO GIVE a presentation on Shoghi Effendi[44] as part of a week-long conference at Landegg Academy, a school in Switzerland that offers several degree programs and enrichment seminars. When Hossain Danesh, the rector, asked for a topic, I spontaneously suggested "Shoghi Effendi as Planner." This choice surprised even me. Shoghi Effendi is not widely known as a planner, but rather as the leader of the Bahá'í Faith from 1921 to 1957. Among other things, he is known for his administrative leadership, his authoritative translations from Persian and Arabic to English, his forceful and unique use of the English language in his own writings, his intuitive design and construction of gardens and holy shrines, and his spiritual leadership of the Bahá'ís. He had ample talents and "professions," but planner would not at first glance seem to be one of them.

Preparation for the presentation made it clear that Shoghi Effendi was indeed a "planner," in at least three ways. He "planned" for the administrative order of his religion, by taking its basic spiritual teachings and applying these to the practical governance of Bahá'í communities. He was also a "planner" in that, with no formal training, he designed a collection of gardens and oversaw the construction and restoration of shrines in the Holy Land that illustrate some of the best principles of landscaping and architectural construction. Shoghi Effendi as well oversaw the implementation of outstanding multiyear plans designed to move his global community forward toward key benchmarks of progress. It was this last sense in which he planned that intrigued me the most. In his written guidance about the establishment and implementation of these plans, apparent was a level of insight, wisdom, and capability that had escaped many of the most well known professional "planners" in the world at large.

The term "planning" refers to organized forethought or, according to planning scholar John Friedmann, to the linkage between knowledge and action. At its simplest, planning can merely create a modest plan of action, but planning can also be quite complex, leading some people to specialize in its various aspects. My own professional background is urban and regional planning, which focuses on the planning of urban places, but this field is only one kind of planning. Other planners work in corporations, government, and various types of organizations, and many of the approaches of these various planners overlap.

Two major concerns motivated me to write this book. One was the difficulty people and groups appear to experience with the process of creating and carrying out plans for social progress, and the other was the paucity of role models for effective planners. A wide range of people and groups have trouble planning for a better future. In some urban neighborhoods, for example, it is very difficult for people to envision an alternative future and then to take the practical steps necessary to pull their neighborhoods out of physical decay and social disintegration. Part of the difficulty lies in the conditions that face them, but another serious constraint is not knowing how to tackle a manageable agenda for modest improvement and then how to organize to accomplish it. As a consultant for the City of Detroit during a 1994 sabbatical leave, I was privileged to serve as one of several staff working under the direction of citizens and government decision-makers to develop the strategic plan necessary to create Detroit's Empowerment Zone. In the United States, an Empowerment Zone is a federally designated area of economic distress targeted for social and economic improvements. The city's application process was reasonably successful, leading as it did to a $2 billion commitment from the federal government, local corporations, and financial institutions to help improve economic development, health and safety, neighborhoods, and the environment in the city's target area. In the process, however, it was necessary to spend much time helping citizens, businesses, and government participants understand the basic parameters (goals, objectives, anticipated activities) of planning, as well as helping them work through historic patterns of conflict. City government and the neighborhoods, in particular, had such a history of conflict that cooperation itself proved to be one of their greatest challenges.

Another area of concern was the need to help increase my religious community's comfort with the planning process. I served for nine years in a volunteer position for the Bahá'í Faith, as Auxiliary Board member assigned to serve the propagation efforts of Bahá'í communities in four states located in the United States Midwest. One responsibility was to assist local communities that were supposed to adopt and carry out annual or multiyear plans for community growth and development but that some times did not. Although many communities grew and evolved through their own focused and organized efforts, others either did not link planning and action or adopted overly ambitious plans that succeeded only in intimidating everyone. Surprisingly, these difficulties were taking place in a religious community with a strong tradition of planning, dating back to World War I. Even though Bahá'ís should have understood better than most people the importance of effective planning, some communities did not seem to be able to use such understanding to yield results.

Part of this general problem with planning effectiveness may be the lack of role models. Before beginning this project, if someone had asked me to name one person who was a truly exemplary role model for planning leadership, I would have been at a loss to do so, even after working more than twenty years as a university professor of urban planning. Pressed to respond, one might perhaps refer to England's Ebenezer Howard, whose 1898 book *Garden Cities of Tomorrow* influenced urbanism by setting forth an invention—planned urban communities known as garden cities—that laid the basis for modern new towns. However, Howard did not so much plan as invent basic characteristics of garden cities, many of which new town planners abandoned in later years. Several very good contemporary and historic urban planners have made exceptional contributions, such as Norman Krumholz and Allan B. Jacobs, the former planning directors of Cleveland, Ohio and San Francisco, California respectively; James Rouse, the founder and developer of the multiracial town of Columbia, Maryland; and Walter B. Griffin, architect/planner of Canberra, Australia. For various reasons, however, their approaches could not resolve the more general planning problems that face the population at large.

Perhaps in other planning fields besides urban planning people have emerged as exemplary planners. John Bryson is one of the foremost scholars of strategic planning, and his writings are filled with well-documented examples. People have created important economic, business, or strategic plans for their nations, corporations, or businesses, but how widely is it possible to apply the strategic planning experience as an exemplary model of planning in general?

Looking at Shoghi Effendi from this perspective—as planner of global plans—opens a whole new array of possibilities. First of all, his planning leadership style is well documented and preserved through his instructive letters to various national communities throughout the implementation of their multiyear plans. Second, because he was an individual of diverse talents, a so-called Renaissance man, it is not surprising that several areas of his genius have gone unexplored, as they may have been overshadowed by his other talents. Third, unfettered by professional training in planning or by a structured field such as economics or urbanism, Shoghi Effendi approached the basic process of planning with creative and original ideas, as well as with spiritual insight and drive brought about by sheer dedication and personal will power. Looking with fresh eyes at his plan-related letters, we can see that here indeed is a potential role model. Of particular note are his use of vision as a motivating tool, his masterful selection of audacious goals and objectives, his careful monitoring of implementation, his ability to motivate people to succeed, and other aspects of his leadership that deserved to be unearthed and shared.

Anyone who is concerned about the development of social progress, particularly as this relates to plans, should find something of use in this book. It should prove of value to readers familiar with the Bahá'í Faith, who know much about Shoghi Effendi but may hereby gain greater insights into how he helped plan for community progress and how they might also do so. Such readers may find that references to materials from the fields of planning and organizational development, while perhaps unfamiliar, broaden their understanding of the innate wisdom of his approach.

The reader interested in effective planning who is not familiar with the Bahá'í Faith or with Shoghi Effendi could benefit from exploring this book as well. While that reader may be concerned about the discussion of religious thought and the persistent reference to spiritual matters, particularly in the framework of a religion that might be unfamiliar, this framework should illustrate and illumine rather than obscure the important principles involved. Although it is necessary to understand something about the Bahá'í Faith in order to understand Shoghi Effendi, because after all his plans were focused on the growth and consolidation of that religion, this book has very practical implications for a wide range of applications as well.

The intent was to include dialogue about general planning principles and their role in human progress that many people will find useful, no matter what their national, racial, or religious background.

The format of the book is designed to provide information as well as to suggest specific skills. Various tables summarize the highlights of Shoghi Effendi's approaches to different phases of the planning process, and four of the seven chapters end with bulleted points that offer guidance for practical planning applications. These points offer advice relevant to both religious and secular settings. The last chapter offers a summation that focuses on how Shoghi Effendi's approach could help the broader field of planning. An appendix provides a "primer" on some basic principles and procedures for planning action.

The principal methodology used for this book was not atypical—to read related books, articles, and materials to glean important concepts from these sources. One fairly unusual approach was to carry out a content analysis of writings by Shoghi Effendi. Based in large part on guidance offered in the qualitative research literature, which suggests many creative ways to analyze the meaning implicit in written text, this research approach involved looking systematically at the key ideas and themes that emerged in Shoghi Effendi's plan-related letters, postscripts, and cables to North America. One of the first tasks was to read carefully the two main books[45] that collected these letters and to mark each paragraph—and in some cases several sentences within each paragraph—with a draft topical area. This method enhanced the "discovery" of the rich variety of means by which Shoghi Effendi promoted the successful execution of plans. In the final analysis, the draft classifications of topical areas proved less reliable than anticipated, since his writings in many ways defied simple classification. Furthermore, it was not possible to present all of the examples that the process yielded or to tally them in any meaningful sense. However, this procedure did force the researcher to examine the primary source materials rigorously and to organize themes in some coherent fashion. Sorting this material through the lens of my professional training in planning theory and practice helped provide a framework for the text and also allowed a few interpretations to emerge; it is hoped that these have clarified rather than veiled the work of this great planner.

Acknowledgments

ALL PRAISE IS DUE FIRST to the forces and forebears who inspired Shoghi Effendi, and then to Shoghi Effendi himself, whose keen intellect and natural leadership abilities, as expressed through transcendent and robust letters and other writings, will stand the test of time. Special thanks to Shoghi Effendi's widow, Rúḥíyyih Rabbani, for her many services over the years, including authorship of the most complete biography of her husband.

As for help in bringing this book into being, Hossain Danesh was instrumental in initiating the project, encouraging its expansion, and serving as a source of scholarly inspiration through his own myriad writings. For working through the minutiae of early drafts and offering excellent commentary, special kudos to fellow planning professor Anna Vakil, who provided the foreword, and to organizational development specialist Kirk Weigand; both of these extraordinary people offered fact-filled, intelligent critiques that somehow managed to combine insightful and frank appraisal with loving encouragement. Thanks as well to Andy Tamas, whose keen insights enabled several important revisions. Billy Roberts lent incalculable moral support, as did Kiser Barnes, resident in Haifa, Israel, who helped in ways only possible for someone living in that locale. Barbara Johnson's early praise for the manuscript opened passageways that she cannot imagine, and support by people such as Marsha Ritzdorf, Caswell Ellis, Jena Khodadad, Melanie Smith, Lynn Barnes, Mehdi and Ursula Samandari (Cameroon), and Washington Araujo (Brazil) will always be appreciated. Several anonymous reviewers were also very helpful, as were archivist Roger Dahl and interviewee Paul Pettit.

Actual production rested upon the able shoulders of the Association for Bahá'í Studies' managing editor Christine Zerbinis, who is as multitalented an administrator as one could hope to find and whose capable editorial signature is apparent on every page of this book. Thanks also to assistant editor Danielle Christensen for her extensive work on proofreading, page layout, and reading for common sense. Stan Phillips is a wonderful graphic designer who has created a beautiful book cover. Several of the Association's editorial board members offered important aid as well, in particular Peter P. Morgan. At Michigan State University, graduate assistant Chantalle Verna carried out indispensable tasks, including proofreading and preparing the first draft of the index. Bets Caldwell and Fran Fowler provided key secretarial assistance, including in Bets' case transferring balky text files from one word-processing program to another.

Husband Richard's firm optimism and unwavering esteem were indescribably essential, from the very beginning, and throughout every day and every phase of research, writing, and book production. Children Kemba and Ali offered enthusiastic and loving encouragement as well.

None of the worthy people listed above can be held responsible for errors, which are entirely the author's.

Chapter I

Planning for Human Progress

> Whatever happened to Progress through Planning? In fact, what happened to Progress?
> —Lisa Peattie, *Planning: Rethinking Ciudad Guayana*

EVEN THOUGH THE HUMAN RACE was "created to carry forward an ever-advancing civilization"[1] and has produced miracles of technology, it has not solved the fundamental problems of hunger, poverty, homelessness, war, ecological destruction, and political strife. If progress occurs in one area, it appears to be counterbalanced by backwardness in another. Many nation states remain unable to undertake fundamental improvements in such important areas as education, health care, transportation, and pollution control. Municipalities, governments, corporations, communities, and other organizations struggle to adapt to the changing world in which they must survive and to carry out the purposes for which they were created.

Bringing about desired change, that is, planning for a better future, is a difficult task. Concerned individuals despair of seeing their institutions or their governments generate effective and long-lasting social, economic, political, or environmental reforms. Some nations are now floundering in the aftermath of well-meaning but flawed central planning, and even smaller organizations fail to plan for their own growth and development, instead choosing to survive day-to-day, accepting change as it occurs.

The purpose of this book is to explore (by focusing upon the ethos and leadership of one person who is a potential role model for people who plan) some basic concepts that make it possible to plan effectively for human progress. Over a period of thirty-six years, Shoghi Effendi, who was born in Palestine in 1897 and lived mainly in Haifa until his death in 1957, carried out plans that greatly expanded the membership and scope of the Bahá'í Faith, using the concept of global plans to help move the Bahá'í Faith toward fulfilling a vision of worldwide transformation. This book will examine some of the sources of Shoghi Effendi's inspiration and his methods of helping implement the plans he also supervised. While he encouraged the commonly known functions of envisioning change, setting goals and objectives, assuring their implementation, and following through with successive action, his creativity, style, and natural leadership—and the extraordinary results he achieved—offer valuable lessons to all of us. This is true because we are all planners in some sense.

Planning and Human Progress

We are all planners because, as author Ervin Laszlo points out, one of the hallmarks of human beings is that we "are capable of thinking, planning, and envisioning alternative courses of action."[2] This remarkable trait distinguishes people from the rest of nature, in which the parts cannot consciously influence the destiny of the whole. In contrast, human beings can indeed influence the destiny of society. To do so, however, people need to become more adept at choosing actions that benefit human society.

Planning is a necessary, essential aspect of social change. Part of the normal capacity of the average human being is the ability to undertake "organized forethought"—that is, to assess a situation, to think through procedures necessary to change that situation or to bring about a desired result, and then to act in a systematic way to implement them. This process is necessary whether the situation is simple or complex. A simple example of such planning is preparing for a community meeting or other basic event, which planning scholar Melville Branch has called "functional planning." More complex effort is needed to construct a house or a new city, which Branch calls "project planning." In each case, someone has to think through the necessary tasks and attempt to implement them in some systematic fashion.[3]

Even at the individual level, planning is difficult. Time-management experts have made millions of dollars training corporate executives and employees to plan their daily activities, rather than to address issues as they arise. The idea that it was more productive to sit down at the beginning of each day or week and determine what should be done and in what order of importance was so revolutionary that it spawned a mega-empire of training sessions, day-calendar systems, computer software, and accompanying paraphernalia. Many corporations gladly pay for their employees to attend training sessions that teach daily planning, because they know that chaos and lack of direction in the workplace reduce productivity. Obviously, such training would be unnecessary if individual planning were commonplace.

The larger the entity or system involved, the more difficult the process of planning becomes. To plan a local community meeting is challenging but manageable. One would have to find sufficient resources, establish a place and a program, and perhaps advertise to assure attendance, but all these steps can be fairly easy to accomplish. However, as anyone who has planned a community meeting well knows, lack of proper preparation could make even the simplest meeting collapse. It does not take long to move up the ladder of complexity. The same organization that can plan a successful meeting might fail to plan for a year's worth of activities and programs. Planning a new city or subdivision, or any large construction project, involves an even larger outlay of resources, time, and effort.

Top authorities of large organizations carry out the "most complex and potentially controversial" planning.[4] Planning the activities of a large corporation or provincial/state government can be challenging, but planning to revise a nation's health-care system or to implement a national economic development plan is significantly more difficult. Planning for multinational or global changes—such as countering global warming, ensuring equitable food distribution, merging monetary systems, or coordinating defensive military action—involves a number of unconnected organizations and individuals, and can therefore seem almost impossible.

Nevertheless, human beings have undertaken large-scale planning activities for thousands of years. Branch suggests that "[e]very event of consequence during historical times, which was the result of human action rather than forces of nature or capricious chance, would not or could not have been carried out without planning of some kind."[5] To build major monuments, undertake military campaigns, or establish school systems, someone had to link conscious planning thought with deliberate action so as to get results. To conquer the world as it was known in his time, Genghis Khan pursued a canny strategy of conquest and terror. His movements from city to city were far from random, but rather a part of his overall scheme to conquer much of the world's then-known territory. In building a city, the emperors of ancient China made sure to pick an auspicious spot, laying out the parameters in an appropriate orientation and determining where the rulers and the privileged would live.

Although the human race has innate abilities to plan and has been doing so for thousands of years, many of us hesitate to plan for the future. Several reasons explain why. One is our natural tendency to avoid the necessary work and effort, since it often seems easier not to plan than to plan. "Planning presupposes that rationality triumph over irrationality, order over disorder, constructive hope over discouragement and fatalism, action over inaction. It requires extra energy. It is much easier to continue as is and change only when necessary than to struggle for improvement," Branch indicates.[6] Some may think it is more attractive to drift through the days and years, meeting demands as they arise, not attempting to take control of the future; but what is seemingly easy—not bothering to plan—may generate other difficulties. Failing to project annual budgets for a business, for example, may cause serious financial trouble.

Some groups spend weeks or months creating a plan, or preparing to create a plan, all to no avail. Sometimes the plan is set aside, laid on the proverbial shelf, collecting dust, to no effect at all. It may have offered some initial direction but provided little relevant guidance for daily or monthly activities. Or its creation may have caused so much conflict that the cohesion of the group suffered irreparable damage. Part of the problem is that group planning requires cooperation. "Coordination requires less selfishness, less egocentrism, willingness to work with others cooperatively attributes which are neither widespread nor readily acquired," according to Branch.[7] "[M]any of the most critical problems requiring planning today involve cooperative interaction among the people of different nations, ethnic backgrounds, political systems, and religious faiths."[8] If cooperative action is needed for future improvement, then it will be necessary to over come problems with joint planning.

Perhaps we dare not hope that it is possible for humanity to envision, and then move cooperatively toward, a better future because such promises have in the past proven so empty. A well-known example is the multiyear economic planning of China, the former U.S.S.R., and other communist allies. Those national plans often attempted to coordinate thousands of details of industrial and agricultural production but failed to create an effective and efficient economic system. Indeed, the false appearance of control sometimes caused more problems than benefits, since the governments failed to harness other motivating forces (such as workers' ambition or the profit motive). In reaction, many other peoples in the world have prematurely rejected the idea of national or international planning. Fear of communist influence was a key factor, for example, in the United States's rejection of several national planning initiatives that arose during the 1930s, such as the National Resources Planning Board, which argued for organizing human settlement around planned regional cities rather than around sprawling suburbs. This board proposed many good ideas that, if implemented, would have prevented many contemporary urban problems.

Descriptions of planning efforts gone wrong (not just in the communist world) fill libraries. Several urban planning examples relate to poorly conceived new cities, such as New Delhi, Brasilia, and Ciudad Guayana. Venezuela's Ciudad Guayana, for example, was supposed to illustrate the best of urban planning, by showing that it was possible to build a completely new city and to make of it a showpiece. According to Lisa Peattie, an anthropologist who worked at the project site and watched the story unfold, national and foreign "experts" had no idea how to build a new city at the location they had chosen. They failed to acknowledge the preexistence, very close to the location, of a de facto city—the low-income settlement in which Peattie lived—and did not coordinate their efforts with those residents. They did not know how to link the massive amount of economic and design-oriented data they collected with a realistic vision of a new city. Encouraging social-class segregation, they created a two-headed metropolis that chained its workers to an insane commute from affordable living quarters in the old city, to their jobs on the other side of the newly constructed city. Yet Ciudad Guayana's planners were supposedly some of the best architectural and economic planning experts of Venezuela and of the United States, imported as foreign advisors.

Perhaps when people consider "planned progress," they remember such poor examples and cringe. How is it possible to plan for global progress when we cannot plan for an organization or a city or a national economy? Many positive examples of planning for progress do exist, but we need to search for them. Positive role models help show the possibilities.

Consider Britain's new town program, for example. Great Britain expanded upon the traditions of garden cities, which visionary Ebenezer Howard first promoted at the beginning of the twentieth century, in a new town program the government launched after World War II to assist people to move out of bombed-out London. Britain's latest generation of new towns shows that it is possible to design and build sensible, pleasant, and reasonably efficient modern settlements. Japan has built new towns complete with employment, commercial, and recreational facilities, thus drawing people away from overcrowded Tokyo. While far from perfect, these projects indicate the potential for alternative types of human settlements.

Some countries have begun to master national planning. France has successfully launched several five-year national development plans, and the Netherlands, Italy, Spain, and Germany have developed strategic plans for national growth and development.[9] An entire literature has arisen documenting the remarkable experience with economic planning in India. The Indian example deserves some commentary because it is a significant illustration of national socioeconomic planning in developing countries that arose from internal rather than external forces (e.g., pressure from international aid organizations). In 1937, almost a decade before national independence, a working committee of Indians formed a National Planning Committee to prepare for post-independence economic planning.[10]

Modern India began national planning for social improvement under its first prime minister, Jawaharlal Nehru, whom one author has called the "chief architect of Indian planning." Nehru viewed planning as "a positive instrument for resolving conflict in a large and heterogeneous subcontinent" and saw planning as a sensible way to guide progress within a democracy.[11] Nehru came to power after decades of British colonial rule had left the country impoverished and lacking in basic technological capacity. Although sixteenth-century India had been one of the world's richest countries, at the end of colonialism, the technology did not exist in the country to manufacture even the most basic household goods. Nehru gathered around him economists who initiated plans that became models for development planning in developing countries. Beginning in 1950, India adopted a series of five-year plans that set specific goals and strategies for improving various sectors, such as agriculture or industry.

Although the first three plans "fell short of expectations," particularly in the area of effective land reform, they helped diversify the industrial structure. They also helped upgrade workers' skill levels and prodded the country's agricultural sector out of stagnation.[12] These plans were "especially important as attempts at giving concrete shape to the vision of transformation, social and economic."[13] After the first three plans, however, enthusiasm waned, particularly in the 1960s, when the nation suffered through two droughts, leading to a temporary cessation of multiyear planning. Other challenges also arose, such as political change and, some observers have charged, the blatant misuse of planning for less than altruistic political aims.[14] However, for nearly fifty years India has operated under the canopy of sequential five-year plans, producing positive growth in several important economic indicators.[15]

Of course, the issue is not merely improvement in social indicators. Planning leaders should be capable and trustworthy, leading people toward admirable goals, not toward negative ends such as totalitarianism. Clearly, "successful" plans achieved by a murdering despot are not good, but some times the choices are not so obvious.

The problem can be illustrated using the example of India. While Nehru was a well-respected man of outstanding character whose selfless devotion to the betterment of India was widely recognized, it was difficult for subsequent leaders to live up to his stellar reputation. In some quarters, cries of concern arose over the seeming ascendancy of personal political aims over goals designed for the benefit of greater India. Under the circumstances, could the citizens be sure that the national planning experts' targeted goals were best for the country as a whole? In Ciudad Guayana, Venezuela, how was it possible for the official planners to be so far out of synchronization with the existing and future population's needs? Where was the flaw in their thinking?

In general, people's hesitance to see planning as an attainable process for ensuring the social progress of humanity is due not just to our natural tendency to avoid planning because of the work involved. Neither is the existence of major counterexamples of plans gone wrong the only barrier. While it is clear that, in selected instances, planning for progress does indeed lead to progress, simply carrying out planning activities that lead to visible results is not sufficient. Over time, other issues arise, such as: How trustworthy are our planning leaders? How closely do our goals match our true needs? How can we assure ourselves that implementation of our plan is in keeping with the highest standards of human attainment?

Rather than greater exposure to the technical aspects of successful planning, perhaps we need more careful analysis of the ethical and spiritual dimensions involved. We need to examine the planning process within the context of a worldview that is based on noble goals-such as global cooperation, the unity of humanity, and the perfectibility of human society. Those who guide and participate in that planning process should manifest an innate understanding of what motivates human beings to sacrifice their personal time and resources to help carry out plan-related tasks. In this context, it makes perfect sense to look closely at Shoghi Effendi, a religious leader who believed in and acted on the basis of higher social values, and who seemed to generate uncommon personal sacrifices for the sake of plans.

Shoghi Effendi as Planner

Shoghi Effendi, like Nehru, faced a highly challenging situation. Shoghi Effendi was the international leader of the Bahá'í Faith, a religion founded in Persia in 1844 by the "Twin Manifestations of God," transcendent and charismatic personalities known by their respective titles of "The Báb" and "Bahá'u'lláh." They had brought to humanity many beautiful sacred writings and teachings, which thousands of people adopted as their personal ethos, but by the time Shoghi Effendi became leader in 1921, much work remained to be done. The religion was still in its infancy, its numbers were small, and its institutions needed extensive development and expansion.

The Bahá'í teachings focused on the need to create unity and true affection among the various religions, races, and nationalities of the world and to move toward building institutions that would create a firm foundation for a global society. Even at great personal risk, hundreds of thousands of former Muslims, Zoroastrians, and Jews declared their belief in the new religion in its home country of Persia. Religious persecution led to the slaughter of thousands of followers of the Báb in the mid-nineteenth century.[16] Still the religious community survived; by the time Bahá'u'lláh died in exile in 1892 in Palestine, followers of the religion, Bahá'ís, lived in fifteen different countries, concentrated in the Middle East. Bahá'u'lláh's son, 'Abdu'l-Bahá, a remarkable person in his own right, then became the international leader of the Bahá'í Faith. When he died in 1921, the number of countries, colonies, or mandated territories in which adherents lived had expanded to thirty-five, and membership included many former Christians in the West.[17] However, in many cases, only a few isolated Bahá'ís lived in each of several places, and they were weakly organized.

Shoghi Effendi, grandson of 'Abdu'l-Bahá, was twenty-four years old and a student at England's Oxford University when his grandfather died in 1921. Raised in a household where Persian was the dominant language, Shoghi Effendi had already distinguished himself as a brilliant translator and writer of English as well as a person of outstanding character and dignity. The challenges immediately facing him included the need to strengthen the spiritual and administrative foundations of his religion, translate many more of its key writings into English, and plan for the more effective global expansion of an as yet small religious community that strongly valued internationalism. He did all of these things extraordinarily well. To offer just a few of many indicators: during the thirty-six years of his leadership, he oversaw the expansion of the Bahá'í Faith from thirty-five countries to 219, simultaneously building up several strong national spiritual assemblies (national governing bodies) and effectively laying the groundwork for an internationally governed community.[18]

These facts, while important, seem inadequate to the task of explaining the sort of person Shoghi Effendi was. His exceptional talents in a wide range of fields, his obvious self-sacrifice and willingness to live in utter poverty even as he spent with generosity for the cause of the religion, and his brilliant leadership confirmed that 'Abdu'l-Bahá had made a wise choice in selecting Shoghi Effendi as worldwide leader to succeed him. When in turn Shoghi Effendi died in 1957, many Bahá'ís marked the day as one of the most tragic of their lives and recalled every detail of what they were doing when they heard the news.

Not surprisingly, much has been written about his life and his influence. The most important book about him is *The Priceless Pearl*, an insightful biography written by his widow, Rúḥíyyih Rabbani, née Mary Maxwell. Another book, *The Vision of Shoghi Effendi*,[19] offers diverse perspectives on Shoghi Effendi's influence in such spheres as English translation, spiritual growth and development, administration, and American race relations. *Shoghi Effendi: Recollections*[20] gives author Ugo Giachery's personal account of Shoghi Effendi's brilliant supervision of construction projects in the Holy Land and would be particularly attractive to architects, urban planners, engineers, stonemasons, or anyone in the construction trades. *The Spiritual Conquest of the*

Planet: Our Response to Plans,[21] prepared in workbook format, allows readers to think about major themes apparent in the plans led by Shoghi Effendi and by the Universal House of Justice, which now oversees the affairs of the worldwide Bahá'í community.

For the first few years of his administrative leadership, Shoghi Effendi focused on laying the foundation for the growth, stability, and consolidation of his global community. He translated key documents and writings, explained their essence, and encouraged creation of spiritual assemblies (governing bodies) at both the national and local level. He also began to communicate systematically with both individuals and communities throughout the world, developing a particularly close relationship with the Bahá'ís of North America. As part of his written communications, he urged those national communities capable of doing so to develop national plans for action, and he often suggested various goals and procedures for them to undertake.

Because of the Bahá'í world's admiration and respect for Shoghi Effendi, records of his mailed and cabled communications were carefully preserved, particularly those sent to national spiritual assemblies. The North American Bahá'í community not only kept his letters and cables but also published many of these in several news magazines and then in several books, as did the Bahá'ís of Great Britain, Australia, India, and other nations. Most of the cables, letters, and postscripts to letters that he wrote to the North American community during the three global plans (see Table 3.1) are published in three books: *The Advent of Divine Justice*,[22] *Messages to America: Selected Letters and Cablegrams Addressed to the Bahá'ís of North America, 1932-1946*, and *Citadel of Faith: Messages to America, 1947-1957*. These plan-related missives offer an extraordinary opportunity to see and assess, firsthand, the "planning style" of an exceptional planning leader. These communications form much of the primary source material for this book.[23]

Chapter 2

Spiritual Principles of Planned Progress

The plans of the heart belong to man, but the answer of the tongue is from the Lord. All the ways of a man are dean in his own sight, but the Lord weighs the motives. Commit your works to the Lord, and your plans will be established.
—Solomon, Proverbs 16:1-3

Can humanity conceive a plan and policy better and superior to that of God? It is certain that no matter how capable man may be in origination of plan and organization of purpose, his efforts will be inadequate when compared with the divine plan and purpose; for the policy of God is perfect. Therefore, we must follow the will and plan of God. As He is kind to all, we must be likewise; and it is certain that this will be most acceptable to God.
—'Abdu'l-Bahá, *Promulgation of Universal Peace*

BEFORE EXAMINING SPECIFIC CHARACTERISTICS of planning that pervaded Shoghi Effendi's work, it is essential to understand the ethos that guided him. Shoghi Effendi did no more than carry out, as he saw best, the tasks left to him by his forebears, the Báb, Bahá'u'lláh, and 'Abdu'l-Bahá.[1] Certain aspects of their teachings offered important background concepts and understanding for Shoghi Effendi's writings.[2]

Bahá'u'lláh's writings demonstrated remarkable faith in the perfectibility of human society. Bahá'u'lláh may not have used the words *plan* or *planning* in the sense of systematically designing a project, according to a key word search of those writings that have been translated into English, but he wrote extensively about several related concepts. 'Abdu'l-Bahá frequently used the term plan, referring to it as a mechanism for social progress and divine will. He offered valuable concepts and techniques, and spearheaded several innovative approaches later elaborated upon by Shoghi Effendi. During World War I, 'Abdu'l-Bahá sent the North American Bahá'ís a series of letters, collected in the book *Tablets of the Divine Plan*,³ which contained explicit guidance about how to carry out a plan for the expansion and diffusion of the Bahá'í community. These letters, filled with moving words of encouragement and vision, eventually changed the shape of the Bahá'í world.

Guidance from Bahá'u'lláh

Bahá'u'lláh laid the preparatory basis for Shoghi Effendi's concept of planning by stressing that it is important to think about human progress in a way that is purposeful, deliberate, and tied to effective action. Bahá'u'lláh's vision of future society revealed a fundamental belief in the potential for improvement in the human condition. Throughout his writings, he promoted "development" of human society as a spiritual obligation, and he explained several important concepts about effective leadership and decision making.

A Vision of Development

One of the most basic principles apparent in Bahá'u'lláh's writings is the necessity to progress toward a better society. The belief that this is both possible and imperative makes planning for the social good more than an exercise; it then becomes a spiritual obligation. Salvation, in Bahá'u'lláh's view, is in great part a matter of the spiritual growth and development of the individual, but it also hinges upon the increasingly enlightened governance of the general affairs of humanity. This governance, and all the affairs of humanity, rest on the solid bedrock of justice and unity. As humanity grows toward a greater state of unity—which presupposes the equality of men and women, and a lack of racial, ethnic, or national prejudice—war will become a thing of the past, and the nations and peoples of the world will interact in peace, harmony, and prosperity.

As a great spiritual leader, Bahá'u'lláh emphasized the role of spiritual growth in creating this better society. Bahá'u'lláh exhorted humanity to pray and meditate daily, for example, and he revealed hundreds of beautiful prayers and meditations designed to assist this process. He offered guidelines for principled living that highlighted such issues as treating fellow human beings with love and friendship, respecting one's parents, and cultivating such human virtues as courtesy, honesty, trustworthiness, and humility.

In addition, however, Bahá'u'lláh created a vision of global society that extended far beyond widespread personal virtue. For someone writing in the mid- to late-1800s, Bahá'u'lláh had a remarkably clear and revolutionary vision of the future of the world. He foresaw a future world society where communication would be simplified, commerce facilitated, and world disputes settled. Shoghi Effendi at one point summarized some of the pivotal components of Bahá'u'lláh's vision. Here are key portions of Shoghi Effendi's summary, presented in such a way as to highlight the sequence of steps:

> The unity of the human race, as envisaged by Bahá'u'lláh, implies the establishment of a world commonwealth in which all nations, races, creeds and classes are closely and permanently united, and in which the autonomy of its state members and the personal freedom and initiative of the individuals that compose them are definitely and completely safeguarded.
>
> This commonwealth must, as far as we can visualize it, consist of a world legislature, whose members will, as the trustees of the whole of mankind, ultimately control the entire resources of all the component nations, and will enact such laws as shall be required to regulate the life, satisfy the needs and adjust the relationships of all races and peoples. . . .
>
> A world tribunal will adjudicate and deliver its compulsory and final verdict in all and any disputes that may arise between the various elements constituting this universal system.
>
> A mechanism of world inter-communication will be devised, embracing the whole planet, freed from national hindrances and restrictions, and functioning with marvellous swiftness and perfect regularity.

A world metropolis will act as the nerve center of a world civilization, the focus towards which the unifying forces of life will converge and from which its energizing influences will radiate.

A world language will either be invented or chosen from among the existing languages and will be taught in the schools of all the federated nations as an auxiliary to their mother tongue. A world script, a world literature, a uniform and universal system of currency, of weights and measures, will simplify and facilitate intercourse and understanding among the nations and races of mankind....

The economic resources of the world will be organized, its sources of raw materials will be tapped and fully utilized, its markets will be coordinated and developed, and the distribution of its products will be equitably regulated.

National rivalries, hatreds, and intrigues will cease, and racial animosity and prejudice will be replaced by racial amity, understanding and cooperation. The causes of religious strife will be permanently removed, economic barriers and restrictions will be completely abolished, and the inordinate distinction between classes will be obliterated. Destitution on the one hand, and gross accumulation of ownership on the other, will disappear.

The enormous energy dissipated and wasted on war, whether economic or political, will be consecrated to such ends as will extend the range of human inventions and technical development, to the increase of the productivity of mankind, to the extermination of disease, to the extension of scientific research, to the raising of the standard of physical health, to the sharpening and refinement of the human brain, to the exploitation of the unused and unsuspected resources of the planet, to the prolongation of human life, and to the furtherance of any other agency that can stimulate the intellectual, the moral, and spiritual life of the entire human race.[4]

This is a remarkable vision, sweeping in its scope and implications. As the reader can see, many components of this vision have already begun to appear within the world—such as international systems of communication, currency (in Europe), and, to a limited extent, governance

(United Nations)—although in their current form these elements need much additional refinement. Other elements, such as the elimination of racial and national rivalries, require considerably more effort on the part of humanity in order to bring them into being.

Of Bahá'u'lláh's numerous volumes, letters, and meditations that related to the topics of development and leadership, three letters (known as "tablets") offer particularly rich guidance. These three letters—the Tablet of Maqṣúd (the name of the person to whom the letter was addressed) and the two tablets entitled "Splendours" and "Words of Paradise"—summarized many of Bahá'u'lláh's teachings concerning the basic requirements for the governance and progress of humanity. They covered several key points that 'Abdu'l-Bahá later expanded upon in the book *The Secret of Divine Civilization* and that Shoghi Effendi referred to during his time as Guardian of the Bahá'í Faith.

Each of these letters exhorts humanity to take deliberate steps toward purposeful social improvement. In the letter to Maqṣúd, Bahá'u'lláh appealed to "every diligent and enterprising soul" to help bring about development and progress, that is, "to exert his utmost endeavour and arise to rehabilitate the conditions in all regions."[5] Bahá'u'lláh did not stop with the call to "rehabilitate" one's own region. He also indicated that everyone had the responsibility to promote peace and well-being in the world at large and exhorted all to "seize upon every means which will promote security and tranquillity among the peoples of the world."[6] Indeed, "[g]reat is the station of man. Great must also be his endeavours for the rehabilitation of the world and the well-being of nations."[7] In the "Splendours" letter, Bahá'u'lláh stated even more forcefully the sacred obligation to promote visionary development: "the progress of the world, the development of nations, the tranquillity of peoples, and the peace of all who dwell on earth are among the principles and ordinances of God."[8]

Bahá'u'lláh provided specific guidance about how to move humanity toward "the progress of the world" and "the development of nations." One suggestion that emerged throughout his writings as a pragmatic "strategy" for world unity was adopting a common, universal language. In the "Words of Paradise" letter, he indicated that one of the ways to create a world that is like "one city" is to encourage each of the world's citizens to read and write a "universal" language that all would learn in addition to their mother tongue, so that everyone would speak two languages. From two, however, "efforts must be made to reduce them to one, likewise the scripts of the world, that men's lives may not be dissipated and wasted in learning divers languages. Thus the whole earth would come to be regarded as one city and one land."[9] A related passage from "Splendours" promoted "the light of unity" and promised that "the greatest means for the promotion of that unity is for the peoples of the world to understand one another's writing and speech."[10]

A second major strategy for development, according to this nineteenth century prophet, was to promote world peace, since "[t]he purging of such deeply-rooted and overwhelming corruptions" as the accumulation of weapons of destruction "cannot be effected unless the peoples of the world unite in pursuit of one common aim."[11] Thus, in the late 1800s, Bahá'u'lláh urged that the nations of the world convene in order to "consider such ways and means as will lay the foundations of the world's Great Peace amongst men" and to "resolve, for the sake of the tranquillity of the peoples of the earth, to be fully reconciled among themselves." This voluntary effort to resolve international differences was no panacea, however; renegade nations might still cause trouble. In that case, Bahá'u'lláh counseled, the other nations should take corrective action: "Should any king take up arms against another, all should unitedly arise and prevent him."[12]

These passages offer only a glimpse into Bahá'u'lláh's spiritual yet practical vision, which was based on the fundamental view that human society is perfectible. The concept of social improvement is so intrinsic to Bahá'u'lláh's teachings that its various manifestations defy summary. Essentially, the Bahá'í Faith sees human progress, ultimately manifested in a future Golden Age of human prosperity and happiness, as a necessary part of its ethos. Each and every diligent person should value and support social improvement, according to this view, but the leaders of the world have a special obligation to do so.

ENLIGHTENED LEADERSHIP

Good leadership was key to Bahá'u'lláh's vision of human progress because leaders have greater responsibilities than other people. According to Bahá'u'lláh, "[i]f the learned and wise men of goodwill were to impart guidance unto the people," then "the whole earth would be regarded as one country."[13] His view of leadership was that both political and religious leaders have responsibilities to improve the world, to "unitedly arise for the reformation of this age and the rehabilitation of its fortunes." Bahá'u'lláh suggested that the world's leaders first come together and assess humanity's needs, in the following manner: "Let them, after meditating on its needs, take counsel together and, through anxious and full deliberation, administer to a diseased and sorely-afflicted world the remedy it requireth."[14]

These writings suggest that leaders reflect upon and assess their own daily activities and be consciously aware of the status of the affairs of their charges. The importance of individual responsibility is clear in the "Tablet of Maqṣúd" statement that "[i]t behoveth every ruler to weigh his own being every day in the balance of equity and justice and then to judge between men and counsel them to do that which would direct their steps unto the path of wisdom and understanding. This is the cornerstone of statesmanship."[15] This matter of "weighing" is surely a matter of conscience, but it also suggests a constant vigilance and determination to assess one's self on a daily basis and then use that assessment to guide action, such as "judging" or "counseling." Two passages from "Splendours" further explain the need to assess information—one of the first steps necessary to planning action. In that letter, Bahá'u'lláh indicated that "[g]overnments should fully acquaint themselves with the conditions of those they govern, and confer upon them positions according to desert and merit."[16] Similarly, they need to "enquire into the conditions of their subjects and to acquaint themselves with the affairs and activities of the divers communities in their dominions."[17]

Also evident in these writings is the need for the process of consultation to inform decision making. Bahá'u'lláh advised the world's leaders, after meditating on humanity's needs, "take counsel together "In other passages, Bahá'u'lláh declared that consultation "is a shining light which, in a dark world, leadeth the way and guideth." He noted, "[i]n all things it is necessary to consult. This matter should be forcibly stressed by thee, so that consultation may be observed by all."[18]

These passages on leadership and consultation laid the groundwork for the leadership style of Shoghi Effendi, who understood not only the constraints but also the potential of his worldwide community. In part, this wisdom emanated from his personal character and stature in the community, suggesting a constant regimen of self-correction and spiritual discipline, qualities Bahá'u'lláh indicated were absolutely necessary for leaders. In addition, however, a very practical way in which Shoghi Effendi developed the knowledge necessary to lead wisely was to acquaint himself, quite thoroughly, with the "affairs and activities" of the communities under his charge. He did so by corresponding with numerous individuals and communities, and by constantly asking them to keep him updated concerning their various activities. This lent his global plans firm grounding in reality, since he knew who had the capacity and potential to carry out the tasks associated with various goals. Such constant communication also exemplified one form of the important principle of consultation, which in this case was carried out through extensive dialogue between a leader and his worldwide community of fellow believers.

Goals and Actions

Bahá'u'lláh's writings also provided the foundation for planning concepts related to goals and actions in at least two important ways. He exhorted people to keep in mind the usefulness of all of their activities. The "Tablet of Maqṣúd" urged humankind to teach those arts and sciences "which will result in advantage to man, will ensure his progress and elevate his rank." In general, according to this letter, "[a]t the outset of every endeavour, it is incumbent to look to the end of it."[19] This reference to the "end" of any endeavor is one of the clearest statements in Bahá'u'lláh's writings that efforts should be goal directed and that people should consciously think about the end products of their activities before undertaking them.

Another relevant principle is that intellectual knowledge and good intentions must turn into meaningful action. Bahá'u'lláh noted that "[t]he day is approaching when all the peoples of the world will have adopted one universal language and one common script." Rather than wait passively for this to happen, however, "[i]t is incumbent upon every man of insight and understanding to strive to translate that which hath been written into reality and action."[20] We should, therefore, strive for deeds rather than words, since "deeds exert greater influence than words."[21] This theme was also apparent in the successive writings of both 'Abdu'l-Bahá and Shoghi Effendi, who on many occasions stressed that planning without action was fruitless.

Guidance from 'Abdu'l-Bahá

With the background of the creativity and fecundity of Bahá'u'lláh's divinely inspired writings, it is not surprising that 'Abdu'l-Bahá was able to contribute great understanding about how to bring such concepts into practice. He expanded upon the concepts of development, leadership, consultation, and goals and action as important components of Bahá'u'lláh's writings. 'Abdu'l-Bahá also made several unique contributions to this line of discourse. One was his tendency to speak directly of the need for social reform and spiritual transformation in terms of "plans." Another was his ability to develop a unique and path-breaking model for Bahá'í plans for progress, via letters published in *Tablets of the Divine Plan*.

As did Bahá'u'lláh, 'Abdu'l-Bahá wrote extensively about the concepts of development and leadership. He summarized these concepts in *The Secret of Divine Civilization*, a book written in 1875. This book is a compelling treatise on the conditions of backwardness then facing Persian society and the need for improved governance and reform. It laid out a set of principles that ostensibly addressed Islamic Persia, but in fact apply to a wide range of civilizations and cultures. First published without the author's true name—to protect his ideas from the immediate hostility that would have been generated by the fact that he was a Bahá'í—this book urged Persians to value enlightened and capable government as a means toward attaining good society, not as an antireligious, foreign invention. *The Secret of Divine Civilization* made it clear that good leaders have a major role to play in improving the overall quality of society. To do so, however, leaders must be well informed about the processes and skills needed in statecraft. Knowledge about how to plan for social improvement is just such a skill.[22]

The framework for all of 'Abdu'l-Bahá's advice concerning development and leadership was fleshed out by spiritual wisdom and insight. His writings do not suggest a mechanical set of skills divorced from the acquisition of such spiritual attributes as justice, equity, and humility. Rather, he urged people to understand that religious fervor and tradition were no excuse for lack of competence and awareness of how to govern well. While today's contemporary challenges are different from those of nineteenth-century Persia, it is still evident that, in all levels of governance, it is beneficial to adopt competent and principled leadership.

While development and leadership were significant themes in 'Abdu'l-Bahá's writings, he also provided important insights into the topics of consultation, goals, actions, and strategic reform. These topics are essential to a clear understanding of the basic principles of social improvement.

Consultation

Bahá'u'lláh counseled people to make decisions about social progress by consulting together. 'Abdu'l-Bahá confirmed the importance of this concept and greatly expanded upon Bahá'u'lláh's explanations about the nature of consultation. 'Abdu'l-Bahá indicated that "[t]he question of consultation is of the utmost importance, and is one of the most potent instruments conducive to the tranquillity and felicity of the people." He also indicated that "[m]an must consult on all matters, whether major or minor, so that he may become cognizant of what is good. Consultation giveth him insight into things and enableth him to delve into questions which are unknown." In fact, he urged, "Settle all things, both great and small, by consultation. Without prior consultation, take no important step in your own personal affairs."[23]

'Abdu'l-Bahá provided cogent descriptions about how consultation operated as a force of cohesion and guidance for groups and explained the prerequisites for consultation to take place. For example, he indicated that when a person is "uncertain about his affairs, or when he seeketh to pursue a project or trade, the friends should gather together and devise a solution for him. He, in his turn, should act accordingly. Likewise in larger issues, when a problem ariseth, or a difficulty occurreth, the wise should gather, consult, and devise a solution."[24] In another instance, he again emphasized that this principle applied for all groupings, saying, "should the people of a village consult one another about their affairs, the right solution will certainly be revealed. In like manner, the members of each profession, such as in industry, should consult, and those in commerce should similarly consult on business affairs."[25]

Of utmost importance, 'Abdu'l-Bahá suggested, was the way in which consultation took place. He repeatedly emphasized that the attitude of the participants and the manner of deliberation were of prime importance. He highlighted, "The prime requisites for them that take counsel together are purity of motive, radiance of spirit, detachment from all else save God, attraction to His Divine Fragrances, humility and lowliness amongst His loved ones. . . ." "The members thereof must take counsel together in such wise that no occasion for ill-feeling or discord may arise." Those consulting, he noted, "must be wholly free from estrangement" and must manifest unity. They should proceed with "utmost devotion, courtesy, dignity, care and moderation to express their views." Once these views were expressed, those who voiced them should not hold stubbornly to their opinions, but rather should yield to the will of the group.²⁶

Seldom does the literature on management or "the planning process" deal with such issues as how people talk to each other about their plans and activities. According to the above writings, however, cooperative dialogue is important when undertaking any group endeavor. Furthermore, that dialogue must be characterized by moderation, love, and respect.

GOALS, ACTION

'Abdu'l-Bahá also provided insight into the nature of goals and action. As did Bahá'u'lláh, 'Abdu'l-Bahá advised people to focus on a particular end or goal, and he offered practical advice about how to obtain such focus. Consider, for example, his image-laden advice about the importance of mental concentration. As he noted:

> So long as the thoughts of an individual are scattered he will achieve no results, but if his thinking be concentrated on a single point wonderful will be the fruits thereof.
>
> One cannot obtain the full force of the sunlight when it is cast on a flat mirror, but once the sun shineth upon a concave mirror, or on a lens that is convex, all its heat will be concentrated on a single point, and that one point will burn the hottest. Thus is it necessary to focus one's thinking on a single point so that it will become an effective force.²⁷

This analogy using the convex lens applies perfectly to the process of planning, since much of what we call planning is merely focusing and acting upon the most important issues at hand. As noted in this passage, a person must concentrate in order to develop effective, focused thinking. The same principle applies to groups of people. They too must concentrate and direct efforts to achieve results. Here is a simple example. Suppose that a community decided to focus its deliberations and activities on two key goals, such as building or refurbishing a community center and educating the community's children. A community that targeted these concerns would be very busy, as these goals encompass many tasks within them. If a community instead chose to do too many things in relation to its size, or if even these two goals were too large for its capacity, its energies could become "scattered" and "achieve no results."

An allied set of concepts relates to the importance of action, perhaps one of the most key ingredients of an effective plan. In several passages 'Abdu'l-Bahá stressed, as had Bahá'u'lláh, the need to translate thoughts, ideas, and desires into action, as opposed to empty talk. 'Abdu'l-Bahá noted in a talk delivered to a Paris audience in 1911:

> What profit is there in agreeing that universal friendship is good, and talking of the solidarity of the human race as a grand ideal? Unless these thoughts are translated into the world of action, they are useless.
>
> The wrong in the world continues to exist just because people talk only of their ideals, and do not strive to put them into practice. If actions took the place of words, the world's misery would very soon be changed into comfort.
>
> A man who does great good, and talks not of it, is on the way to perfection.
>
> The man who has accomplished a small good and magnifies it in his speech is worth very little.[28]

In this and several other recorded public addresses, 'Abdu'l-Bahá portrayed action as a complement to character development, as well as a way to strive to translate ideals into reality. As he noted in another talk delivered in Paris, "Some men and women glory in their exalted thoughts, but if these thoughts never reach the plane of action they remain useless: the power of thought is dependent on its manifestation in deeds."[29] 'Abdu'l-Bahá went beyond discussing action as a personal spiritual requirement; he also firmly connected the concepts of planning and of divine assistance to the need for action. Therefore his use of the concepts of "action" and "volition" directly translated into plans for social progress. The analogous image he used was that of constructing a house:

> mere knowledge is not sufficient for complete human attainment. The teachings of the Holy Books need a heavenly power and divine potency to carry them out. A house is not built by mere acquaintance with the plans. Money must be forthcoming; volition is necessary to construct it; a carpenter must be employed in its erection.

It is not enough to say, "The plan and purpose of this house are very good; I will live in it." There are no walls of protection, there is no roof of shelter in this mere statement; the house must be actually built before we can live in it.[30]

The layers of meaning contained in this passage (as in all those quoted) are such as to require each individual to contemplate them thoroughly for himself or herself, since many interpretations are possible. In one sense, this quotation is a confirmation of what psychologist Daniel Jordan has highlighted as "knowledge, volition, and action," which are essential strategies for purposeful self-improvement. In an especially perceptive article on this subject, Jordan elaborated at some length about 'Abdu'l-Bahá's advice that we link these three attributes as a potent means for transforming ourselves spiritually.[31] Another possible inference from this passage concerns social, as opposed to individual, transformation. Plans, it would seem, are necessary but not sufficient means for human attainment. Divine power is an essential part of human attainment, as are a series of practical steps: getting material resources (money), desiring to accomplish the task (having volition to construct), and engaging human resources (employing a carpenter). These are important for a wide range of social accomplishments, including implementation of plans.

A final example of the need to connect plans and actions—and of their powerlessness without divine influence—is a story that 'Abdu'l-Bahá told about a conversation with a military officer:

Many years ago in Baghdád I saw a certain officer sitting upon the ground. Before him a large paper was placed into which he was sticking needles tipped with small red and white flags. First he would stick them into the paper, then thoughtfully pull them out and change their position. I watched him with curious interest for a long time, then asked, "What are you doing?" He replied, "I have in mind something which is historically related of Napoleon I during his war against Austria. One day, it is said, his secretary found him sitting upon the ground as I am now doing, sticking needles into a paper before him. His secretary inquired what it meant. Napoleon answered, 'I am on the battlefield figuring out my next victory. You see, Italy and Austria are defeated, and France is triumphant.' In the great campaign which followed, everything came out just as he said. His army carried his plans to a complete success. Now I am doing the same as Napoleon, figuring out a great campaign of military conquest." I said, "Where is your army? Napoleon had an army already equipped when he figured out his victory. You have no army. Your forces exist only on paper. You have no power to conquer countries. First get ready your army, then sit upon the ground with your needles." We need an army to attain victory in the spiritual world; mere plans are not sufficient; ideas and principles are helpless without a divine power to put them into effect.[32]

Here is a common-sense approach to planning: Plans go nowhere with out the resources, both material and spiritual, necessary to carry them out. Again apparent is the theme of the importance of divine power, but getting an "army" ready is also important, because human resources help move a plan from empty gestures, pins upon a map, to the firm grounding of reality and ultimate victory.

STRATEGIC SOCIAL REFORM

Bahá'u'lláh and 'Abdu'l-Bahá, as spiritual leaders, felt strongly that divine will was an important factor in all activities. 'Abdu'l-Bahá sometimes referred to the teachings of God as "plans" that superseded lesser "plans." Here is a remarkably clear example:

> To use a metaphor, when an army is placed under various commanders, each with his own strategy, they will obviously differ as to battle lines and movements of the troops; but once the Supreme Commander, who is thoroughly versed in the arts of war, taketh over, those other plans will disappear, for the supremely gifted general will bring the whole army under his control.[33]

According to this view, the plan of God is supreme, and God has both a plan and a strategy. This passage reminds us of the need to view humanly devised plans with humility.

Yet, as 'Abdu'l-Bahá noted, this does not mean humans should not make plans. Plans indeed are useful theoretical constructs for implementing social reform. When speaking of universal peace, 'Abdu'l-Bahá confirmed Bahá'u'lláh's suggestion that humanity establish a Supreme Tribunal (an overarching world court) to help bring about world peace. In a remarkable passage, 'Abdu'l-Bahá described the route toward creating a Supreme Tribunal as a series of steps that he called a "Plan." Excerpts are presented in such a way as to highlight the sequence of steps:

> And His plan is this: that the national assemblies of each country and nation—that is to say parliaments—should elect two or three persons who are the choicest men of that nation, and are well informed concerning international laws and the relations between governments and aware of the essential needs of the world of humanity in this day.
>
> The number of these representatives should be in proportion to the number of inhabitants of that country.
>
> The election of these souls who are chosen by the national assembly, that is, the parliament, must be confirmed by the upper house, the congress and the cabinet and also by the president or monarch so these persons may be the elected ones of all the nation and the government.
>
> From among these people the members of the Supreme Tribunal will be elect ed, and all mankind will thus have a share therein, for every one of these dele gates is fully representative of his nation.
>
> When the Supreme Tribunal gives a ruling on any international question, either unanimously or by majority rule, there will no longer be any pretext for the plaintiff or ground of objection for the defendant.
>
> In case any of the governments or nations, in the execution of the irrefutable decision of the Supreme Tribunal, be negligent or dilatory, the rest of the nations . . . of the world are the supporters of this Supreme Tribunal.
>
> Consider what a firm foundation this is![34]

A firm foundation indeed. As is clear from this and several similar passages, the precepts of universal government extend far beyond vague platitudes. This vision is a very sophisticated series of purposeful steps toward social reform and is in that sense a "plan," but it also takes into account the importance of the appearance of justice. This prescription for peace is the very opposite of haphazard social reform; it is instead quite deliberate.

'Abdu'l-Bahá also tapped into a very practical aspect of planning as a technique for encouraging the growth and consolidation of the Bahá'í Faith. He created a plan shaped to specific geographic target areas, with clear procedures and goals, all within the context of spiritual principles and needs. He offered this innovation in a series of letters written to the Bahá'ís of North America, in 1916 and 1917, and collected in *Tablets of the Divine Plan*. This compendium of "Divine Plan" letters demonstrated conclusively that 'Abdu'l-Bahá saw planning as an essential element of social progress and divine will. This slim volume, sometimes referred to as one of the basic "mandate" documents of the Bahá'í Faith, is most certainly its "mandate" planning document.

'Abdu'l-Bahá was not unfamiliar with North America. He had traveled extensively in North America in 1912, had maintained an active correspondence with many people there, and had received several of these people in Palestine as visitors. His missives were therefore based on firsthand knowledge and information about the conditions and potential of the areas in which they lived. During World War I, 'Abdu'l-Bahá wrote a series of fourteen letters, asking Bahá'ís to carry out specific activities. He addressed some of these letters to the Bahá'ís of Canada, some to those of the United States, and others to Bahá'ís in specific regions, such as the southern United States. These letters, which contained many striking features, laid the groundwork of a new way for Bahá'ís to think about transforming their community.

One of the clearest innovations of the Divine Plan letters is their geographic structure and targeting. In this first century of the Bahá'í Faith, it was not uncommon for the central figures or leaders of the religion to give specific travel instructions to individuals, asking them to go to certain lands and carry out various tasks. 'Abdu'l-Bahá carried this tradition to new heights, organizing instructions and requests for believers residing in select regions of North America, such as the northeastern, southern, central, and western states in the United States, and in Canada and Greenland. This practice allowed him not only to address concerns tailored to subregions but also to refer directly to stirring examples of local history, as with his extensive references to the City of Chicago's noble history in one of the letters addressed to believers in the "Central States." He encouraged those living in multistate subregions to travel to underrepresented states, and he identified extensive lists of places to settle and "illumine" far beyond the borders of North America. This farsighted characteristic of the Divine Plan made it ongoing, because the number of countries named meant that it could take many years to carry out the plan.

A second striking feature of the Divine Plan letters is the consistent reference to the major goal of arising to spread belief in the teachings of Bahá'u'lláh. As noted previously, 'Abdu'l-Bahá believed that it was important to focus thoughts and translate these into action. The Divine Plan letters gave such focus and opportunity to the Bahá'ís of North America by offering specific guidance about what they should do. These instructions were couched in beautiful, confirming language, but they were instructions nonetheless.

As an illustration: In the first letter, addressed to "Northeastern States" residents, 'Abdu'l-Bahá first stated the existing conditions—in some cities of certain states "people are not yet illumined"—and then he asked that "whenever it is possible for each one of you, hasten ye to those cities and shine forth like unto the stars with the light of the Most Great Guidance."[35] The variations are slight; to the southern states, he instructed readers "either go yourselves or send a number of blessed souls to those states"; to the central states, he listed strong areas and weaker ones, and then suggested that the stronger areas send to those areas with fewer members "teachers who are severed from all else save God"; in similar fashion, he asked people in stronger western communities to "travel yourselves, personally, throughout those states or choose others and send them, so that they may teach the souls"; believers of Canada and Greenland were encouraged to "become self-sacrificing and like unto the candles of guidance become ignited."[36]

These consistent exhortations gave structure and unity to the Divine Plan letters. It was not necessary for Bahá'ís to wonder what they were supposed to do. They were to travel, to settle in unsettled places—or to send other travelers in their stead—and then to "shine forth." In terms of clarity of approach and focus upon individual initiative, this was a sterling example of a plan.

Inspiration and Encouragement

Another characteristic of these Divine Plan letters was their stirring references to heroes and heroines who would be familiar to Bahá'ís and thus capable of evoking memories of valor and courage. 'Abdu'l-Bahá also effectively referenced the inspiration of sacred writings, including the Bible, and he offered prayers that could be recited as sources for assistance and power. In the first five of the fourteen letters, 'Abdu'l-Bahá offered various analogies and words of encouragement. In the case of the nine letters received in 1919, we see supportive language used even more extensively than before, largely through the addition of a special prayer at the end of each letter. These prayers taught the Bahá'ís to beseech divine blessings and support for their efforts and simultaneously lent a rarefied atmosphere of detachment, trust, hope, and courage that could only have had a galvanizing effect on the letters' recipients.

Perhaps the most striking and noteworthy feature of these letters is their language and tone. It is this feature that most distinguishes them from the ordinary plans one finds today in corporations, cities, and communities, even religious ones. The tone was one of absolute love and support for the accomplishments that the author, 'Abdu'l-Bahá, was sure would be forth coming. Note how this passage from one letter to the central states mixes praise with instruction:

> Although in the states of Illinois, Wisconsin, Ohio, Michigan and Minnesota—praise be to God—believers are found who are associating with each other in the utmost firmness and steadfastness—day and night they have no other intention save the diffusion of the fragrances of God, they have no other hope except the promotion of the heavenly teachings, like the candles they are burning with the light of the love of God, and like thankful birds are singing songs, spirit-imparting, joy-creating, in the rose garden of the knowledge of God—yet in the states of Indiana, Iowa, Missouri, North Dakota, South Dakota, Nebraska and Kansas few of the believers exist. . . . Therefore, if it is possible, send to those parts teachers.[37]

It is, of course, possible that the letter's recipients were as wonderful as 'Abdu'l-Bahá claimed, and were indeed "burning with the light of the love of God." If they were not, however, this missive must have surely spurred them to rise to meet these luminous expectations. Offering effusive praise and spiritual allusions was but one means of encouragement that 'Abdu'l-Bahá used. He gave instruction in the required conditions for success, referred to the spiritual bounties that were theirs, and otherwise inspired his North American readers. 'Abdu'l-Bahá suggested that the Bahá'ís should manifest certain qualities if they wanted their plans to be successful. Three such qualities were firmness in the Covenant, another way of characterizing "faith";[38] absolute love and unity among themselves; and the ability to travel without attachment to material comforts, a form of "detachment." Other personal characteristics were important too, such as luminosity or radiance—the ability to shine as a person of resplendent character.

Ponder for a moment the advice given about the importance of love and unity, the basic glue that would hold the community together and help them to become the "armies of God."[39] By stressing these and other social and spiritual qualities, 'Abdu'l-Bahá infused spirit and insight into what could have been a dry series of exhortations and list of places to which they should travel. In contrast, 'Abdu'l-Bahá emphasized that, to be successful, they must show forth

> [f]ellowship and love amongst the believers. The divine friends must be attracted to and enamored of each other and ever be ready and willing to sacrifice their own lives for each other. Should one soul from amongst the believers meet another, it must be as though a thirsty one with parched lips has reached to the fountain of the water of life, or a lover has met his true beloved. For one of the greatest divine wisdoms regarding the appearance of the holy Manifestations is this: The souls may come to know each other and become intimate with each other; the power of the love of God may make all of them the waves of one sea, the flowers of one rose garden, and the stars of one heaven.[40]

'Abdu'l-Bahá did not want a series of automatons carrying out his exhortations with blind obedience but without joy or fellowship. Rather, he wanted them to be a spiritual army, guided by absolute belief in the teachings of God, by love and unity among themselves, and by a willingness to detach themselves from material pursuits and comforts. All of the passages from the Tablets of the Divine Plan offer inspiring lessons about how to ask people to do audacious things, whether in relation to formal plans or for other purposes.

TABLE 2.1
A FEW SPRITUAL PRINCIPLES FOR PLANNING HUMAN PROGRESS

Visionary development	Systematic social reform
Enlightened leadership	Inspiration and encouragement
Consultation	Firm faith*
Goal-directed behavior	Love and unity among participants
Meaningful action	Detachment from materialism

* For nonreligious groups, this is simply faith in the organization and its mission. For members of religious communities, this refers to firmness in the Covenant, which is the belief in the agreement between God and humanity, and between Manifestations of God and their followers, who must in turn believe, trust, and obey religious laws and institutions.

CONCLUSION

In conclusion, the writings of Bahá'u'lláh and 'Abdu'l-Bahá yield several implications (summarized above in Table 2.1) for planning human progress. From Bahá'u'lláh's writings, we see an abiding faith in the perfectibility of human society, as manifest in his vision for a better world. According to Bahá'u'lláh, spirituality is not remote from the affairs of human development and governance, nor is fundamental and far-reaching improvement of life and society on this planet impossible. For such betterment to take place, however, each of us must understand that working toward social progress is part of the life of a spiritually mature person. Leaders must understand that they have a particular obligation to promote such progress and that several practical steps, such as adopting a world language and forming consultative institutions to establish and maintain world peace, will help move the world toward global tranquillity. At the same time, they should also take care to nourish their own growth and knowledge by assessing their behavior on a daily basis, by becoming familiar with the conditions facing those they govern, and by making choices based upon equity and justice. Moreover, all of us must understand that all such efforts will be facilitated if we "look to the end" of our activities, making goal-directed action part of our movement toward global improvement. It will also be important to consult about matters in order to understand how to proceed, because consultation is a "shining light" in a dark world.

'Abdu'l-Bahá confirmed these concepts and principles. His book *The*

Secret of Divine Civilization is an especially complete treatise on development and the importance of enlightened governance. He elaborated at length upon the nature and importance of consultation, highlighting the human virtues that must characterize dialogue between consulting parties. His analogies and wise exhortations about the importance of concentrating on a single point, translating words into action, and building projects such as military campaigns or houses not "by mere acquaintance with the plans," but rather with resources, volition, and divine inspiration, offered valuable guidance about how to plan.

In addition, 'Abdu'l-Bahá wrote a series of letters that offered plan related spiritual guidance to the Bahá'ís of North America. Characterizing these letters were effective geographic targeting, focused exhortation toward an overarching goal, and a tone of transcendence and loving encouragement. The example of 'Abdu'l-Bahá's "Divine Plan" strongly suggests that we "planners" should reconsider how we create, present, and talk about plans with fellow human beings. The best lessons to be learned from these letters are probably not the mechanics and components of the planning process. Rather, they best indicate how to use planning as a tool for spiritual transformation and how to treat the people with whom, and for whom, we plan. The level of gentleness, support, and encouragement is such that one could read these letters as meditations rather than directives, and yet they gave explicit directions, some of which were, indeed, extremely difficult to carry out. Perhaps key ingredients for those who would encourage successful promulgation of difficult plans are love and encouragement, as well as appeals to spiritual attributes rather than material limitations.

Another implication of this chapter's discussion is that the lives and writings of Bahá'u'lláh and 'Abdu'l-Bahá provided the foundation for the work of Shoghi Effendi, who, as their descendant and interpreter in both a literal and a spiritual sense, was intimately familiar with their writings. One could argue that Shoghi Effendi's considerable capacities in designing and promulgating audacious plans only reflected his superior understanding of the concepts described by 'Abdu'l-Bahá and Bahá'u'lláh. Although, as will become obvious, Shoghi Effendi contributed his own special touch to such endeavors, he had a firm framework upon which to build. The writings of his forebears provided concepts and approaches that apply just as much to planning today as they did to Shoghi Effendi's plans more than forty years ago. According to these writings, planning for social progress, which is a spiritual endeavor, requires belief in the perfectibility of humanity, understanding of the principles of good leadership and governance, creation of goals connected with purposeful action, and loving, effective encouragement of focused efforts.

It is important to note, however, that in the ethos of Bahá'u'lláh and 'Abdu'l-Bahá, these factors were merely ornaments to the central task, which was the perfectibility of human society in a spiritual as well as a material sense. They considered the spiritual growth and development of the individual necessary (but not sufficient) for creating a better world. Their principles for social development depended not merely on enlightened governance, but also on personal morality and the cultivation of human virtues such as devotion, courtesy, purity of motive, and radiance of spirit. Within the supportive framework of a socially progressive religion, Bahá'u'lláh and 'Abdu'l-Bahá aimed for the same goals as other great spiritual leaders, all of whom exhort some personal code of morality and salvation. Their belief in the essential role of divine power—as exemplified in 'Abdu'l-Bahá's comments on the inadequacy of "mere knowledge" without "a heavenly power and divine potency"—was unshakable. What was particularly notable about their perspective was the marriage of these age-old concerns with broader questions of human progress and social justice.

This spiritual context gave their followers unique powers to carry out plans and other efforts designed to bring about social improvement. Those followers were quite literally believers, followers of teachings that highlighted the power of divine forces in their lives. This situation gave their plan-related activities a deep ideological dimension that added strength to their commitment to plan success. Therefore, not only was the belief system of the planning leaders an important element, so too was the belief system of ordinary members. Without such steadfast commitment, all plans would be futile and many initiatives would fail, no matter how exemplary the technique.

Chapter 3

Envisioning Change

Where there is no vision [Bible notation: or revelation], the people are unrestrained, but happy is he who keeps the law.
—Solomon, Proverbs 29:18

This is not a Cause which may be made a plaything for your idle fancies, nor is it a field for the foolish and faint of heart. By God, this is the arena of insight and detachment, of vision and upliftment. . . .
—Bahá'u'lláh, Kitáb-i-Aqdas

IN MANY CIRCLES, THE "NEW" FASHION IS TO PLAN for the future of one's self, geographic area, or organization by first enunciating a vision, which is a clear idea of where one wants to go. Consciously identifying a vision can break open the dull old parameters of the present and the past that confine and oppress, and can offer new possibilities, prospects, and paradigms. Numerous books have appeared that focus on the concept of vision and how to get it. Burt Nanus's book *Visionary Leadership* informs readers that "there is no more powerful engine driving an organization toward excellence and long-range success than an attractive, worthwhile, and achievable vision of the future, widely shared."[1] A good "vision of the future," Nanus suggests, is one that is appropriate for the organization. This vision is important because it clarifies purpose and direction, and helps to inspire enthusiasm for "excellence and long-range success." He instructs his readers to carry out a "vision audit" and to build a constructive image of the future that allows the organization to grow and change. He offers examples of visions, such as Walt Disney's original concept of Disneyland, which propelled their creators to do bold and innovative things, such as creating a microcosm of small-town America.

The concept of vision is anything but new. This chapter's first epigraph is the proverb: "Where there is no vision, the people are unrestrained." In the King James translation, the proverb warned that without vision "the people perish."² Numerous historic leaders had "vision," ranging from Hammurabi's vision of a just Mesopotamian society governed by a consistent code of laws, to the vision Moses held of the "promised land" of Canaan, to the vision of justice and freedom articulated by leaders such as Mahatma Gandhi, Martin Luther King Jr., and Nelson Mandela. Vision—of a better society and of better human beings—is also an inherent characteristic of the world's major religions.

Considering how important vision is for human progress, we know remarkably little about it as a tool for inspiration and motivation, even with useful books such as *Visionary Leadership*. For example, it is one thing to state that Martin Luther King Jr. had a vision; it is quite another to understand how he managed to tap into that vision to motivate his followers. To do so, we would need to do more than quote his famous "I Have a Dream" speech, even though that is an important visionary statement. We might ask King's colleagues whether his everyday conversations referred to his vision or ask his followers how King's vision moved them. Although his books offer some tangible insights, one might still not fully understand how King's vision motivated people to act.

This chapter offers some broader thoughts on the "planning process" and its relation to vision, and explores how Shoghi Effendi used vision to help motivate people. It is possible to begin to document his visionary leadership through examining those books, letters, and cables explicitly designed to help his followers visualize successful plans. Shoghi Effendi was a remarkably apt "teller of the dream," and his frequent letters provide unique source material about one leader's visionary planning.

THE PLANNING PROCESS: THE PROFESSIONAL LITERATURE

Since developing a vision is a part of the planning process, it is useful to review what that process is and to determine how the concept of "vision" fits into it. Two modern scholars best known for their work about planning as a method for thinking and acting are John Friedmann and Melville Branch, both urban planners by training. Friedmann's book *Planning in the Public Domain: From Knowledge to Action* is required reading for many thousands of urban planning students around the world. It presents the planning process according to several main schools of thought.[3] According to Friedmann, the intellectual forebears of planning—ranging from Karl Marx to Robert Owen, from John Dewey to Amitai Etzioni, from Donald Schon to Aaron Wildavsky—are extremely diverse but do have something in common. They all assume the need for social improvement, and they all propose planning or action that involves most of the following components:

- "Futurity"—or some concept of the future, involving goals and objectives, forecasts, or educated guesses about probable outcomes of action;
- Space—some orientation to particular locations or spatial organizations;
- Resource requirements—assessments of physical resources or costs;
- Implementation procedures—ways that society or organizations can actually carry out planned improvements, based on action; and
- Feedback and evaluation—assessment of whether the planned changes are actually happening and working, and adjustment of action as necessary.[4]

This list looks remarkably similar to one developed by Melville Branch as he tried to explain planning as a "universal process" that applied to a wide range of fields of human endeavor. Branch also spoke in terms of steps and phases, supposedly sequential:

- Information-the first step, needed to gather information about "the current state and future potential of the organism involved in planning";
- Analysis—processing of information to reach conclusions about what can be done and how this can be accomplished;
- Reaching conclusions, making decisions, and preparing a plan—three steps based on information and analysis;
- Implementation, feedback, and modification or revision—three steps that ensure that the plans are carried out and revised as necessary.[5]

With these readings, similar opinions about an overall process begin to emerge. To carry out planned social improvements, it is apparently important to gather some ideas or information about the future. It is also necessary to gather or tally resources for the plans and to analyze relevant information. At some point, it is necessary to undertake action, to implement related tasks, and to evaluate the effectiveness of those activities.

Strategic planning, a form of the planning process, may be more familiar to many readers. Strategic planning involves targeting a few key areas of focused endeavor before acting. John Bryson, author of *Strategic Planning for Public and Nonprofit Organizations*, has helped many people bring about focused change in their corporations, municipalities, organizations, or government agencies. Bryson does not hesitate to prescribe ten steps, which he believes are largely sequential. First, he suggests initiating and agreeing upon the process, then identifying organizational mandates, and next clarifying mission and values. Then he counsels groups to assess their external and internal environments, identify strategic issues, formulate strategies appropriate for these issues, and adopt the plan. Finally, he urges organizations to establish an effective organizational vision, develop an implementation process, and then reassess the whole process.[6]

This list shows that the supposedly "new" strategic planning is, in essence, very much like the old planning process. The order is different, as are the specifics, but the focus is still on some process of gathering information, deciding on courses of action, carrying out those actions, and assessing them. The role of ideas about the future may vary according to different authors—Bryson suggests determining the "organizational vision" near the end of his list of steps instead of at the beginning—but it is still very much part of the whole process.

Given this overall agreement as to the components of planning activities, if not the process and the sequence, obviously vision is a critical issue. Everything we plan for involves the future. Karl Marx aimed for a future based on the ascendancy of the proletariat and the abolition of industrial capitalism. His nineteenth-century vision of communism was very different from the vision of the contemporary communitarian Amitai Etzioni. Etzioni suggests that North American democracies can develop social values necessary to survive in the twenty-first century without resorting to class struggle or revolutionary upheaval. Both authors, however different their approaches, base their ideas on visions of a better future.

An excellent contemporary statement of vision, Ervin Laszlo's *Vision 2020*, advises that visions be based upon noble values and lack of individual or social oppression. Laszlo suggests the need to safeguard the individual and the need to achieve global cooperation. He notes that, to safeguard the individual, it will be necessary to restrain the power of nation-states and politicians. To achieve global cooperation, Laszlo argues for international agreements in the three crucial arenas of defense, the environment, and development.[7] He acknowledges that religions may help move us toward this vision of a "post-critical world," and he lists Judaism, Christianity, Islam, and the Bahá'í Faith as among several potential contributors to social progress.[8] Even religions, however, must safeguard the individual and move toward global cooperation.

We might also add that visions must be inclusionary, widely accepted, and based not on the fancies of a few but on the needs of the many. Lest this sound too abstract, consider the case of Ciudad Guayana, the Venezuelan city mentioned earlier in which the foreign designers brought "not only an art of designing the future city but also a vision of the future city as well." But their future city was to be "a city of sweeping avenues, orderly public places, urban amenities for the well-to-do, and orderly settlements for the poor. This was a vision derived from a tradition of design for wealthy individual patrons and well-endowed public clients."[9] This was not a vision derived from the reality of the actual people who lived in the region, who needed flexibility, the ability to build their own housing and erect their own community institutions, and the right to live near their jobs. The "real" residents gradually remade the planned city into one of their own image, better suited to their needs, but "ruining" the careful designs of the designers, who had been careless about some crucial things.

As another example of the power of inclusionary vision, consider a story retold by author Peter Senge in his book *The Fifth Discipline*. Senge argues that "shared vision" is essential if a group of people is to progress. Of the numerous examples he offers, his first is about the movie *Spartacus*, based on the experiences of an army of slaves who rose up against the Roman Empire in 71 B.C. According to the screenwriter's reenactment, the vanquished army stood before Roman general Marcus Crassus, who ordered their leader Spartacus to step forward and identify himself. If he did not, the general warned, the Roman soldiers would crucify every one of them. Spartacus did step forward and declare "I am Spartacus," but then so did the man next to him, and the man next to him. Soon, everyone in the defeated army was clamoring that he was Spartacus. By standing up in this way, these men chose death, but their loyalty was not so much to their leader Spartacus as to the vision which he had inspired—the idea that they could be free men. They were so committed to this vision that they refused to give it up and return to slavery, even if it meant sacrificing their own lives.[10]

This story illustrates the fact that it is not enough just to establish a good vision. Rather, this vision must be shared to the extent that people in the organization feel committed to it. When people throughout the organization become truly committed to a vision, they are willing to do whatever is necessary to make it happen.

THE PLANNING PROCESS ACCORDING TO SHOGHI EFFENDI

Although Shoghi Effendi was not a student of planning as a field of scholarly study, he was probably exposed to many of the same intellectual streams of thought. As a student at American University in Beirut from 1914 to 1918, and at Oxford University from 1920 until 1921, Shoghi Effendi surely read some of the great thinkers that Friedmann cites in his book *Planning in the Public Domain*. Shoghi Effendi was acutely aware of communism and must have known of the multiyear plans that arose in Europe and in Asia during his mature adulthood. His intellectual tastes, according to his widow, included such "big thinkers" as Gibbon, whose book about the rise and fall of the Roman Empire always lay near Shoghi Effendi in the room where he slept and was usually with him when he traveled as well.[11]

His most influential source of knowledge, however, was the religious writings of the world, particularly those written by the Báb, Bahá'u'lláh, and 'Abdu'l-Bahá. These writings gave Shoghi Effendi excellent guidelines about how to lead his religious community into the future. They also gave him the inheritance of a vision that was indeed noble, inclusionary, and grand. This was a vision of the new global civilization described by Bahá'u'lláh.

Shoghi Effendi's "planning process" emerges more from his letters and testimony from his companions than from his own explicit explanation. A microcosm of his planning style can be found in Shoghi Effendi's oversight of the construction of gardens and shrines on and near Mt. Carmel. Alain Locke, famed African-American writer and educator, noted after his personalized tour of one garden project that

"Shoghi Effendi is a master of detail as well as of principle, of executive foresight as well as of projective vision. But I have never heard details so redeemed of their natural triviality as when talking to him of the plans for the beautifying and laying out of the terraces and gardens."[12] Ugo Giachery, who supervised the purchase, cutting, carving, and shipping of hundreds of tons of Italian marble used to build beautiful Bahá'í shrines, highly praised Shoghi Effendi's supervision of those challenging construction projects. However, one of his most telling stories is not about magnificent buildings but about a garden. For many years, Shoghi Effendi had waited for the courts to grant access to all of the property surrounding the burial place of Bahá'u'lláh. After the courts had confirmed ownership, Shoghi Effendi announced one morning that he needed the help of every able-bodied man. On that day, Shoghi Effendi

> followed a plan preconceived in his mind. Assisted by [an assistant], who carried a ball of string and some wooden pickets, he traced all the paths, nine in number, which like a fan were to radiate from the Shrine of Bahá'u'lláh. . . . Shoghi Effendi was moving about directing, counselling, cautioning, encouraging, explaining, demonstrating how to do apparently impossible things, and rejoicing in the transformation of the land under our very eyes.[13]

Shoghi Effendi took much the same approach to leadership of his community. He spent many years "encouraging, explaining, demonstrating how to do apparently impossible things," just as he did for those gardens, which eventually became world renowned for their beauty, attracting thousands of visitors every year from Israel and from around the globe.

Shoghi Effendi's widow also noted that his oversight of the construction of key shrines and gardens is one way to discern Shoghi Effendi's planning skills. As did Giachery, she spoke about the parallel manifestation of those skills in his administration of the Bahá'í Faith. She has said that Shoghi Effendi went about such tasks as building up the administrative order or implementing plans

> very much as the great Renaissance painters created their vast frescoes and canvases. First came the cartoon, the whole idea, scale, colour, proportion; then it was quartered, divided into a grid of

squares; this was transferred to the permanent surface and the great guiding lines filled in, the outlines, the figures in shadow; then came the detail and colours, applied with infinite patience until perfection was achieved. Such was the method of Shoghi Effendi and he allowed no one to start painting in figures or details before the canvas was ready to take them.[14]

This is an amazingly compelling portrait of a visionary planner. Shoghi Effendi had the complete fresco of a worldwide community in mind, and he spent his entire adult life systematically planning for its final, beautiful, color-filled appearance, just as he did for the gardens. Here is one major example. Some Bahá'ís initially felt that, at twenty-four years of age, Shoghi Effendi was too young when his grandfather died to be able to lead the global community. They urged him to bring into being, immediately, the worldwide Bahá'í governing body that was presaged in Bahá'u'lláh's writings. Shoghi Effendi, understanding the broader framework, knew that such a body must rest on the foundation of strong national or multinational governing bodies, the national spiritual assemblies. These institutions did not yet exist in sufficient numbers to support an international governance system. Shoghi Effendi carried out the many tasks needed to fill in the details of the broader framework. He translated writings explaining how these assemblies should operate and nurtured particularly apt students of the Bahá'í administrative order such as the North American national spiritual assembly. He sent people to dozens of other countries to help erect other strong local and national spiritual assemblies, and in this way slowly and painstakingly erected the necessary international infrastructure.

It was with the same deliberate care that he approached global plans. Shoghi Effendi referred often to the *Tablets of the Divine Plan* as "'Abdu'l-Bahá's unique and grand design."[15] Nothing in the text of these letters, written during World War I, suggested that 'Abdu'l-Bahá expected it would take decades to implement this plan. However, Shoghi Effendi did not rush the North American Bahá'ís and worked instead to build institutional maturity. He did not initiate a major undertaking for the successful prosecution of the grand design until twenty years after 'Abdu'l-Bahá's death, when the Bahá'í administrative institutions were ready for "its efficient, systematic prosecution."[16] Once he started urging this plan's completion, however, his pace was fast and unyielding. When Shoghi Effendi urged the North Americans to accept their first global plan, timed to extend for seven years beginning in 1937, he was very much like a general. In his particular version of war, his widow indicates, "He fought for the future, with its radiant age of peace and unity, a world society and the Kingdom of God and earth." He fought, that is, for the establishment of a civilization governed by principles of unity and peace.[17]

In attempting to connect Shoghi Effendi's style of operation with the traditional professional planner's understanding of the planning process—a difficult task, since Shoghi Effendi's style was in many ways unique—we should first of all note that he believed in a strong vision, which guided all of his efforts and rested upon an ironclad sense of purpose or mission. This sense of purpose or mission was, for the North American Bahá'ís, inextricably tied with their "mandate" planning document, 'Abdu'l-Bahá's *Tablets of the Divine Plan*. Shoghi Effendi believed in careful institutional preparation for plans designed to carry out this mandate, even if this preparation took years; he also believed in clear and attainable objectives and in effective strategies for action. During implementation he urged immediate action, and he encouraged the Bahá'ís to send a constant stream of information about the progress of the plans. Although Shoghi Effendi operated as a spiritual and administrative leader and had the authority to do so, he depended heavily upon the power of inspiration and upon his community's willing cooperation and heartfelt attachment to the success of these goals and plans. Another way of summarizing this process is as follows:

- Building institutional capacity and gathering information about the state of the community;
- Clarifying the vision and gaining heartfelt commitment to that vision;
- Choosing clear objectives and effective strategies and encouraging sustained action;
- Monitoring implementation, throughout the plan, and indicating subsequent action.

Because this stripped-down list is inadequate to reflect the multifaceted beauty of his approach, several chapters will be devoted to discussing these points, with one chapter for each of the last three points, beginning later in this chapter with "vision." Shoghi Effendi acted with authority, spiritual insight, and an impeccable sense of how to motivate people to do their best. His objectives were extraordinary and reflected a wise assessment of the capacity and potential of his followers, stretching them in innovative ways to do the seemingly impossible. His monitoring was no simple receipt and acknowledgment of reports, no automatic gathering of numbers, but a wholehearted devotion to understanding each success and focusing in upon each unmet goal to help identify what needed to be done. His assessments of plan accomplishments were glorious letters, filled with luminous encouragement and praise, as well as loving but frank identification of duties yet undone.

No evidence suggests that Shoghi Effendi categorized his plan-related letters and cables into the areas of concern or endeavor listed here, either in the four bulleted points above or elsewhere in this book. While several of his communications had dominant themes and while whole paragraphs or pages addressed such identifiable topics as the vision or mission or objectives of a plan, on the whole his communications appeared to be all of one piece. Although this book divides discussion somewhat into chapters and sections, dealing with vision here, and strategies or monitoring elsewhere, the only purpose of this division is to make it easier for readers to understand implications for planning in other contexts.

The uniqueness of Shoghi Effendi's "planning process" was neither in his overall steps nor in their order, but rather in how he participated in that process, infusing it with a spiritualism and strong sense of purpose that guided all his actions. His planning leadership was noteworthy because vision and spiritual wisdom pervaded that leadership, because he took on an audacious set of tasks, and because he succeeded in creative ways in helping people do what they set out to do.

SHOGHI EFFENDI AND THE GLOBAL PLANS

To understand why the tasks were so challenging, observe the state of the community that Shoghi Effendi led. When Shoghi Effendi took over the worldwide leadership of the Bahá'í Faith in 1921, the total number of countries in which Bahá'ís lived was thirty-five. In North America, although a few valiant believers arose in response to the *Tablets of the Divine Plan*'s directive to travel and spread throughout the country and the world, in general the national community did not have the capacity to support the individual initiatives. By 1953, after strenuous exertion to expand, the United States Bahá'í community had just over 175 local spiritual assemblies, which were the local governing bodies in communities where at least nine adult Bahá'ís resided. This was the largest number in any country, including Iran (formerly Persia), but this modest number of United States assemblies in 1953 suggests that during the 1920s the number of North American assemblies must have been far fewer than that.[18]

Most national groups of Bahá'ís were organized in only rudimentary fashion; in the 1960s Rúḥíyyih Rabbani indicated that "[i]n 1922 there cannot have been, throughout the Bahá'í world, more than one body—the American one—which remotely resembled a [modern] nationally elected National Assembly"[19] Even that assembly was not formally established until 1925. The four other national spiritual assemblies established during the 1920s—in the British Isles, Germany-Austria, Egypt-Sudan, and Pakistan-Burma—sometimes faced internal or external crises, as did the Persian and Iraqi national spiritual assemblies, established in 1934 and 1931 respectively.[20]

The need for more deliberate, planned action within the Bahá'í world became obvious by the mid-1930s. The North American and other national communities had specific projects that needed to be completed, such as the construction of the House of Worship in Wilmette, Illinois. Moreover, the Bahá'í Faith needed to grow and spread throughout the world. It was, after all, a global religion, based on a vision of a world governed by principles of progressive development and social improvement. Bahá'u'lláh had created a structure of world governance for the global community that assumed Bahá'ís resided throughout the world, but they did not. Before 1892, practically all members of the religion lived in the Middle East. By 1921, Europe had become well represented, as had North America (the United States and Canada), but only one sub-Saharan African nation (South Africa) had members of the Bahá'í Faith. The Asian nations included only China and Japan, and Brazil alone represented South and Central America. Between 1921 and 1932, only five countries were added to the list of places where Bahá'ís lived.[21] Clearly, it was time to grow, to push forth deliberately with the *Tablets of the Divine Plan*'s call for North Americans to settle throughout the world. Thus, in the mid-1930s Shoghi Effendi began to push for national plans of action.

It might be useful here to expand upon the reasons why Shoghi Effendi—and, by extension, this book—centered attention upon plans carried out by the North American community of Bahá'ís. Much of the focus upon North American Bahá'ís was due to the fact that 'Abdu'l-Bahá had sent them the Tablets of the Divine Plan, even though most Bahá'ís at the time lived in the Middle East. Through the act of giving this plan to the North Americans, 'Abdu'l-Bahá conferred upon them a special mandate, since he turned to the North American believers to be responsible for tasks important for the entire Bahá'í world.

'Abdu'l-Bahá constantly encouraged the North American readers of his letters by referring to their special destiny and to the favorable conditions facing them, including their relative religious freedom. Speaking to the Bahá'ís of nine states in the northeast United States, he promised that "[l]ikewise, the continent of America is, in the eyes of the one true God, the land wherein the splendors of His light shall be revealed, where the mysteries of His Faith shall be unveiled, where the righteous will abide and the free assemble. Therefore, every section thereof is blessed"[22]

Shoghi Effendi further explained the focus on North America. As he indicated, in the 1930s much of the world was torn by strife, particularly in Europe, Asia, and the Holy Land. He called the North American Bahá'ís "[t]he one chief remaining citadel, the mighty arm which still raises aloft the standard of an unconquerable Faith "This community had earned its station, moreover, "[b]y its works, and through the unfailing protection vouchsafed to it by an almighty Providence, this distinguished member of the body . . . bids fair to be universally regarded as the cradle, as well as the stronghold, of that future New World Order." He counseled anyone inclined "to either belittle the unique station conferred upon this community, or to question the role it will be called upon to play in the days to come," to consider the promises offered by his grandfather 'Abdu'l-Bahá, who had given such a special mandate to the North American Bahá'ís.[23] Shoghi Effendi then posed a remarkable series of rhetorical questions, asking "what other community" had fixed the pattern of the original Bahá'í administrative institutions, "what other community" had demonstrated with such consistency the determination and zeal necessary to erect these nascent institutions, "what other community has shown the foresight, the organizing ability, the enthusiastic eagerness" that the North American Bahá'í community showed in its "establishment and multiplication, throughout its territory," of the first schools of Bahá'í learning? He also praised the North American Bahá'ís for sending numerous pioneer families to other parts of the globe, providing funds and resources for the translation of Bahá'í materials into forty languages, and framing the first Bahá'í national and local constitutions. "Such a matchless and brilliant record of service," he indicated, made them the likeliest community to lay the groundwork for the further global expansion of the faith of Bahá'u'lláh.[24] Hence, their plans, among all the national plans, had first priority. This did not mean North Americans were in any sense superior by nature. Tempering this high praise, the North Americans knew, were an extensive number of other communications which warned against the flaws rampant in North American society, such as materialism, racism, and moral laxity. Shoghi Effendi presented the Bahá'ís' tasks as responsibilities, not privileges.[25]

North American Bahá'ís remained important in Shoghi Effendi's planning initiatives throughout his life. As Rúḥíyyih Rabbani indicates, "For twenty years, under the guidance of Shoghi Effendi, to a design he provided, the Bahá'ís wove the tapestry of the three great Crusades of his ministry."[26] The next passage indicates the importance of these "Crusades," and the essential role of the North American plans:

> With Shoghi Effendi everything was clear: there was The Plan, and then there were plans and plans! There were, after the inauguration of the first Seven Year Plan, in the course of many years, and in various parts of the world, a Nineteen Month, Two Year, Three Year, Forty-five Month, Four-and-a-Half Year, Five Year, Six Year and other plans; but whether given by him, or spontaneously initiated by the Bahá'ís themselves, he knew where to place them in the scheme of things. There was a God-given Mission, enshrined in a God-given Mandate, entrusted to the American believers; this Mission was their birthright, but they could only fulfill it by obeying the instructions given them in the Master's *Tablets of the Divine Plan* and winning every crusade they undertook: the other plans "are but supplements."[27]

The first Seven Year Plan referred to above was the first of the three crusades that Shoghi Effendi personally helped the North American believers to accomplish. In 1936, one year before the beginning of the first Seven Year Plan, Shoghi Effendi asked the North American Bahá'ís to create "[a] systematic, carefully conceived, and well-established plan," to be "rigorously pursued and continuously extended."[28] One year later he asked for a formal Seven Year Plan, based on the same objective he had suggested the year before, plus one more. The North Americans succeeded in accomplishing these objectives within the time frame of the plan. After a two-year interlude, he suggested a second Seven Year Plan, beginning in 1946 and associated with four objectives. In 1953, he launched a third global plan, the Ten Year Plan or Global Crusade, that delineated clear areas of responsibility for several national spiritual assemblies but gave the bulk of the work to the United States Bahá'ís.

The overall accomplishments were noteworthy. From 1921 to 1952, near the end of the second Seven Year Plan, the Bahá'í Faith was established in ninety-three new countries and territories, including several African, Asian, and South American nations. By that time, Bahá'í literature had been translated into seventy-one languages, and Shoghi Effendi proudly noted that at least thirty races were represented within the Bahá'í ranks, plus twelve African tribes.

TABLE 3.1
THREE KEY GLOBAL PLANS LED BY SHOGHI EFFENDI

PLAN	RESPONSIBLE NATIONAL SPIRITUAL ASSEMBLY
First Seven Year Plan (1937-1944)	American (United States and Canada)
Second Seven Year Plan (1946-1953)	American (United States and Canada)
Ten Year Plan (Global Crusade 1953-1963)	Twelve national spiritual assemblies (major responsibilities given to United States*)

NOTE: Shoghi Effendi also helped oversee many additional national plans, some of which had international implications.

* The National Spiritual Assembly of the Bahá'ís of the United States and Canada had divided into two separate national spiritual assemblies in 1948, as one of the objectives of the second Seven Year Plan, which aimed for the formation of three new national spiritual assemblies, including one in Canada.

By 1953, the Americans had completed building their first and holiest House of Worship and the nearby administrative headquarters of their national community. Bahá'ís lived all over the world, and several national spiritual assemblies were functioning at a high enough level to become part of the third plan. By the time the Ten Year Plan ended in

1963, the number of countries in which Bahá'ís lived had doubled, the number of languages into which literature had been printed had tripled, and the number of national spiritual assemblies had quadrupled, to a total of fifty-six.[29] Under the capable leadership of Shoghi Effendi, the Bahá'í community had become truly global.

It is in large part because of these accomplishments that Shoghi Effendi deserves to be called a "successful" planner, but other reasons indicate success as well. Three reasons stand out in particular. First of all, the Ten Year Plan, indeed the entire administrative structure of the Bahá'í Faith, survived Shoghi Effendi's 1957 death intact and without schism, which is testimony to his guidance and strong emphasis during his lifetime on community unity and cohesion. The plan proceeded from 1957 to 1963 without Shoghi Effendi, the last eligible descendant of Bahá'u'lláh to serve as Guardian of the Bahá'í Faith; other leaders arose who jointly oversaw the affairs of the global community but then humbly stepped aside with the first election of the nine-member Universal House of Justice in 1963.[30]

A second sign of success is the continued evolution of the physical development projects that were always a part of Shoghi Effendi's global plans. This is true not only in the national communities but also in the international community. The Universal House of Justice has continued to add to the improvements of the gardens, administrative headquarters, and sacred shrines. These are clustered on the slopes of Mt. Carmel in Haifa and on the plains near 'Akka, Israel, where Bahá'u'lláh is buried, near the prison city where he was last exiled from his homeland of Persia (now Iran).

The third and perhaps most telling indication of success is that the worldwide Bahá'í community has learned how to plan. Since the end of the Ten Year Plan in 1963, the community has continued to create and promulgate multiyear global plans, which strive to emulate the best principles of Shoghi Effendi's plans. Although the Universal House of Justice takes overall leadership and sets broad goals and time frameworks, the national and local communities create and implement thousands of plans for their own growth and development.[31] Furthermore, the planning process has become increasingly democratic and decentralized, with more authority and self-determination placed in the hands of national and local governing bodies. This has become a remarkably grand experiment: A global religious community plans, in synchronized multiyear phases, for its expansion, spiritual development, and administrative improvement. This is due to the planning leadership of 'Abdu'l-Bahá and Shoghi Effendi, and later the Universal House of Justice.

THE VISION OF SHOGHI EFFENDI

The vision Shoghi Effendi held of the Bahá'í community was a powerful one, for he foresaw this multinational and multiracial fresco, and worked diligently to complete its creation. The Bahá'í world has only begun to tap the true extent of his vision.

Shoghi Effendi's most basic vision was Bahá'u'lláh's vision of a world populated by spiritually mature individuals, governed by peaceful means, and characterized by unity and cooperation. Shoghi Effendi used this vision to motivate the widely dispersed followers of his religion. One of his most notable talents was his ability to offer, in a few paragraphs, a fresh and compelling portrait of Bahá'u'lláh's vision of a world civilization and then to refer to components of that vision in his everyday communications.

In March of 1936, one year before the first Seven Year Plan, Shoghi Effendi summarized the future of the world as envisioned by Bahá'u'lláh in the space of a few single-spaced pages (see summary on pages 13-14 above). The basis of all development was to be the spiritual improvement of human beings, through spiritual education and maturation, and through such means as acquiring human virtues. Also important was the vision of societal improvement, "the establishment of a world commonwealth in which all nations, races, creeds and classes are closely and permanently united," with a world tribunal, world legislature, world system of intercommunication, and world language. Bahá'u'lláh's divinely inspired vision also foresaw that national and racial rivalries and hatreds would cease, that a world metropolis would serve as the center of world civilization and radiate unifying guidance, and that the economic resources of the world would be in order and more evenly distributed.[32]

This was obviously an extremely powerful vision, one of a future world many years beyond the times of Bahá'u'lláh and Shoghi Effendi. This "big vision" served to guide all action, but Shoghi Effendi held up smaller visions before the community as well. For the North American Bahá'ís, chief promulgators of his global plans, the smaller vision was often quite simply the successful completion of their plans, or the fulfillment of the Divine Plan goals, or some point in the not-so-distant future when the current and future plans had been accomplished.

For example, *The Advent of Divine Justice* was a plan-related document in the sense that its major purpose was to prepare the North American believers to carry out the goals of the first Seven Year Plan. Written in 1938, it started with a vision that was more near-term than the "big vision" previously discussed:

> the possibilities of the future: The election of the International House of Justice and its establishment in the Holy Land . . . ; the gradual erection of the various dependencies of the First Mashriqu'l-Adhkár [House of Worship] of the West, and the intricate issues involving the establishment and the extension of the structural basis of Bahá'í community life; the codification and promulgation of the ordinances of the Most Holy Book, necessitating the formation, in certain countries of the East, of properly constituted and officially recognized courts of Bahá'í law . . .[33]

An even nearer-term example of visioning is a cable that Shoghi Effendi sent the North Americans in July, 1936, during the preparatory phase before the first global plan. "Founded on the unity and understanding so steadily achieved, functioning within the framework of the Administrative Order so laboriously erected, inspired by the vision of the Temple edifice so nobly reared," (referring to the House of Worship in Wilmette, Illinois, several years before anything other than the foundation had actually been built), "the American Bahá'í Community should rise as never before to the height of the opportunity now confronting it."[34] Thus, he was holding up a visionary image of the future completion of their magnificent House of Worship, which was to become one of the key objectives of their first Seven Year Plan.

The special mission of the North American Bahá'ís was part of the vision, since it was they who would usher in "that promised World Order, the shell ordained to enshrine that priceless jewel, the world civilization, of which the Faith itself is the sole begetter."[35] While acknowledging their impediments, including fewness of Bahá'ís and paucity of material resources, he praised them for being able to raise "in so short a time and in the course of such crucial years, an edifice that can well deserve to be regarded as the greatest contribution ever made by the West to the Cause of Bahá'u'lláh."[36] He also expressed absolute confidence in their ability to rise to their potential.

Thus, Shoghi Effendi's vision went beyond offering a vision of the future. He addressed the North American Bahá'ís as responsible for that vision. He also indicated that they had the capacity to succeed but that they would need to arise to carry out whatever was necessary. One of the most startling examples of this strong focus was one of the cables he sent in response to congratulations concerning his 1937 wedding: "Deeply touched. . . . Noblest contribution individual believers can make at this juncture to consecrate newly acquired tie is to promote with added fervour unique plan conceived for them by 'Abdu'l-Bahá."[37] Even his wedding, then, was an occasion to turn attention to the plan.

For Shoghi Effendi "vision" was not just an initial step taken at the beginning of the plan, but rather an ongoing theme used as a reminder at frequent intervals. This must have been a powerful tool for encouragement. In a letter written in April of 1938, Shoghi Effendi indicated that the Seven Year Plan "is in itself but an initial stage in the unfoldment of 'Abdu'l-Bahá's vision of America's spiritual destiny—a destiny which only those who will have successfully accomplished this preliminary task can enable the rising generation who will labor after them to fulfil in the course of the succeeding century."[38] In 1939, referring again to the Divine Plan, he assured them that "a fresh revelation of Divine light and strength will guide and propel it forward until it consummates, in the fulness of time and in the plenitude of its power, the Plan inseparably bound up with its shining destiny."[39] These are just two of many letters and cables in which Shoghi Effendi made brief, but effective and frequent, reference to the vision.

In his shorter letters and cables, three additional tendencies stand out that further reinforce this theme of the power of vision to motivate. He made the vision concrete through connecting it to the world at large, to the times in which they lived, or to the inspiring activities taking place in the Holy Land.

The context of world events was not so much a vision as a barometer, to ensure the Bahá'ís understood the importance of their actions when the world—sliding into yet another war—was falling down around them. One 1938 letter noted that "[t]he marked deterioration in world affairs, the steadily deepening gloom that envelops the storm-tossed peoples and nations of the Old World, invest the Seven Year Plan, now operating in both the northern and southern American continents, with a significance and urgency that cannot be overestimated."⁴⁰ In 1940, he cabled that

> [t]he long-predicted world-encircling conflagration, essential pre-requisite to world unification, is inexorably moving to its appointed climax. Its fires, first lit in the Far East, subsequently ravaging Europe and enveloping Africa, now threaten devastation both in Near East and Far West, respectively enshrining the World Center and the chief remaining Citadel of the Faith of Bahá'u'lláh. The Divinely-appointed Plan must and will likewise pursue undeflected its predestined course.⁴¹

Even after the war ended, Shoghi Effendi continued to talk about the world context, referring to such issues as the setbacks suffered with the United States's disengagement from the League of Nations, and the fortunate selection of New York as the headquarters for the United Nations.⁴² His usual approach was to indicate that twin processes were at work, one of disintegration and another of integration. On the one hand, destructive world events were evidence of the decline of the old ways of doing things, which were dysfunctional. On the other hand, the Bahá'ís were helping to build a new world civilization built upon the foundations of unity and justice.⁴³

Shoghi Effendi also very frequently referred to the context of time. It was as if he were keeping a calendar or chart of where his followers were in history and constantly reminding them of their location on the chart. This too served to offer a broader framework in which to operate and carry out the vision. He indicated that during the "Formative Age of the Faith," which was the multi-epoch period that followed the death of 'Abdu'l-Bahá and could last several centuries, multiple things will have been accomplished. Among the first, the Universal House of Justice will have been elected, but later "the Lesser Peace will have been established, the unity of mankind will have been achieved and its maturity attained, the Plan conceived by 'Abdu'l-Bahá will have been executed, the emancipation of the Faith from the fetters of religious orthodoxy will have been effected, and its independent religious status will have been universally recognized." Thereafter, following the Formative Age, would come "the Golden Age," when "the birth and efflorescence of a world civilization, the child of that Peace, will have conferred its inestimable blessings upon all mankind."⁴⁴

Thus Shoghi Effendi reminded the letter's readers that the purpose of the current and future global plans was no less than to contribute to "the efflorescence of a world civilization," which would assure the maturity of humanity. Throughout his letters, he constantly reminded his fellow believers of this vision. He thereby helped them realize the overall purpose of their work, as well as its importance.

Another vision-related strategy that followed naturally was for Shoghi Effendi to connect the Bahá'ís with events taking place in the Holy Land, at the center of their administrative order. Shoghi Effendi's intense enthusiasm for the development and expansion of the sacred places on and near Mt. Carmel was contagious.[45] In a region of the world characterized by desert temperatures, on the side of a mountain remarkable for its stony soil and lack of natural water, Shoghi Effendi's plans for shrines and formal gardens truly were visionary. Because these precincts were so sacred and because they also served as the site for the administrative headquarters of the Bahá'í Faith, Shoghi Effendi could point to their development as symbolic of the development of the Bahá'í Faith. He understood the importance of giving the Bahá'ís tangible and visible goals to accompany the more abstract areas of endeavor such as increasing the number of local spiritual assemblies. Here is one passage from a December 15, 1947, letter which clearly refers to the importance of such projects:

> Happy to announce completion of plans and specifications for erection of arcade surrounding the Báb's Sepulcher, constituting the first step in the process destined to culminate in construction of the dome anticipated by 'Abdu'l-Bahá and marking consummation of enterprise initiated by Him fifty years ago according to instructions given Him by Bahá'u'lláh.[46]

Many of the messages were shorter updates that gave specifics about the progress of construction, such as the announcement that "six hundred tons of stones destined for the arcade of the Báb's Shrine, received in successive shipments to the Holy Land, have been safely transported to its precincts despite repeated accidents."[47] The overall effect of these updates was to help Bahá'ís feel a part of the tremendous effort needed to carry out these projects and to offer them a tangible connection with the evolutionary progress of their young religion.

Table 3.2 below summarizes some of the points covered thus far. An additional theme—Shoghi Effendi's constant "caveats" or warnings that the Bahá'ís should not let the vision of a better world in the future obscure their resolve to act in the present—is listed at the bottom of Table 3.2. A 1939 letter indicated that it was "not ours to attempt, at the present moment, a survey of the distant scene, or to seek to visualize its glories, or to dwell on the consequences of the eventual attainment of an as yet far-off goal." It was, instead, the time to work hard to carry out the plan. In a 1947 letter written during the second global plan, immediately after a beautiful passage that described how their administrative order would evolve and their world move toward peace, he brought them back to the present day. "Not ours, however, to unriddle the workings of a distant future, or to dwell upon the promised glories of a God-impelled and unimaginably potent Revelation. Ours, rather, the task to cast our eyes upon, and bend our energies to meet, the challenging requirements of the present hour."[48]

TABLE 3.2
SHOGHI EFFENDI'S USE OF THE CONCEPT OF VISION

OVERALL CATEGORY	SHOGHI EFFENDI'S APPROACH
The Vision Defined	• Bahá'u'lláh's vision of world unity, peace, and prosperity • Visions of more near-term future accomplishments
Style of Referral	• References to the special mission of his readers • Summary but complete statements of the vision in longer letters • Constant referrals, in letters and cables, to shortened versions of the vision
Broader Context	• Context of world events • Context of time, ages, epochs • Context of the Holy Land
Caveat	• Warned not to dwell upon the vision, neglecting action; instead work for the vision through plan-related tasks

All of the points described thus far explain only a small part of the reason why Shoghi Effendi was able to tap into the power of vision. It is indeed true that he used several "techniques" that were effective, such as clarification of the broader vision, constant reminders, and referrals to context. This still does not completely explain why his fellow believers became committed to the vision he promoted. This commitment, while different than that shown by the slave army led by Spartacus who were willing to die for their vision, was in some cases of no less intensity. Commitment to the vision, that is, extended far beyond what could have been generated by any technique.

Several additional factors may have made a difference. First of all, Shoghi Effendi was expounding not only a noble vision but also one given quite clearly by a personage regarded by his religious community as their leader. Shoghi Effendi did not whimsically invent an image of a future world; rather, this vision was of sacred origin. Therefore, in some sense it was incumbent upon loyal fellow believers to adopt this vision as their own.

As Peter Senge pointed out in his book, however, obligatory visions have no power to generate true commitment, which must come from within the heart of each individual. Such commitment is only possible if people truly believe in the power of the vision, as well as love, respect, and admire the leader who enunciates it. This was certainly the case with 'Abdu'l-Bahá, whose exemplary personage inspired fierce loyalty and devotion. Part of Shoghi Effendi's power to lead people to the vision must have come not because of his "position" or "strategies," but because of his own personal qualities and his attempt to exemplify the virtues specified by his forebears as necessary for leadership. Ugo Giachery listed some of Shoghi Effendi's most outstanding personal virtues: his great faith, humility, selflessness, generosity, spiritual discipline, eagerness, and perseverance. Giachery offered convincing illustrations of the manifestations of each of these virtues in Shoghi Effendi's character.[49]

Consider as well the difference between Shoghi Effendi's conceptual framework and others from the same era. In the 1930s, the world was indeed being torn apart by strife, particularly nationalistic rivalry. Although "vision" was not unknown as a concept at the time, it was not commonly referred to in the management or corporate literature, as it is now by writers such as Senge and Nanus. The most publicized visions available in the world news were nationalistic, based on ascendancy of a race or people or nation over everyone else. In Hitler's Germany, the vision was of an ascendant Aryan race, dominant over Jews and taking its supposed place as leader of the world's peoples.

In contrast, Shoghi Effendi was holding up a vision of a world that was characterized by human beings who were spiritually well developed and who had undertaken purposeful reform of the human condition for all peoples. In this worldview, all nations and races would come together in peace and harmony. Although North America was singled out for leadership in bringing about this new world civilization, this was not a right by birth or race, but rather a privilege of circumstance and an opportunity to serve through constant sacrifice, travel, and focused development. Their special mission was not a license to rule over others, but rather an opportunity to serve them.

To motivate and inform Bahá'ís about this special privilege, Shoghi Effendi constantly reminded them of "the big picture." Understanding human nature, however, he also held out before them smaller visions of success that could be more easily attained. It was as if a master city planner were constantly holding up to his fellow workers the vision of a shining city upon a hill, characterized by love, peace, harmony, achievement, and beautiful buildings, a city that would possibly take generations to build. It was an article of faith that this city would emerge even though war raged around it and the time of its full emergence was far distant. While he continued to hold up this vision of the bigger city and to lay out its overall pattern of development, the planner also turned their attention to the one small section of the city and its gardens that could be constructed in their lifetimes, if they worked hard. That this section would help set the pattern for the city as a whole made their work of utmost importance.

Summary

Experts agree that being able to look to the future is an important step in the process of planning for social change. Diverse schools of thought offer competing definitions about what the planning process is or should be. Although "lists" from the professional planning literature indicate some overlap, they also show a lack of a completely shared understanding of this phenomenon. Yet advocates and scholars of the planning process who agree on little else do agree on the need to include "futurity," which means either a strong organizational vision, or goals, or at least a clear understanding of the mission and values of the groups involved. Many famous leaders would not have been able to succeed without compelling visions of a new and just society. How these leaders made these visions operational is somewhat of a mystery, however. How did Martin Luther King Jr. tap into his vision in order to lead and encourage his followers? How is it possible to make sure that leaders' visions are good ones, based on principles of individual freedom and global cooperation, as Laszlo suggests, or at least high ideals "widely shared," as Nanus suggests?

Shoghi Effendi was a natural leader, gifted with broad intellectual skills and a firm grounding in spiritual writings. He consistently operated in the context of a big picture that provided the framework for his endeavors; his widow refers to this as a "fresco" similar to that of the great Renaissance painters. As he began to help generate global plans, he followed a process that included several steps: building institutional capacity and gathering information, clarifying the vision, choosing goals and activities, monitoring implementation, and indicating subsequent action.

The three plans described here were important because they helped the Bahá'í community to become truly global, rather than confined merely to one region or to a few countries. They effectively strengthened the Bahá'í administrative order so that it survived Shoghi Effendi's death. The plans also set in motion physical development projects that have continued to the present, and they established a tradition of multi-year global plans. All of this evolved in the context of a breathtaking vision. The long-term vision of Bahá'u'lláh was one of a world protected from disunity and strife by a global governance system based on justice and equity. More limited visions held power as well, particularly those that brought to life the future accomplishments of the current plan. In numerous letters and cables, Shoghi Effendi referred to these visions and to his followers' special mission as part of an ongoing process that spurred activity and gave it meaning. He used several strategies that other "planners" might well consider as they encourage themselves and others to succeed with their plans. These strategies would suggest the following approaches:

- Remind participants in your plan of their special mission and station. Let them know, if this is indeed true, that they have the capacity necessary to carry out the objectives of the plan.

- Refer to the vision constantly and consciously, as a means of inspiration, throughout the implementation of your plan. "Visioning" was not a separate process for Shoghi Effendi. Although at the outset of the process of global planning he wrote communications that laid out a compelling vision, more notable was his tendency to make brief references to the overall vision throughout his communications about the plans, as a means of motivation and encouragement.
- Refer, if not to the context of world or national events or time, then to some other broad context of importance, to help people understand the potential and importance of their tasks and therefore succeed. Such referrals let the Bahá'ís of Shoghi Effendi's time see their role as valuable within the "big picture." These references helped them understand that the challenges they faced would indeed matter in the evolution of their religion and of the world.
- Link, if possible, the everyday activities of your plan with a visible symbol of progress. The extent to which this symbol embodies the hopes and dreams of the planning population may be the extent to which it has the power to motivate. The symbols that Shoghi Effendi chose most frequently were the sacred shrines and properties in the Holy Land, on and near Mt. Carmel. These projects tapped into the innermost yearnings of the Bahá'ís, whose efforts then became connected with the creation of sacred places of beauty and nobility.
- Remind everyone constantly that it will take work and purposeful effort to bring the vision into being. Do not allow the beauty of the vision, however, to suppress action.
- Exemplify the best qualities of visionary leadership, if you are in position to be a leader, whether as an individual or as a part of a group. Offer inspirational guidance toward the vision, but also strive to generate true commitment to that vision in the hearts of the wider community.

Chapter 4

From Goals to Action

> Promote ye the development of the cities of God and His Countries. . . . We have assigned to every end a means for its accomplishment; avail yourselves thereof, and place your trust and confidence in God, the Omniscient, the All-Wise.
> —Bahá'u'lláh, Kitáb-i-Aqdas

> At the outset of every endeavour, it is incumbent to look to the end of it.
> —Bahá'u'lláh, *Writings of Bahá'u'lláh*

> Some men and women glory in their exalted thoughts, but if these thoughts never reach the plane of action they remain useless: the power of thought is dependent on its manifestation in deeds.
> —'Abdu'l-Bahá, *Paris Talks*

IF VISION WERE ALL THAT WAS NECESSARY, if merely identifying our goals were enough to attain them, how perfect the world would be! It would be at peace, it would be conflict-free, it would be a paradise of social reforms. The same thing holds true for our visions of organizations, communities, and individuals. If wishful thinking were enough, everyone could rest and take it easy, for no work would be required. Often, the problem is not that we have no vision, but that we do not know how to reach our goals. Figuring out exactly what we want, in small enough increments to make sense but in large enough increments to make a difference, is hard enough.

Becoming sufficiently motivated, focused, and organized to do these things is even more challenging. Therefore, people everywhere wish for accelerated social progress but fail to make that happen.

This chapter's first epigraph from Bahá'u'lláh's writings commands humanity to promote development and promises the means to accomplish this noble endeavor. What are these means, and what exactly is the end? Many things are involved in the concepts of means and ends, more complicated and philosophical than can be addressed here. Some people debate whether good ends justify perfidious or dishonest means. When "means" refers to the principles underlying action, surely those who would argue that good ends justify bad or corrupt means are mistaken. The problem is that the issue of "good" or "bad" is not always at stake. In many planning contexts, the debate is not over the moral rectitude of the means; rather, it is over what strategies and actions to choose when a range of morally acceptable alternatives is possible.

Good leadership not only helps clarify the vision but also helps identify attainable goals and possible means, in the form of principled action, for reaching those goals. This is what has happened with several famous individual leaders whose efforts we intuitively admire. Mahatma Gandhi operated with a compelling vision of an India free of British colonial rule and able to make its own decisions. Gandhi articulated this vision well and was able to identify means for making it come true. He and his compatriots believed in several goals: dependence on simple means of production and consumption, political independence, and nobility of national character. He chose means, i.e., strategies and actions, which were adopted widely enough to make his efforts a social movement rather than an individual's eccentric protest. Some of these means included adoption of simple, non-Western clothing; efforts to create economically self-sufficient villages; and nonviolent resistance to the forces of the British military and police. All of these strategies had the power to help bring about the goals. The means and ends were so close, in fact, that they were basically the same thing.

Many people find it difficult to negotiate goals and means so successfully. It is not uncommon for groups or organizations to fail to identify adequately what they are aiming for, or to neglect to design effective strategies for reaching those aims, or to botch efforts to carry out their own strategies. Such problems can lead to plans that either remain unused or fail.

This chapter offers various writers' suggestions about the linkage between goals and action. A small sample of their comments provides back ground for examining the means that Shoghi Effendi employed to help the Bahá'ís surmount difficult obstacles to their plans. The simple but effective mechanisms he identified as necessary for successful implementation are much the same ingredients needed today to promote social progress.

FROM GOALS TO ACTION: PROFESSIONAL LITERATURE

Teachers of planning often recommend choosing general goals and more specific objectives as part of "the rational planning process." Sometimes this choice of goals happens after individuals or groups gather basic information about the phenomenon for which they are planning; in other instances, sufficient information is already known, and the immediate task is to develop a vision or to set goals and objectives toward which to work. However, choosing goals can be extremely difficult, and for some groups, it can be virtually impossible. Goal-setting may be difficult because people have trouble identifying appropriate targets to aim for, or because they are not used to the concepts of goals and objectives, or simply because they cannot agree on what they want to accomplish. For example, in a city where business owners, neighborhood groups, and city government officials suffer from strong disagreements and conflicts, it can be impossible to agree upon as simple a goal as what to aim for when improving a specific city area, even if the area is as small as a city block.

Author John Bryson warns that establishing goals within an organization requires "a fairly broad and deep agreement"[1] on the organization's direction. Goal-setting works best where the organization has an existing vision of success, a clear system of authority, and few "powerful stakeholders" pulling it in different directions. When these conditions do not exist, it might be simpler to skip over the concept of goal-making and return to it later. Some planning theorists reject the entire concept of rational goal making linked to planned action, suggesting instead a continual dialogue about change and action, or constant reflection and learning by practitioners.[2] However, if a group or groups can come together well enough, identifying goals can create a succinct framework for working toward implementing the vision. Both goals and objectives can help make it possible to reach the desired ends of a plan.[3]

Goals or objectives by themselves mean little or nothing without accompanying strategies or plans of action. Bryson defines a strategy as a pattern of "purposes, policies, programs, actions, decisions, and/or resource allocations" that defines what an organization is, what it does, and why it does it. This is no static process, where a strategy is put in place and then followed rigidly; instead, what happens "typically involves highlighting what is good about the existing pattern, reframing or downplaying what is bad about it, and adding whatever new bits are needed to complete the picture."[4] What emerges is a fluid process of assessing the effectiveness of action and then changing as necessary. Even though the process is fluid, nonetheless, laying out the strategy in the context of a plan is helpful. Among the benefits of strategy and plan development are emotional bonding to the new reality or vision, enhancement of organizational creativity, and the ability to offer "[a] fairly clear picture . . . —from grand conception to many implementation details—of how the organization can meet its mandates, fulfill its mission, and deal effectively with the situation it faces. This picture provides a measure of clarity about where an organization is going, how it will get there and why; this is an important part of most successful change efforts."[5]

This process all seems clear. For some reason, however, getting the plans to work, that is, getting through the stages of strategy making and implementation, has proven particularly difficult. This difficulty is so pervasive that an entire genre of books and articles has arisen about the problems encountered when trying to carry out plans. From the urban planning literature, one article indicates that various European nations have not been able to implement plans designed to improve urban regions. Translating the plan into action stalled in part because most professional urban planners are trained to produce a plan, but not to implement it. Many European regional strategic plans have become unworkable for this reason.[6]

Outside Europe, people also experience problems with implementation. Recently, a pair of authors reviewed twelve case studies demonstrating failure to implement public policy reforms, in places ranging from Jamaica to Indonesia. Noting that international agencies often assume that good analysis translates into good policy, the authors found instead that the connection between analysis of appropriate policy options "and their adoption cannot be assumed. Moreover, even after the decision to adopt a new policy is made, considerable evidence suggests the real work of turning reform into reality is still ahead." Because of such dilemmas, they found that "implementation is often the most crucial aspect of the policy process and that the outcomes of implementation efforts are highly variable." They give the example of an attempt by the World Bank to impose a particular pricing system on development projects in India that were designed to improve the urban water supply. Local bureaucrats refused to implement the new "water charges," however, because they knew the charges would be unpopular and unenforceable. And so the policy failed. (Or it failed appropriately, depending upon one's perspective.)[7]

Having plans imposed from the outside is not the only problem. The Indian experience shows that creating plans from the inside rather than the outside does not alone ensure their success. One of the most respected commentators on these national economic plans, the Indian economist Sukhamoy Chakravarty, offered his opinion about the mixed success of his nation's successive five-year plans. He noted that any plan which does not propose reasonable or feasible means for implementation cannot be successful:

> It has been widely held among observers of the Indian planning experience that Indian plans may be good on paper but are rarely good in implementation. This is a point of view which deserves serious consideration. What can this proposition mean? A simplistic interpretation is that while Indian plans project a desired state of affairs with some precision, and may also succeed in indicating directional changes that may be required in consonance with the objectives, they do not pay enough attention to issues of feasibility. If this is indeed the case, Indian plans cannot be good even on paper. Without question, a good plan must minimally attempt a proper appraisal of the feasibility of what it normatively postulates.[8]

Chakravarty pointed out that many reasons could explain a plan's failure to meet such aims as an increased growth rate for employment. Perhaps flawed information or erroneous models of thought underlay the thinking behind the plan, or coordination among different actors was simply faulty. Perhaps the agencies expected to carry out the plans did not have the capacity to do so. Any number of things could have gone wrong, but as far as possible these factors should have been anticipated.

A good plan should specify feasible actions and workable ways to carry out those actions. The literature on unimplemented plans, in a wide range of countries and localities, is extensive and potentially discouraging. Plans do succeed, and this is why people still use them. Less is known about successful plans, apparently because they are not as interesting to write about, and so they suffer from a lack of publicity. However, this cannot be the only problem—plans really can easily fail, in whole or in part, particularly if they have inappropriate goals, inadequate strategies for action, or inadequate assessment of the outside factors.

Shoghi Effendi's Use of Goals, Objectives, and Strategies

Shoghi Effendi's situation, compared with that of many of the planners listed earlier, had both disadvantages and advantages. His disadvantages included a widely dispersed worldwide community in the earliest stages of organizational development. Also challenging were his massive job responsibilities, since human resources were extremely limited at the religion's world headquarters. Shoghi Effendi's relative advantages included a community with absolute faith in his leadership, as well as personal faith in the vision and processes entrusted to him by Bahá'u'lláh and 'Abdu'l-Bahá. Shoghi Effendi operated under optimal conditions for cohesive goals. These conditions included a widely shared vision, organizational self-discipline, authority granted to him by the founders of his religion to carry out a divinely inspired mission, and fellow believers who followed his guidance not just because of duty but also because of genuine respect for his dedication, talents, and virtues.

Shoghi Effendi held a unique position. He was "chosen" as leader in 'Abdu'l-Bahá's last will and testament, in part on the basis of the fact that Shoghi Effendi was a direct descendant, but also because of the young man's superior capacities. In addition, the Bahá'í writings indicated that eventually global leadership was to be shared with the Universal House of Justice, once this body of nine members was elected from the worldwide community. Until this body could be brought into being, however, an unusual amount of decision making rested on Shoghi Effendi's shoulders.

He was obliged to exemplify the requirements for good leadership, such as wisdom, self-examination and self-discipline, knowledge of conditions in regions of responsibility, and consultation. Many of the ways he exercised that leadership, furthermore, could easily apply to both religious and secular contexts. For example, Shoghi Effendi resided in a then fairly remote part of the world and did not travel extensively. He never even visited North America, yet he was able to overcome these barriers and still gather information and consult with his community. The consultation came not so much through taking no step without the approval of "constituents," which is the misguided concept of "leadership" that public polling surveys have given some modern political leaders, nor through authoritarianism, which is the opposite extreme. Rather, he made decisions according to his own conscience, his study of related guidance, and his perspective on the "whole picture." Shoghi Effendi set the pace, gave the broad guidelines or goals, and then entered into extensive dialogue about the nature of these guidelines and how to apply them. He evidently talked about these plans and activities with the steady stream of visitors to the Holy Land, with whom he established "the example of free and open consultation."[9]

Chapter three listed information gathering as an important component of Shoghi Effendi's "planning process," along with institution building. This information gathering was part of his inquiry into the conditions of his charges, one of the principles of good leadership and a part of his style of consultation. Shoghi Effendi's extensive correspondence with the Bahá'ís around the world began soon after he assumed leadership of the worldwide community. In 1922, he asked all North American local spiritual assemblies to send him a detailed report of their activities, "the character and organization of their respective assemblies, accounts of their public and private gatherings, of the actual position of the Cause in their provinces and of their plans and arrangements for the future."[10] He made similar requests of other national groups, ranging from Germany to Australia.

While it is not clear that he kept up the system of receiving reports and plans from all local spiritual assemblies, he did maintain correspondence with all the national spiritual assemblies, as well as some of their committees. Shoghi Effendi also corresponded with thousands of individuals and local communities. Many of those letters are preserved in various archives, books, and compilations. This voluminous correspondence gave Shoghi Effendi an intimate understanding of his widely dispersed community's needs and assets. When, in the mid-1930s, he began to suggest specific objectives and strategies for the North American community to help them carry forth the Divine Plan outlined in 'Abdu'l-Bahá's *Tablets of the Divine Plan*, that community benefited from considerable prior preparation. The value of that preparation showed in Shoghi Effendi's suggestions for each of the three global plans and in his suggestions for additional national plans in various places besides North America.

J. Jameson Bond, an anthropologist who, with his equally dedicated wife, Kathleen Gale Bond, moved to the Canadian Arctic Islands to help meet the goals of the Ten Year Plan, has explained the importance of Shoghi Effendi's letters about the plans:

> One of the qualities of a great general is the capacity to motivate the troops under command to achieve heroic levels of service. Shoghi Effendi demonstrated this capacity in a number of different ways. One of the most important ways lay in his skill as a master communicator. His messages to the friends appealed to both the mind and the heart. Closely reasoned explanations set in penetrating, analytic language clarified objectives, processes, and priorities for the friends.[11]

The communications from Shoghi Effendi aimed at the heart but also stimulated the mind with penetrating writing and analytical thinking. These missives laid the groundwork for Shoghi Effendi to identify inspiring objectives that people could understand and adopt.

The first objective[12] for the first Seven Year Plan, cabled to the North American annual convention in 1936 (a year before the plan started), was stunning in its simplicity: "Would to God every State within American Republic and every Republic in American continent might ere termination of this glorious century[13] embrace the light of the Faith of Bahá'u'lláh and establish structural basis of His World Order." This request for North American Bahá'ís to settle, by the end of the plan, in every state in the United States and in every country on their continent where no Bahá'ís lived, had an immediate impact. The convention delegates, chosen by their home communities to attend the annual convocation, embraced Shoghi Effendi's vision as their own and entered an extensive consultation about the implications of this request.[14]

A follow-up letter from Shoghi Effendi dated May 30th emphasized the "supreme immediate objective should be the permanent establishment of at least one center in every state of the American Republic and in every Republic of the American continent not yet enlisted under the banner of His Faith." That letter went on to talk about the need to extend efforts gradually to Europe, and so it might have seemed that Europe was part of the plan's goals.[15] The message to the 1937 convention first referred to a Seven Year Plan and as a second major objective added the need to complete the exterior ornamentation of the House of Worship in Wilmette, Illinois. After back-and-forth communications between Shoghi Effendi and the national spiritual assembly, it gradually become clear that the objectives were separate and that these were largely confined to North and South America and to the House of Worship. The expansion objective widened the boundaries of the Bahá'í community's "territory" in accordance with the boundaries of their continent, and the construction objective offered a tangible product. Both objectives would certainly be easy to measure. At the end of the Seven Year Plan, either Bahá'ís would reside in every state in the United States and every country in North, Central, and South America, or they would not. Either the exterior ornamentation of the House of Worship would be completed, or it would not.

To complete the exterior ornamentation of the House of Worship being built in Wilmette, Illinois, was no small feat. The building was not to be used only for local worship services; it was to be the "mother temple of the West," the holiest House of Worship among many to be built around the world. Although the foundation hall upon which the exterior would rest was in place, that unique ornamentation required entirely new ways of casting and placing concrete panels, which were to appear perforated almost as delicately as if they were handcarved "lace."

Understandably, for a time the correspondence from the national spiritual assembly to Shoghi Effendi was filled with questions concerning his advice about carrying out this difficult construction job. Finally, Shoghi Effendi pointedly began to refer to the "twofold" plan. Hence, a June 4, 1937, letter from his secretary reminded them of the "twofold plan of completing the ornamentation of the Temple, and of establishing the Faith in every State within the American continent." A postscript in Shoghi Effendi's handwriting mentioned the "twofold task" yet again, and an August cable referred to the first stage of their "dual task."[16] In these ways, Shoghi Effendi brought their attention to the fact that they had two major objectives and were not to neglect one for the sake of the other, even though the details of constructing the outer dome of the House of Worship must have seemed all-consuming. They responded positively; a 1938 letter from the assembly secretary indicates that at a recent meeting "[t]he most serious consideration was also given to the matter of teaching plans and policies." Furthermore, "[t]here is no doubt but that the significance of your messages to the N.S.A. and to the Convention will become more apparent as they are continuously studied by the members and by the believers in general."[17]

Shoghi Effendi's April, 1946, letter listed a suggested first set of objectives for the second Seven Year Plan. For that plan, he asked the North Americans to:

1. Consolidate victories already won, by multiplying the number of Bahá'í centers and more boldly proclaiming the Bahá'í Faith;
2. Complete the interior ornamentation of the House of Worship;
3. Form three national spiritual assemblies, in Canada, Central America, and South America;
4. Initiate a systematic teaching activity in war-torn Europe, aimed at establishing assemblies in the Iberian Peninsula, the Low Countries, Scandinavia, and Italy.[18]

But this list needed adjustment as well. Thus, in a cable sent two months later, he offered a set of strategies that were strong enough to be, in fact, new objectives. He asked the national teaching committee, an arm of the national spiritual assembly, to "enable thirty groups having six or more members speedily attain Assembly status," which could be gained with nine adult members each. Furthermore, he noted that he was "[d]evoutly praying number of Assemblies functioning in North America will reach one hundred and seventy-five ere expiry of second year of second stage of Divine Plan."[19]

This second Seven Year Plan is the only plan of the three for which he suggested objectives for the next plan just before the last plan ended. The third plan, for ten years, was the culmination of his global planning efforts, since it involved coordinating the activities of twelve separate national spiritual assemblies. The four objectives, therefore, were particularly global in scope. These were, according to a cable sent in October, 1952:

1. Development of the institutions at the World Centre, in the Holy Land;
2. Consolidation of the twelve territories to serve as administrative bases for the operation of the twelve national plans;
3. Consolidation of all new territories already opened to the Bahá'í Faith;

4. Opening of the remaining chief virgin territories on the planet, via allotments to each of the functioning national spiritual assemblies.[20]

These objectives offered a general picture of global aims for the Bahá'í Faith. Shoghi Effendi had much more specific duties in mind for each national community. Evidently confident in the Bahá'í of the United States, he gave them a total of twenty-four tasks for their share of the Ten Year Plan. Here is a part of his summary of these tasks:

1. To create nuclei of future assemblies in eleven territories and islands of Africa, eight of Asia, six of Europe, and four of America;
2. To start to build the dependencies [associated institutions] of the House of Worship in Wilmette, and complete its landscaping;
3. To consolidate administration in twenty-three territories and islands in four continents;
4. To assist in the development of thirty-six "pillars" of national spiritual assemblies, including twenty in Latin America, twelve in Europe, two in Asia, one in North America, and one in Africa;
5. To help finance land acquisition for four Houses of Worship, two in Europe, one in Africa, and one in Central America;
6. To establish 300 local spiritual assemblies and 100 incorporated local spiritual assemblies in America, as well as found a publishing trust and make greater use of the press and radio;
7. To enroll members of the Indian, Basque, and Gypsy races; to translate writings into twenty languages; to help consolidate eight European goal countries via local incorporations, as well as quadruple their number of local assemblies and treble the number of local centers in each one.[21]

Again he was careful to explain the importance of these tasks, making it clear that the most important task was for Bahá'ís to move to territories around the globe where no Bahá'ís yet lived. The response of the community was wholehearted; many left comfortable jobs and homes, and moved to distant, often inhospitable states and countries. True leaders by example and not just words, several members of the United States National Spiritual Assembly resigned their positions and left as well.

The beauty and power of these objectives shines forth. These objectives and tasks were all truly challenging, but they were also attainable, simple, and easy to grasp. They allowed the community members to picture themselves taking appropriate and purposeful multiyear leaps, such as finishing the exterior of the Wilmette House of Worship (first plan), then the interior (second plan), then the gardens and auxiliary buildings (third plan). In the objectives requiring them to spread outward, they were first supposed to send people to every state and country in their continent (the first plan), then specific areas of war-torn Europe (the second), and then four continents and many additional countries of the world (the third). For each of the three plans, the over-all number of objectives was limited to a manageable three or four; only with their third plan and after considerable planning experience were the Americans given a more complex list of twenty-four tasks.

With each of these three global plans, almost all of the objectives were essentially won by the time the plan ended. All of the objectives were won for the first two plans, and all objectives were accomplished during the Ten Year Plan except for those affected by unavoidable circumstances, such as political barriers to immigration into certain "closed" territories. This record of achievement is remarkable considering the small size of the North American Bahá'í community, custodians of the first two global plans and prime actors in the third. That community, for the first Seven Year Plan, scrambled to send members to each state in the United States. For the second Seven Year Plan, it had to strive hard to get at least 175 local spiritual assemblies established throughout North America. But time and time again, Shoghi Effendi was able to encourage, convince, and compel them to complete their tasks successfully. Somehow, he set the levels of the objectives so that they required considerable effort, yet were not impossible to accomplish. How was this possible?

One way he did so was himself to demonstrate the powers of concentration and careful planning. According to his widow, Shoghi Effendi was able to carry out his enormous responsibilities "by practising intense concentration and by the efficient use of highly focussed energy. Because of the great sense of urgency that impelled him and his awareness of the irretrievable opportunities of each passing hour, she likened his concentration to the action of a blowtorch. Perhaps the best measure of a leader is the example of his own life."[22] It requires considerable concentration to think through the implications of plans. Shoghi Effendi did not merely specify what objectives needed to be won; he suggested ways for the Bahá'ís to accomplish them. What we have seen in some quotations was his tendency to offer helpful strategies for success, but he also provided guidance by suggesting standards of success. Together, these two broad categories gave the Bahá'ís much-needed direction and guidance.

An early example is particularly striking. The first plan included calls to send forth "pioneers," the term used to describe people willing to settle elsewhere (with their own financial support) to begin to build new Bahá'í communities, as well as specific instructions for the national bodies responsible for rallying the people to prosecute the plan. Here are strategies suggested in a letter written two years after the first plan had begun:

> Whether through the frequency of their visits, the warmth of their correspondence, the liberality of their support, the wisdom of their counsels, the choice of the literature placed at the disposal of the pioneers, the members of the community should, at this hour when the sands of a moribund civilization are inexorably running out, and at a time when they are preparing themselves to launch yet another stage in their teaching activities, insure the security and provide for the steady expansion, of the work initiated in those territories so recently set alight from the torch of an inextinguishable Faith.[23]

Pause here to consider the remarkable warmth and spiritual insight that this passage offers, since it is no mere list of dry strategies, but rather a luminous lesson in encouragement. Noteworthy are the stirring tones and spiritually insightful suggestions, which indicate, for example, that wise counsel and liberal support of the pioneers were important keys to success. Here, Shoghi Effendi illustrated the fine touch with which he handled the substance of strategies.

Evidence of his capabilities in this area are apparent throughout all of the global plans. Here is another example, from a letter written in 1946, with strategies emphasized:

> Through the prompt settlement of nine wholly dedicated souls, aglow with enthusiasm and keenly aware of the plight of the peoples for whose sake they are abandoning the comfort and security of their homeland . . . ; through the dispatch of itinerant

teachers who, either delegated by the American National Spiritual Assembly or of their own accord, will cross and re-cross the vast distances, now providentially shrunk, which separate the old and new worlds, who will assiduously water the seeds sown by these pioneers, consolidate the work already started by isolated believers, and act as intermediaries between the various groups . . . ; through the vigorous dissemination of literature, properly translated, promptly printed, and comprehensive in range, in French, Italian, Spanish, Portuguese, German, and Dutch and each of the Scandinavian languages; through a steady process of concentration on a few receptive souls, who can be relied upon to embrace, wholeheartedly and with alacrity, the truth of the Faith, identify themselves unreservedly with its tenets, actively support its institutions, and join in forming its initial Assemblies.[24]

Again we see the hand of a person who understands not only effective strategy but also the high standards necessary. Another important point to notice about these strategies is that Shoghi Effendi left little to chance. He instructed the Americans in several aspects of their duties, and the instructions were quite extensive. Here are some excerpts, set in a string of clusters to make them easier to read:

the enterprise associated with the completion of the first [House of Worship] of the West . . . must be strenuously pushed forward. . . . The necessary modifications of the design chosen for its interior ornamentation should be adopted, the plans and specifications prepared, the preliminary contracts for its execution placed, and actual construction work started, if possible, ere the expiry of the present year.

The utmost effort by the National Teaching Committee and its auxiliary Regional Teaching Committees, aimed at raising the number of spiritual assemblies in the North American continent to no less than one hundred and seventy-five . . . should be exerted. The eighty cities newly opened to the Faith should, likewise, be reinforced. The two hundred and eighteen groups already constituted should be continually encouraged to evolve into assemblies, while the vast number of localities, totalling over nine hundred, where isolated believers reside, should . . . be enabled to attain group status. . . .

... a resolute attempt should be made by the national elected representatives of the entire community, aided by their Public Relations, Race Unity, Public Meetings, Visual Education, College Speakers Bureau and Radio Committees, to reinforce the measures already adopted for the proclamation. ...

National advertising and publicity should be further developed, the contact with seven hundred and fifty newspapers, magazines and trade papers should be maintained and the public relations programs amplified.[25]

The list continues and includes the need to establish local endowment funds, to develop the summer schools further, and to expand publications. He then turned to tasks directed specifically to the Alaskan, Canadian, Latin American, and European initiatives.

These passages illustrate how thoroughly Shoghi Effendi advised the Bahá'ís about how they could succeed with the objectives of their plans. Based on a firm understanding of what they had accomplished in the first global plan and what institutions or committees existed (some of which he had suggested forming) to help carry out the work, he was able to give clear and compelling suggestions about what to do next.

The important tasks were not to be accomplished in a mechanical manner or with half-hearted desire for success. He counseled that the quality of interaction and support be the warmest, most loving, most genuine possible. He was also sensitive to issues such as self-determination and lack of domination by non-native pioneers. For the second Seven Year Plan, the fourth objective was to launch a systematic teaching campaign in ten countries of war-torn Europe. Shoghi Effendi wanted the Americans to go as pioneers to Europe to help get this started but not to take over or to perceive their mere presence as meeting the objective. He instructed them in how to make their presence most effective and most respectful of the native population:

The ten countries ... must each evolve into strongholds from which the dynamic energies of that Faith can be diffused to neighboring territories in the course of the unfoldment of the Plan. The nuclei that are now being formed, and the groups that are beginning to emerge, must be speedily and systematically reinforced, not only through the dispatch and settlement of pioneers and the visits paid them by itinerant teachers, but also through the progressive development of the teaching work . . . among the native population in those countries. Any artificially created assembly, consisting of settlers from abroad, can at best be considered as temporary and insecure, and should . . . be supplanted by broad-based, securely grounded, efficiently functioning assemblies, composed primarily of the people of the countries themselves.[26]

Such passages have enormous implications. They suggest that planners should consider giving much more attention to detail, to the means of implementation, and to the quality of that implementation, than is now customary. Here was a set of directions developed far beyond the mere recitation of objectives. How was Shoghi Effendi able to convince people to carry out these most difficult assignments? What gave him the ability to specify strategies with such power and confidence and then to point out what standards of success were expected?

We have already indicated that clear vision, assiduous information gathering, keen insight, and mental discipline helped Shoghi Effendi identify objectives and strategies appropriate to his audience. However, these were not the only ways that Shoghi Effendi was able to motivate his fellow believers to succeed in carrying out these very difficult plans. Although one cannot completely dissect Shoghi Effendi's natural abilities to motivate and lead, the next two sections describe some of these ways.

TABLE 4.1
MOVING FROM GOALS TO ACTION: OBJECTIVES AND STRATEGIES

OVERALL CATEGORY	SHOGHI EFFENDI'S APPROACH
Objectives	• Received and processed information (correspondence) necessary to understand the circumstances
	• Based on that information, identified clearly understandable objectives, appropriate to the implementing population
	• Added or clarified objectives as appropriate
Strategies	• He himself demonstrated powers of concentration and careful planning
	• Specified strategies for success of the objectives, based on information about current status of implementing population
	• Specified standards for success, based in large part on spiritual principles

Levels of Responsibility

Something often missing from regular plans in both religious and nonreligious contexts is clarity about varying levels of responsibility. Surprising as it might sound, many plans fail to succeed because it is not clear who is supposed to carry them out, or because those who are supposed to carry out specific tasks do not receive resources or suggestions about what to do and how to do it.

Clarify Roles. In contrast, Shoghi Effendi used his plan-related letters to help clarify who was responsible for the success of the plans. He encouraged the maturation and evolution of two main audiences. The first audience was made up of the institutions associated with Bahá'í administration and their various committees and task forces. Continuing the process he had begun long before the plan, he suggested what kinds of activities and initiatives they should undertake. In *The Advent of Divine Justice*, he explained the importance of "rectitude of conduct" as a broad rubric for the overall principles that must govern their work. This explanation confirmed that values do count and that the means of moral conduct are even more important than the ends of plan accomplishment:

> Such a rectitude of conduct must manifest itself, with ever-increasing potency, in every verdict which the elected representatives of the Bahá'í community, in whatever capacity they may find themselves, may be called upon to pronounce.
> ... It must be made the hallmark of that numerically small, yet intensely dynamic and highly responsible body of the elected national representatives of every Bahá'í community, which constitutes the sustaining pillar, and the sole instrument for the election, in every community, of that Universal House.[27]

The responsibilities and processes of the institutions were in fact a common theme. In another 1938 letter, he suggested that the local spiritual assemblies were responsible for admitting new believers into the community and that with each one they should try, "by their patience, their love, their tact and wisdom to nurse, subsequent to his admission, the new comer into Bahá'í maturity, and win him over gradually to the unreserved acceptance of whatever has been ordained in the teachings." As for the national spiritual assembly, its "responsibility is to guard the integrity, coordinate the activities, and stimulate the life, of the entire community," and also to "anxiously deliberate on how best to enable both individual believers and local Assemblies to fulfil their respective tasks."[28]

Encourage the Individual. While all of these specific suggestions surely helped encourage appropriate institutional behavior, the truly remarkable aspect of Shoghi Effendi's discussions of responsibilities is the obvious emphasis he placed upon personal behavior. Unlike many "secular" plans, when plan makers are content to name the various institutions and their roles, if they go that far, Shoghi Effendi (and, before him, 'Abdu'l-Bahá) explained that all activities depended upon mature and motivated individuals. Thus, he devoted much time and energy to talking directly to the audience of individuals who made up the Bahá'í community and provided the human resources necessary to carry out the plans. In the passages aimed toward individual action, he counseled spiritual growth and development, exemplary lifestyles, freedom from prejudice, and other personal qualities. He also offered practical advice about how individuals could help with the success of the plan.

The most important components of *The Advent of Divine Justice*, for example, are suggestions addressed to individual Bahá'ís, particularly those who might travel to South America. Most of the passages referring to "rectitude of conduct" relate to the importance of good conduct for individuals rather than for institutions. In addition to rectitude of conduct, Shoghi Effendi indicated that two more qualities were essential if North Americans truly desired a successful plan. These two qualities, chastity and freedom from racial prejudice, lay largely in the domain of the individual. Shoghi Effendi explained that the individuals could succeed (the "end") only if they lived exemplary lives (the "means"). Personal chastity was an important factor that would "contribute its proper share to the strengthening and vitalization of the Bahá'í community, upon which must in turn depend the success of any Bahá'í plan or enterprise." All men and women must "pause to examine themselves, scrutinize their conduct, and with characteristic resolution arise to purge the life of their community of every trace of moral laxity that might stain the name, or impair the integrity, of so holy and precious a Faith."[29]

Freedom from racial prejudice very likely had not previously been associated with the requirements for the success of a multiyear plan. It was a very prominent component of Shoghi Effendi's advice because he knew that racism threatened the very fabric of North American society. In a religion that so highly valued diversity of nationality and race, particularly in a region of the world where race so thoroughly divided people, prejudice was a significant barrier to community unity and therefore to community growth. He indicated that "[f]reedom from racial prejudice, in any of its forms, should, at such a time as this when an increasingly large section of the human race is falling a victim to its devastating ferocity, be adopted as the watchword of the entire body of the American believers, in whichever state they reside, in whatever circles they move, whatever their age, traditions, tastes, and habits." He then went on to make several specific recommendations about how to overcome the lingering effects of prejudice within the Bahá'í community.[30]

The remainder of this masterful book-length letter went on to identify specific strategies for those who traveled to foreign lands. These strategies included learning the fundamentals of their own religious principles, mastering the languages of the populations they would visit, approaching new people via several avenues of approach, paying particular attention to contacting racial minorities, and forming first small local groups and then national spiritual assemblies. Other passages talked about the roles of youth and of women. By the end of the letter, he had created a virtual spiritual handbook for the individual's role in the successful execution of the global plans.

As was the case with his statements of vision, Shoghi Effendi was not content to state the role of the individual once and leave it at that. Throughout his letters and notations for the next twenty years, he constantly returned to the themes of the important role of individual standards of personal conduct and spiritual development, as well as the role of wellfunctioning, morally based institutions. During the first global plan, he counseled the North Americans to demonstrate the truth of their message "[t]hrough the clearness and steadiness of their vision, through the unvitiated vitality of their belief, through the incorruptibility of their character"[31] In similar phrasing used in a subsequent letter, he called for them to triumph "[b]y the sublimity and serenity of their faith, by the steadiness and clarity of their vision, the incorruptibility of their character, the rigor of their discipline, the sanctity of their morals, and the unique example of their community life."[32]

Individual spiritual development was not an abstract, internal process divorced from the need for positive action. Shoghi Effendi continued to call upon the individual to arise and assure the success of the plans:

> This challenge [Ten Year Plan], so severe and insistent, and yet so glorious, faces no doubt primarily the individual believer on whom, in the last resort, depends the fate of the entire community. He it is who constitutes the warp and woof on which the quality and pattern of the whole fabric must depend. He it is who acts as one of the countless links in the mighty chain that now girdles the globe. He it is who serves as one of the multitude of bricks which support the structure and insure the stability of the administrative edifice now being raised in every part of the world. Without his support, at once whole hearted, continuous and generous, every measure adopted, and every plan formulated, by the body which acts as the national representative of the community to which he belongs, is foredoomed to failure.

He then went on to address a target audience in words and phrases that were certain to get a reaction:

> It is therefore imperative for the individual American believer, and particularly for the affluent, the independent, the comfort-loving and those obsessed by material pursuits, to step forward, and dedicate their resources, their time, their very lives to a Cause of such transcendence that no human eye can even dimly perceive its glory. Let them resolve, instantly and unhesitatingly, to place, each according to his circumstances, his share on the altar of Bahá'í sacrifice . . .[33]

No wonder the global plans succeeded. The numbers of people involved were few, but even if just a portion took these letters to heart, each individual member of that portion felt responsible for increasing personal capacity through spiritual growth and development, and for arising to help these audacious plans to succeed, committing both themselves and their other resources. Therefore, the power of their small numbers was multiplied.

SPECIAL TECHNIQUES OF ENCOURAGEMENT

Shoghi Effendi also motivated people to succeed with the plans in several additional ways. It is this key issue of motivation that is most glaringly missing from much of the existing literature on planning. How is it possible to motivate people to proceed to carry out the vision of the plan? Although it is difficult to capture the essence of Shoghi Effendi's process, it is possible to continue to explore his technique by reading and rereading his plan related letters and postscripts, classifying various paragraphs and sentences, and trying to discern patterns. Several key patterns emerge.

Evoking Divine Guidance. The original source of inspiration for all of these letters and exhortations, and indeed for all of these efforts, was Shoghi Effendi's belief that he and the community were following the pathway of God's guidance. Frequently, Shoghi Effendi reminded his charges of the importance of divine guidance and support for their efforts from the realms on high, reinforced by the quintessential guidance offered by the Báb, Bahá'u'lláh, and 'Abdu'l-Bahá. Therefore, Shoghi Effendi often linked his references to the spiritual origins of the change they were promoting with the Divine Plan. This took the plan out of the realm of the mortal—where it was at the mercy of human frailty and mishap—and placed it in the realm of the immortal, where all things were possible.

Near the beginning of the first Seven Year Plan, in 1939, the same year that World War II began, Shoghi Effendi indicated that they were moving toward a "divinely-appointed goal." He stated that "[t]he stage is set. The firm and irrevocable Promise is given. God's own Plan has been set in motion. It is gathering momentum with every passing day. The powers of heaven and earth mysteriously assist in its execution. Such an opportunity is irreplaceable."[34]

In the same year, he offered much the same assurance: "As the days roll by, as the perturbations of an imperiled civilization are more alarmingly manifested, the potentialities of God's creative Plan correspondingly unfold." Moreover, he promised, with every successful effort, they would gain "a fuller measure of celestial strength."[35] Shoghi Effendi made similar references throughout all of the global plans, as he encouraged Bahá'ís to think of their efforts in the context of divine support for their Plan.

This God-centered path is probably difficult for the reader to emulate if he or she is not involved in a spiritually motivated planning endeavor and is not convinced of the role of divine guidance in that endeavor, or even in everyday human affairs. This is all the more reason to acknowledge that Shoghi Effendi was a religious leader and that the recognition of divinity, and its role in plans, must surely provide an assurance and certainty of purpose that would be otherwise hard to match. Shoghi Effendi felt comfortable assuring the North Americans that God's guidance was an important ingredient for their success. This is no more than a repetition of the approach so masterfully used by 'Abdu'l-Bahá, who integrated prayer and spiritual exhortations into so many of his plan-related letters.

Reference to Heroes and Heroines. Another pattern evident throughout these letters is Shoghi Effendi's reference to examples of valor and courage by the heroes and heroines of the Bahá'í Faith. This approach was bound to encourage, because it tugged at the heartstrings of all of those who remembered the tremendous sacrifices their spiritual ancestors endured for the sake of spreading their religion. This association also elevated their current plan out of the realm of the mortal and mundane.

Speaking to those who had traveled to Latin America and to those Latin American recruits to the Bahá'í Faith, Shoghi Effendi noted "theirs is the opportunity, if they but seize it, to adorn the opening pages of the annals of the second Bahá'í century with a tale of deeds approaching in valor those with which their Persian brethren have illuminated the opening years of the first, and comparable with the exploits more recently achieved by their North American fellow-believers."[36] Yet another letter urged the American believers to emulate "exploits of their spiritual progenitors, the dawn-breakers of the Heroic Age, which immortalized the dawn of the first Bahá'í century."[37]

He placed even completion of the House of Worship in a noble context. In a 1949 letter, Shoghi Effendi named several people that Bahá'ís would recognize as having died during the violent persecutions that so characterized the early years of their religion in the mid-1800s:

> No lesser tribute can be paid the memory of the glorious Báb, the immortal Quddús, the lion-hearted Mullá Ḥusayn, the erudite Vaḥíd, the audacious Ḥujjat, the illustrious seven martyrs of Ṭihrán and a host of unnumbered heroes whose lifeblood flowed so copiously in the course of the opening decade of the first Bahá'í century, by the privileged champion-builders of the World Order of Bahá'u'lláh during . . . His Dispensation, than a parallel outpouring of their substance by the builders of the most holy House of Worship.[38]

In a passage that was bound to move all but the hardest of hearts, with its image of a blood-soaked torch, he called for the American believers

> to rededicate themselves and resolve, no matter how great the perils confronting their sister communities on the European, Asiatic, African and Australian continents, however somber the situation facing both the cradle of the Faith and its World Center, however grievous the vicissitudes they themselves may eventually suffer, to hold aloft unflinchingly the torch of the Faith impregnated with the blood of innumerable martyrs and transmit it unimpaired so that it may add luster to future generations destined to labor after them.[39]

These passages reconfirm the importance of plans that help meet noble ends. Certainly, it would make little sense to make such powerful evocations for the sake of minor or frivolous or ignoble causes. Those involved in the successful prosecution of noble plans must constantly acknowledge that they owe much to the sacrifices of those who have gone before, that is, to local heroes and heroines, in the secular world as well as the religious. Shoghi Effendi did not allow the deceptively "ordinary" nature of many of the Bahá'ís' tasks—such as raising money to build a House of Worship—to diminish their importance. The tasks were not, after all, ordinary; they were this era's version of heroism in fulfilling a divinely inspired mission. Their success was, he signaled, of paramount importance.

Issuing Inspiring Calls to Action. Shoghi Effendi's letters contained numerous inspiring calls to action. This is something that might seem obvious but is not. One would think that for leaders to help plans succeed, they would have to exhort their followers to succeed. At the very least, near the beginning of a plan, one would expect stirring calls of encouragement, referring to the importance of winning the goals set before the group. On the contrary, in many circumstances people mistakenly expect plans to succeed without direct inspiration to carry them out, and perhaps even without mention. Such plans truly "sit on the shelf." In this context, Shoghi Effendi's approach stands in striking contrast.

Here are a few examples of how Shoghi Effendi called people to action. As before, these passages often combine several techniques. Here is one excerpt from a letter written near the beginning of the first Seven Year Plan. It gives a stirring call to arise, but it also refers to the special station of North Americans and places key responsibility upon the individual:

> All should arise and participate. Upon the measure of such a participation will no doubt depend the welfare and progress of those distant communities which are now battling for their emancipation. To such a priceless privilege the inheritors of the shining grace of Bahá'u'lláh cannot surely be indifferent. The American believers must gird up the loins of endeavor and step into the arena of service with such heroism as shall astound the entire Bahá'í world. Let them be assured that my prayers will continue to be offered on their behalf.[40]

Another passage, written near the beginning of the second global plan, stressed the need to persevere:

> Setbacks may well surprise them; trials and disappointments may tax their patience and resourcefulness; the forces of darkness, either from within or from without, may seek to dampen their ardor, to disrupt their unity and break their spirit; pitfalls may surround the little band. None of these, however fierce, sinister or unyielding they may appear, must be allowed to deflect the protagonists of a God-impelled Plan, from the course which 'Abdu'l-Bahá has chosen for them.[41]

In 1953, at the beginning of the Ten Year Plan, the stirring call to action was even clearer. He told the Americans "to arise and, in the course of these fast-fleeting years, prove their worth as gallant warriors battling for the Cause of Bahá'u'lláh."[42] This crusade was going to require even more sacrifice than usual, since it called on Bahá'ís to travel to countries, territories, and islands that many of them had never even heard of previously. Sketching out for them what they would face and why became very important. One passage is so image laden that it is important quote it at length, although what might be the heart of the "call to action" has been italicized:

> Bracing the fearful cold of the Arctic regions and the enervating heat of the torrid zone; heedless of the hazards, the loneliness and the austerity of the deserts, the far-away islands and mountains wherein they will be called upon to dwell; undeterred by the clamor

which the exponents of religious orthodoxy are sure to raise, or by the restrictive measures which political leaders may impose; undismayed by the smallness of their numbers and the multitude of their potential adversaries; placing their whole trust in the matchless potency of Bahá'u'lláh's teachings, in the all-conquering power of His might and the infallibility of His glorious and oft-repeated promises, *let them press forward, each according to his strength and resources, into the vast arena now lying before them*, and which, God willing, will witness, in the years immediately lying ahead, such exhibitions of prowess and of heroic self-sacrifice as may well recall the superb feats achieved by that immortal band of God-intoxicated heroes who have so immeasurably enriched the annals of the Christian, the Islamic and Bábí Dispensations.[43]

It would be hard to find similar examples of stirring language in most documents related to organizational or municipal or community plans. Shoghi Effendi gave new meaning to the descriptive adjective "encouraging." He helped his fellow believers understand the true drama and scope of their initiatives. He in part encouraged action simply by asking them to take action, in terms designed to awaken the sleepiest of souls.

The table below summarizes the three "special techniques" covered thus far, and a fourth technique: the extremely important use of praise, which will be examined in the next section. A fifth area listed, "oversight and monitoring," will be more fully discussed in the next chapter.

TABLE 4.2
MOVING FROM GOALS TO ACTION: RESPONSIBILITY AND ENCOURAGEMENT

Overall Category	Shoghi Effendi's Approach
Levels of Responsibility	• Clarified the various roles of the governing institutions and their subsidiaries • Encouraged the individual to ensure the success of the plan
Special Techniques of Encouragement	• Evoked divine guidance and Divine Plan • Made references to heroes and heroines • Issued stirring calls to action • Praised past successes • Carried out oversight and monitoring

Praise of Past Successes. Chapter two first introduced the concept of "praise," by explaining that 'Abdu'l-Bahá's Divine Plan letters so praised the North American recipients that they surely would have striven to meet such flattering expectations. 'Abdu'l-Bahá's plan-related letters also used some of the other techniques mentioned thus far, particularly his stirring calls to arise and disperse as well as his constant evocation of the need to pray for divine assistance. Shoghi Effendi learned his lessons well from his Master Planner, and so he did not neglect praise.

One might well imagine, upon perusing the passages cited thus far, that these missives must have had two potentially contradictory effects. On the one hand, their exhortations must have been encouraging, telling the North Americans that their efforts fit within a divine plan, that they received divine guidance, and that they operated in the grand tradition of their own heroes and heroines. On the other hand, these letters had the potential to depress action. How many of their readers had utter confidence that they could arise to carry out such audacious plans and that they could befittingly carry and pass on a blood-soaked torch? Although Shoghi Effendi assured them that they had great capacities, at least a few must have doubted this assurance. It became important to lighten the load of tremendous responsibilities with the leaven of praise and assurance. In this way, Shoghi Effendi lent balance and joy to communications that could have been devastating.

As with each of the topics covered thus far, it is impossible to give more than a few examples from one or two letters. In fact, a major dilemma has been which passages to choose, since these highlighted themes and patterns emerge throughout twenty years of correspondence. Shoghi Effendi never wrote more than a few communications without mentioning, at some point (but usually near the beginning of his communication), his appreciation for his readers' efforts and his praise of their capacities and accomplishments. Perhaps it is important to illustrate several distinct but related ways he praised. First, he often mentioned accomplishments in the context of their implications for the plans in general and the world at large:

> The efforts exerted, and the results achieved, by the members of the American Bahá'í Community during the opening months of the two-year emergency period are such as to merit the highest commendation and praise. They will, if the effort be sustained, evoke

the admiration of the entire Bahá'í world, which is now watching, with feelings of wonder and expectancy, the outcome of the tremendous labor of this community now confronted with one of the most challenging, arduous and far-reaching tasks ever undertaken in its history.[44]

A second kind of praise hearkened back explicitly to the relationship of the accomplishment to the hopes and aspirations of the founders and central figures of the Bahá'í Faith, and of its various heroes and heroines. Of all the "praising" communications that Shoghi Effendi wrote, among the most deeply impressive to his readers must have been his cabled response to the completion of the exterior of the Bahá'í House of Worship in Wilmette, Illinois. As he noted on January 18, 1943:

Heart aglow with pride, love, gratitude for superb achievement of completion of exterior of the House of Worship, Mother Temple of the West. Bahá'u'lláh's high behest, enshrined in His Most Holy Book, has been brilliantly executed. The thirty-five year old enterprise, initiated on same day that Báb's sacred remains were transferred to Mount Carmel, has been triumphantly consummated. The unique Edifice, singled out for consecration by the hands of 'Abdu'l-Bahá, has been nobly reared. The Greatest Holy Leaf's ['Abdu'l-Bahá's sister's] last ardent wish has been befittingly fulfilled. The Concourse on high is jubilant. Myself bow head in joyous, reverent recognition of prodigious accomplishment which deserves to rank among the outstanding enterprises launched in the Heroic Age and the most signal victory won since the inception of the Formative Period of the Bahá'í Dispensation.[45]

It was hard to match such lofty acclamations at any time thereafter, but the third category of "praise" communications was effective as well, because it was particularly personal. As indicated in the above quotation, Shoghi Effendi often expressed his own personal joy and satisfaction with the victories already won. This was another characteristic of his letters that served to lift activities well out of the realm of the ordinary. This leader so evidently cared about these plans and so obviously took their success to heart that carrying them forth became a personal privilege rather than an impersonal burden. How else could one interpret a 1940 letter that began by noting that "[m]y heart is thrilled with delight as I witness, in so many fields, and in such distant outposts, and despite such formidable difficulties, restrictions, obstacles and dangers, so many evidences of the solidarity, the valor, and the achievements of the American Bahá'í community"?[46] What must have been the reaction to the opening of the 1943 cable quoted above which indicated "[h]eart aglow with pride, love, gratitude for superb achievement of completion of exterior of the House of Worship"?[47] Or the 1948 communication which indicated that Shoghi Effendi "[j]oyfully acclaim[ed] brilliant achievements transcending fondest hopes and setting the seal of complete victory on the stupendous labors undertaken"?[48]

What made these confessions particularly poignant is that the Bahá'ís knew, from other communications not cited here, that the problems pressing upon Shoghi Effendi were tremendously debilitating. He suffered the calumnies of treachery and oppression caused by several enemies of the Bahá'í Faith, including members of his own family, as well as burdens brought on by his many responsibilities and by strained human and material resources. Practically the only times that he explicitly mentioned his own joy and happiness were those times when he was citing accomplishments of the plans.

One additional form of praise that Shoghi Effendi used was simply to recognize the heroic accomplishments of those individuals and national communities that offered exemplary service in the path of the plans. 'Abdu'l-Bahá had also mentioned, in *Tablets of the Divine Plan*, a few outstanding Bahá'ís who had arisen to carry word of Bahá'u'lláh's message to other parts of the globe. For example, referring to pioneer Agnes Alexander in a 1916 letter, 'Abdu'l-Bahá highly praised her strong efforts in Hawaii, where she had traveled as the first Bahá'í to reach those shores. "Consider ye, what happiness, what joy is this! I declare by the Lord of Hosts that had this respected daughter founded an empire, that empire would not have been so great!"[49] By mentioning and praising such individuals, 'Abdu'l-Bahá encouraged others to arise and follow their lead. After this sentence, for example, was a list of other places to which North American Bahá'ís should travel, including Australia, New Zealand, Tasmania, Japan, and Asiatic Russia, as well as several other Asian, African, and European nations.

Although in the early global plans Shoghi Effendi did not frequently mention individuals, by the third global plan he did so under special circumstances. Shoghi Effendi announced that those who moved to nations and territories where no Bahá'í had previously lived would receive special mention, on a "Roll of Honor." In a May 28, 1953, cable he said that he was

> [p]lanning to inscribe, in chronological order, the names of the spiritual conquerors on an illuminated Roll of Honor, to be deposited at the entrance door of the inner Sanctuary of the Tomb of Bahá'u'lláh, as a permanent memorial of the contribution by the champions of His Faith at the victorious conclusion of the opening campaign of the Global Crusade. . . . Anticipate making periodic announcements of the names of the valiant knights upon their arrival at their posts to discharge their historic missions.[50]

To devoted Bahá'ís, this would be among the highest possible honors: to have one's name inscribed upon a Roll of Honor that would become a part of the tomb of the founder of their religion. As subsequent cables and letters listed the names of these exemplary souls, the effect must have been astounding. Many of these people were quite ordinary from the perspective of the world at large, having done nothing more extraordinary than moving to places where Shoghi Effendi wished them to move. Yet after this simple act, Shoghi Effendi had actually mentioned them as members of the Roll of Honor, one of the highest forms of praise and honor they could hope to receive—a remarkable incentive! No wonder that Shoghi Effendi could warn that "[a]s few as two territories of Europe, six in the Americas, fourteen in Africa and twenty-two in Asia still remain unopened." No wonder that people arose eagerly to help attain "the foremost objective of the initial stage of the Ten Year Plan."[51] No wonder that the plan was successful. Again, it is important to ask an inevitable question: how many people offer generous servings of praise and positive reinforcement to help encourage group action? Do we present and regard plans as mechanical things, mere frameworks for begrudged action, engaging our bodies but not our spirits? Or do we take joy and pride in these road maps to a better future and communicate this joy to others? It is hard to understand how any plan can succeed if the individuals involved in it do not take joyful pride in its potential and accomplishments.

Summary

Although setting goals and objectives seems to be an important common exercise, and although some planning texts explain very sensible means for reaching the ends of goals, in actual practice people and organizations often stumble. Author John Bryson suggests it is not even possible to choose organizational goals without a sense of unity, that is, without broad agreement about purpose and intent. Several examples from around the world show that many urban planners know how to create plans, but not how to implement them; development projects sponsored by funding agencies commonly stall; economic planners sometimes have trouble moving plans from their origins "on paper" to successful implementation in the field.

Shoghi Effendi enjoyed a number of advantages that allowed him to create a planning style that was simple, direct, and effective. As the highly respected leader of the worldwide Bahá'í community, he was able to use his influence to help various national communities identify viable objectives. Familiar with their situations and capacities because of voluminous correspondence and a steady flow of visitors, he offered the North American Bahá'ís a set of inspiring objectives that became the framework for their successful Seven Year Plan. He used much the same approach of suggesting concrete objectives and then helping to lay out necessary strategies for each of the two subsequent global plans.

Many aspects of the strategies Shoghi Effendi suggested were remarkable. Two noted in this chapter were his detailed specification of strategies for success and his clear explanation of standards for success. He went to great lengths to suggest courses of action that would help meet the objectives of the plan. In some passages, he seemed to make direct references to accomplishments that had been won previously and to suggest Bahá'ís build upon these. Overall, the level of detail is staggering.

Even more notable, however, are his suggestions about the standards of success toward which the Bahá'ís should aim. One quotation urged the North American community to support people through "the frequency of their visits, the warmth of their correspondence, the liberality of their support."[52] Such passages lent a radiance to his instructions that came from his own spiritual discipline and from the fact that this was, after all, a spiritual campaign. Another letter frankly explained to the North Americans that, while he expected them to go to Europe to help establish communities, they should work toward the day when the peoples native to those countries ran the affairs of their own communities. Again, one must note how thorough was his guidance, how keen his insights, and how well grounded his common sense.

Several lessons are applicable to planning efforts that readers might have to undertake, whether the "planner" involved is a person, group, or governing institution, and whether the context is a religious one or not. Referring again to Table 4.1, here is a summary of such lessons:

- Understand the population you are planning for or with. Gather information about the values, motivations, and accomplishments that can help assist in the process of choosing reasonable objectives and strategies. Make sure that the relationship remains one of love, trust, and respect.
- Choose clear, understandable, inspiring objectives, perhaps just a few (as with the first two global plans) unless the population is highly experienced with planning. General statements of goals are useful, but it is even more helpful to choose a few specific objectives or "tasks" that have built-in measures of success, so that one can easily see if objectives have been met or not (e.g., complete the outside of the House of Worship; settle in every state). Tailor these to the capacity of the population, but challenge them to grow beyond the usual activities.
- Think through, as far as possible, the strategies that would be necessary to complete these objectives. Although it is important not to emphasize this too heavily, since so many groups stall at this stage, clearly identified strategies are useful and important. These can be revised later, as necessary. Make sure these strategies reflect noble values.
- Keep in mind the standards of success desired. For example, is it sufficient for the group merely to grow in size? Or should it grow in such a manner that everyone maintains a warm and close relationship? Here, it is important to revisit the age-old concerns about ends and means: "progress" is not really progress if it does not proceed according to praiseworthy principles.

Other important points discussed in this chapter are summarized in Table 4.2. In general, the second half of the chapter considered how Shoghi Effendi was so effectively able to motivate people to carry out the strategies necessary for the plans to succeed. Several aspects of his writings were important.

One aspect was his clear delineation of the responsibilities necessary for various parties. Shoghi Effendi, a key advisor to the national spiritual assemblies, used the opportunity afforded by the plans to continue to educate the North American national and local spiritual assemblies about such fundamental matters as the need for "rectitude of conduct." He also indicated which institutions were responsible for which components of the plans. In addition, he was clear in his explanation of the standards and tone with which they should carry out their tasks, so that these did not become mechanical activities devoid of the spirit at the core of Bahá'í belief.

Perhaps the most extraordinary innovation that he offered the world of planning was his repeated tendency to place responsibility for success of the plans upon individuals. His words and exhortations helped give them the strength to arise and ensure the success of the plans. In the final analysis, he noted, it is upon individuals that the success of plans depend.

Finally, several "special techniques" reinforced the encouragement needed to implement the global plans. These included Shoghi Effendi's reference to the overall context of divine will; his affecting references to the heroes and heroines of their religion, which tapped deep emotions of commitment and willingness to sacrifice; his frequent and eloquent "calls to action," so forthright in their purpose and effective in their tone; and his liberal use of praise, that quality so characteristic of 'Abdu'l-Bahá's plan-related letters, which gave a sense of worthiness and accomplishment, and helped lighten what could have been crushing expectations. Here are additional lessons, drawn from Shoghi Effendi's characteristic approaches:

- Clarify which institutions, groups, or committees are responsible for various aspects of the plans. Create new groups or committees if necessary, but make sure they know how important their role is in the overall scheme of the plan.
- Nurture the individual. All groups, organizations, and corporations are made up of individuals. Offering love, support, and encouragement so that each person may contribute as much as he or she can may not motivate everyone equally, but it could help motivate several valiant and capable people to help push important initiatives "over the top."

- Do whatever is necessary to bring a sense of nobility and purpose to the efforts associated with the plans. For religious communities, placing efforts in the context of God's plan for the progress of humanity is always appropriate. Generous reference to inspiring people or incidents is another important part of the approach. All groups, religious or not, function in large part because of inspiration, which by its nature motivates.
- Offer clear and inspiring "calls to action" that make it evident that you want people to play a role and that you value their efforts. Merely creating plans, without asking and inspiring people to carry them out, is not sufficient.
- Make generous use of praise and encouragement for all successes that the plan's implementers are able to attain. This is a basic principle that all effective parents know and understand well: praise of accomplishments won is one of the surest ways to elevate a sense of personal worthiness and to encourage additional appropriate action.

Chapter 5

Monitoring Implementation

It is the glory of God to conceal a matter, but the glory of kings is to search out a matter.
—Solomon, Proverbs 25:2

. . . it is incumbent upon [rulers] to enquire into the conditions of their subjects and to acquaint themselves with the affairs and activities of the divers communities in their dominions.
—Bahá'u'lláh, "Splendours," *Writings of Bahá'u'lláh*

. . . if the vigorous intelligence and superior skill of the nation's great, and the energy and resolve of the most eminent men at the imperial court, and the determined efforts of those who have knowledge and capacity . . . should all be combined, and all should exert every effort and examine and reflect over every detail as well as on the main currents of affairs, there is every likelihood that because of the effective plans they would evolve, some situations would be thoroughly reformed.
—'Abdu'l-Bahá, *The Secret of Divine Civilization*

THE MOST IMPORTANT ELEMENTS OF PLANS include a noble and heartfelt vision; inspiring yet simple and attainable objectives; and appropriate, focused, yet people-sensitive strategies. However, a community could set in place a plan based on all the suggestions proffered thus far, yet still not succeed in carrying out significant improvements.

Any number of reasons could explain why. Consider a hypothetical community that aimed to rehabilitate a community center. Suppose that at the end of the time frame for the plan, the community center was not rehabilitated. What went wrong? It could be that action or implementation began and then waned. Or it could be that the community waited until too near the end of the plan to try to accomplish its goals. Possibly effort was continuous but was misdirected, weak, or simply based on an erroneous understanding of what should be done. Perhaps the group charged with carrying out the rehabilitation became distracted or overburdened, did not understand the mechanics of contracts and building permits, and never sought appropriate help. Without oversight and monitoring, the community might never know what went wrong.

Every major theorist of the planning process cited in chapter three indicated that it is important to evaluate planned action. John Friedmann's review of several authors' writing about social progress led him to identify "feedback and evaluation" as important characteristics of their work. He summarized this as the need to ensure that someone assesses whether planned changes are actually happening and working. Melville Branch counseled that "feedback" and then "modification or revision" of the implemented action were important, for the same reasons: to ensure that planned action is occurring and to adjust it as necessary.[1]

One way Shoghi Effendi encouraged his religious community to carry out audacious plans successfully was to monitor implementation of those plans. Previous chapters did not fully explore the topic of how he monitored the implementation process, largely because this topic deserves much more extensive discussion than possible earlier. However, it is perhaps in this phase of planning that Shoghi Effendi most exemplified extraordinary planning capacity.

Monitoring plan-related activity can be very difficult. It requires conscious assessment of how well plan-related activities are proceeding. Conceivably, a group could develop a vision of where it wants to go and then quickly specify goals, objectives, and strategies to get it there. In contrast, it requires more work and more time to carry out and monitor plans, perhaps week in and week out, year in and year out, throughout the life of a plan.

One example of the positive potential of monitoring action comes from the international development literature. Between 1965 and 1974, over a million illiterate adults in the country of Myanmar (formerly Burma) became literate. This was the result of a national literacy campaign designed as a community-based mass movement drawing upon the services of 200,000 volunteers. Although one dedicated individual (a teacher concerned that he was getting old, who wanted to make an impact before it was too late) initiated the very earliest efforts with the assistance of a group of his students from a teacher-training college, the national government played an important role in setting up the national program. Based on several experimental initiatives between 1966 and 1968, the program was designed as a mass movement, using nonsophisticated techniques and involving youth in the campaign to offer lessons in reading and writing. Campaign leaders also decided to use "continuous monitoring and assessment, so that reinforcement can be brought into areas where interest and tempo have slackened."[2] Armed with their measurable goal, "the total eradication of illiteracy," and their strategies—including recruitment of university students, development of appropriate materials, techniques for inducing people to become literate, and specific teaching methods designed for the campaign—the program implementers soon led a national movement that taught over a million people to read and write. The program did all this, furthermore, with very little financial cost.[3]

One of the reasons for their success was constant monitoring of program activities. This monitoring first began by assessing experimental and pilot programs on a small scale, thus allowing a national committee to set up effective methods for the larger initiative. When issues arose during the program, the national committee or the local village implementers dealt with them as necessary. This was possible because core implementation of the program was decentralized, as was testing. To test the results once total literacy was reached in one village, another village simply tested the people living in the place claiming literacy. The test consisted of reading a current newspaper or writing a simple account of one's thoughts. When it became obvious that some people could not learn to read because of mental retardation or age, a system was devised to leave them out of the count of literate people. When it became evident that some literate people lapsed into illiteracy after instruction ended, the national committee devised follow-up measures, including supplementary "readers" on topics ranging from stories of Buddha's birth to village sanitation. Countless other problems were resolved at the local level through consultation.

Evidently, the "continuous monitoring and assessment" that the program designers put in place worked. For every such story, however, dozens more tell of monitoring that did not take place. In some cases, program designers failed to take into account that the people for whom housing was being built would not wish to live in the houses that were too far from their places of work. In other cases, international agencies planned to improve farming techniques with "green revolution" fertilizers but failed to adjust for the fact that the farmers had neither the money nor the cultural context necessary to support the innovation. Many plans of action fail to succeed not because they are inherently poor plans, but rather because no one monitors and adjusts their implementation.

Monitoring: Professional Literature

Monitoring is one form of program evaluation. Program evaluation is an established, well-known field of study and enquiry. Rossi and Freeman, two of the foremost social scientists in the area of program evaluation, indicate by way of definition that "evaluation researchers (evaluators) use social research methodologies to judge and improve the ways in which human services policies and programs are conducted."[4] As they note, it is often important to distinguish between effective and ineffective programs, and to determine whether planned interventions are reaching their target populations or proceeding as envisioned. They give a number of examples. In a Latin American country, several people created *Plaza Sesamo*, an educational television program based on the model of the United States *Sesame Street* program and designed to raise literacy among schoolchildren. An evaluation study, however, showed that the program was not helping targeted school children read any better. A number of reasons were offered to explain the failure, but the main one was that depressed social conditions and poverty made it unlikely that target children were able to watch the show, suggesting that a more effective strategy would be needed to improve literacy among low-income children in that country.[5]

After World War II, evaluation studies became popular among social scientists and government policy-makers. By the end of the 1950s, evaluators in the United States were studying the effects of attempts to reduce delinquency, provide public housing, and improve public health. Evaluation research also increased in the 1960s because of the rise of new domestic social programs, known collectively as the "War on Poverty," that created many innovative attempts to improve the lives of low-income people. Also studied during this period were family planning in Asia, nutrition in Latin America, and agricultural and community development in Africa. Evaluation research burgeoned as improvements in data collection and the rise of electronic computers made it possible to examine large amounts of information easily.

All of the complex studies and computers did not protect this field of study from critical dilemmas, however. While some researchers argued that scientific models of evaluation would ensure infinite social progress through a series of progressively improved "social experiments," others became disillusioned.[6] Some studies showed that much-vaunted social programs actually did not have any measurable effect. Research funding began to decline rapidly in the 1980s as the evaluation "boom" turned to "bust."[7]

Author Richard Hofferbert argues that this happened in part because scholars claimed evaluation as their exclusive purview and defined it as inquiry into grand social innovations. He argues that a more important, yet less grandiose, type of evaluation monitors action in a way that is useful to the people who are acting. This "monitoring" involves assessing, on an ongoing basis, whether various aspects and phases of programs or plans are working or not, so as to improve them while they are being implemented. (Refer to the second row of Table 5.1 below.)

Program monitoring has been an accepted form of program management and evaluation for some time. Rossi and Freeman count "monitoring and accountability of program implementation" as one of three main categories for evaluation research; the other two focus on planning for implementation before it begins and on assessing the impact of planned programs as implementation concludes. (Each model is represented by one of the three rows of Table 5.1.) They list several reasons to monitor on an ongoing basis. The first is the need "to properly manage and administer human resource programs" by preventing mismanagement. The second reason is the need to provide stakeholders with evidence that "what was paid for and deemed desirable was actually undertaken." Their third reason is to make sure that a program actually took place and served the people it was expected to serve.[8]

While these are all good enough reasons in the context Rossi and Freeman presented, for our purposes, they miss the point. As Hofferbert suggests, the point is that those who are trying to plan for a better future should view monitoring as a positive tool for making a program better, rather than just as a way of checking up on someone else to see if they are mismanaging a program. The people who are carrying out planned programs are the ones most in need of an ongoing system of monitoring

98 Planning Progress

TABLE 5.1
TYPES OF EVALUATION: POLICY RESEARCH

TYPE OF EVALUATION	TIME OF ASSESSMENT	TYPICAL QUESTIONS
Program Design or "Pre-Implementation"	Before the program or planned activities begin	• Is there a need for these activities? • Can we carry out these activities? • What should we do?
Monitoring or Formative or Process Evaluation (In German: *Vollzugsforchung* model)	While the program or planned activities are underway	• Are we actually carrying out the planned activities? • How well are we doing? • Are we reaching the people we need to reach? • Should we adjust activities?
Assessment of Program Utility or Product or Impact Evaluation (In German: *Wirkungsforchung* model)	After the program or planned activities end, or before and after implementation, or over time (time-trend analysis), depending on evaluation design used	• Did the program or planned activity accomplish a reasonable set of objectives? • Did it have a measurable impact on the phenomenon it was supposed to change? • Did it "succeed"?

and feedback. Hofferbert notes that the more dominant model of judging and evaluating program efforts, which looks only at the impact or results of activity—Was the program successful or not? Were the goals won?—often fails to provide the kind of information necessary to make social action work in needed directions.

He calls for a working partnership between those who are carrying out social change and those who are assessing whether such efforts are succeeding. In many cases, in fact, these can be the same people. Hofferbert envisions what is known in German as the *Vollzugsforchung* model of evaluation research (short form: *Vollzui*), which is "more than traditional management or administrative science, in that it focuses rigorously on social targets, that is, on real results and not merely on internal organizational processes." It is a management tool that should be nonthreatening to those who are carrying out program activities. "It can be thought of as analogous to modern fuel injection systems in automobiles, whereby the mixture of inputs is adjusted to external temperature, humidity, and vehicle operation. The adjustment process is automatic and invisible to the external observer."[9]

The processes of assessment and monitoring should be automatic, supportive, inherent, and nonadversarial. According to Hofferbert, this suggests a new approach for those carrying out action programs, as well as for leaders, evaluators, or researchers of implementation:

> Public policy research is useful when it is applied to a current problem faced by both administrators and policy makers. It is useful when the researchers refrain from gratuitous criticism. It is useful when aimed at concrete solutions rather than ideological preaching. Research is useful when there is a basis of trust between the practitioner and the researcher. And it is useful when the recommendations for change are both specific and sensitive to the political and economic realities with which politicians and administrators must live and work.[10]

This approach suggests cooperative effort, unified action, and a short feedback loop between those who implement the plan and those who help monitor its implementation. Necessary are an atmosphere of respect; a warm, perhaps even loving work relationship; and sensitivity to the particular challenges facing implementers.

Shoghi Effendi's Approach to Monitoring

As a planning leader, Shoghi Effendi wanted to ensure that the goals and objectives of the global and national plans he helped oversee were accomplished. That meant he was certainly interested in the "product" or "impact" of plans, as indicated in the bottom row of Table 5.1. He was also interested in the journey on the way to achieving the plan's objectives, however, and so was actively involved in "monitoring" to ensure that the efforts were effective well before the end of the plan, as indicated in the middle row of Table 5.1. Not as a researcher but as a mentor and leader, he helped provide the ongoing feedback and assessment necessary to ensure that well intentioned activities actually do bring progress. Shoghi Effendi's feedback was an inherent part of his fellow believers' planning activities. Although he did not operate as automatically as "modern fuel injection systems," he nevertheless provided an extremely effective example of how it is possible to monitor a plan's implementation with loving support and relationship building, yet with a firm, guiding hand.

General Approaches

Shoghi Effendi wrote many communications that seemed designed for the specific purpose of monitoring action and encouraging necessary adjustments in light of the plans' objectives. Correspondence written to the North American planners sometimes focused on "news" items, but the bulk related in some manner to the global plans, that is, to getting them set up, furthering their execution, or assessing their results. Letters written on Shoghi Effendi's behalf and addressed to the North American national spiritual assembly may have covered a wide range of topics, but his handwritten postscripts almost always focused on prosecution of the plans.

It is also important to note the way that the North American Bahá'ís treated the letters that they received. Not only did they compile and publish these letters and at least his handwritten postscripts in edited books, they also circulated Shoghi Effendi's communications soon after they arrived. The primary source of dissemination in the United States and Canada during most of these years was *Bahá'í News*, a national newsletter/magazine. Throughout the 1940s, Shoghi Effendi's letters were quite often reprinted in full, whether they were addressed to the community at large or to the national spiritual assembly. In some cases, the national assembly published and distributed Shoghi Effendi's letters separately in booklet form.

All of the plan-related communication took place in the 1930s, 1940s, and 1950s. At this time, international communication by necessity took the form of letters, which were very slow, or cables, which were faster but required truncated dialogue ("cable-speak"), since cable companies calculated their charges based on the number of words a communication contained. Still, one is struck by the remarkable frequency, depth, and length of these letters and cables. With great regularity and even greater intensity, Shoghi Effendi called upon the North Americans to succeed with their plans.

It was as if, in his mind, the most important things to talk about were the plans plus the continuous preparation and action needed to undertake such plans. Individuals or groups often wrote Shoghi Effendi seeking advice about various conflicts or disagreements they were having. Rúḥíyyih Rabbani notes that his typical response, when asked to settle disputes, was to turn attention to the plans. He urged all parties "to rise above the situation, to forget the past and forgive, to concentrate on the urgent, the paramount needs of the Faith, which were to fulfill the goals of its current Plans and spread its healing message to all mankind."[11] Communications focused on making these planning efforts succeed were sometimes pure and simple calls to action and success, but many others monitored ongoing action and offered advice. In several cases, he suggested ways to adjust strategies or to help the North Americans decide which actions were of highest priority when they could not undertake them all simultaneously.

The most basic of his strategies for effective monitoring was very simple: To communicate frequently about the progress and status of the plans. On a regular basis, sometimes almost weekly, during all phases of the plan until goals were won, Shoghi Effendi communicated lists of accomplishments, his assessment of which tasks were most urgent, and emergency measures that had to be undertaken to meet those tasks. The implications for his workload must have been enormous: for many years, Shoghi Effendi actually kept up with plan-related reports and letters from individuals, communities, and national spiritual assemblies all over the world, with several sets of communications often arriving from North America alone. This was in addition to his other duties of writing, translating, overseeing construction of holy shrines, designing gardens surrounding the shrines, managing property, advising national spiritual assemblies, and administering the affairs of the world community. Yet he read, assessed, and responded to plan-related information with creativity and drive. Considering his chronic lack of staff and the lack of modern equipment such as computers or even electric typewriters, the immensity of these tasks is awe-inspiring.

Furthermore, it was clear that Shoghi Effendi cared deeply about the ongoing success of the plans. This gave his oversight-related communications an added dimension that must have made his mid-course suggestions particularly effective. At crucial points in the plan, when it was important to stretch just a bit farther to accomplish some objective, it was not unusual for Shoghi Effendi to make a personal plea for the extra effort needed. This personal involvement took "monitoring" to a new level: not only was Shoghi Effendi noticing whether or not they were proceeding according to plan, he was agonizing about this, and he let them know it. The following quotation, from a cablegram sent in 1940, is one illustration of this personal commitment:

> My eyes and heart are anxiously, longingly turned to the New World to witness the evidences of a new, still more heroic phase of enterprise confidently entrusted to vigilant care of the American believers by the ever-watchful, powerfully-sustaining Master. I refuse to believe that a community so richly endowed, so greatly envied, so repeatedly honored, will suffer the slightest relaxation of its resolution.[12]

He sent a similar message in 1948, in a letter that will be quoted more fully later: "The three months' interval is swiftly running out. My heart aches at contemplation of the possibility of failure of the stalwart community to rise to the heights of the occasion."[13]

Obviously, this was a person fully invested, emotionally as well as spiritually and intellectually, in the success of these plans. It was only natural, given this investment, that he was continually helping to assess whether or not the plans were being successfully executed. This intense involvement highly personalized his monitoring efforts.

It is also possible to discern key aspects of his communications that relate to the stage of the plan during which they were sent. Guidance differed slightly depending upon whether it was offered in the beginning, middle, or concluding phase of the plan.

TABLE 5.2
MONITORING ACTION: FEEDBACK

OVERALL CATEGORY	SHOGHI EFFENDI'S APPROACH
Feedback	• Wrote frequent letters and cables focused on specific needs of the plans • Solicited regular reports and letters about the progress of the plans from individuals, committees, and assemblies in the field • Communicated forcefully his personal commitment to the success of the plans

THE BEGINNING PHASE OF THE PLAN

Consider the activities of Shoghi Effendi near the beginning of the plan, defined here as covering approximately the first year of implementation. His activity for this time period was not so much to monitor activities as to help identify key objectives and successful strategies, and to rally his fellow believers to the plan.

Shoghi Effendi sometimes revealed a global plan's overall objectives in stages. This was particularly apparent with his two-part launching of the objectives of the first global plan. A mere two months after he first mentioned the objectives, a gentle message in July of 1936 indicated that he was "eagerly awaiting the news of the progress of the activities initiated to promote the teaching work within, and beyond, the confines of the American continent."[14] Letters and postscripts thereafter, including those following the 1937 launch of the seven-year initiative, offered additional encouragement and reminders.

The first Seven Year Plan ended in the Spring of 1944. For several reasons—including the continuation of World War II and Shoghi Effendi's concern that the successes of the first global plan be consolidated—the North Americans' second plan did not begin until the Spring of 1946. Once it did begin, however, Shoghi Effendi turned full attention to its successful launch. The initial message about this plan came in April 1946, when Shoghi Effendi listed the four objectives previously cited, including one specifically targeted to the European continent. Soon afterward, a veritable flood of communications followed. A May 5th communication appears below in its original cable-speak form ("stop" instead of a period) to indicate how strongly and bluntly it was worded:

OVERWHELMING RESPONSIBILITY RESTS NEWLY ELECTED ASSEMBLY URGE IMMEDIATE MEASURES SET PLAN MOTION ADVISE MORE FREQUENT MEETINGS ASSEMBLY PROMPT FORMATION COMMITTEES CHARGED FURT[H]ERANCE EACH ASPECT PLAN STOP EXERCISE UTMOST CARE SELECTION MEMBERS COMMITTEES STOP FEEL NECESSITY ELIMINATE UNNECESSARY ADMINISTRATIVE DETAILS ENABLING ASSEMBLY MEMBERS FOCUS ATTENTION SESSIONS DIVERS IMPERATIVE REQUIREMENTS PLAN STOP.[15]

Shortly thereafter, a June 5th cable indicated that the "[o]pening phase of spiritual conquest of the old world order under divinely conceived Plan must be speedily and befittingly inaugurated" and asked for the "prompt dispatch of nine competent pioneers to as many countries as feasible charged to initiate systematic teaching work, commence settlement and promote dissemination of literature." This cable also added countries to the North Americans' European campaign, including Luxembourg and Switzerland. Eight days later, Shoghi Effendi asked for an expanded effort, focusing on raising the number of assemblies to 175.[16]

He did not rest there. In a letter dated two days later, June 15, 1946, and extending for fourteen pages in its reprinted form in Messages to America, he wrote yet another statement about the basic rationale and spiritual underpinnings of this second great campaign. He told his readers that their "historic world-embracing crusade" was "unprecedented in religious history" and derived its initial impetus from the Báb's call to those in the West to "issue forth" from their "cities" to aid the Cause of God.[17] He recalled that Bahá'u'lláh had written letters to the kings and rulers of the world, and he made a direct connection between those letters and the work the Bahá'ís were undertaking. He referred to 'Abdu'l-Bahá, the "Center of the Covenant," and the Tablets of the Divine Plan as a charter for their own plan, reminding them again of their special mission and obligations. He indicated where they stood in time, at the opening decade of the second Bahá'í century.

Shoghi Effendi then issued a stirring call to action, assuring his readers that "[t]he objectives . . . which must . . . arouse them to a higher pitch of concerted endeavor, are clearly defined, and by no means beyond their collective power to achieve," but reminding them that the tasks involved must "be relentlessly pursued "The number of administrative centers around the world, numbering perhaps a thousand, "should through resolute effort and careful planning, be continually and speedily multiplied." "Bolder measures designed to proclaim the verities of the Faith, its tenets, its claims and the purpose of its institutions . . . as well as a more convincing presentation of its aims and teachings . . . should, moreover, be seriously and systematically undertaken not only in the mother country but also throughout the Latin Republics."[18] Note that inherent in the wording here was an assessment of the way things had previously been done. The request for bolder measures, or for more convincing presentation, served as a not-so-gentle nudge toward excellence and redoubled effort.

Not yet done, even though this was still only three months after the beginning of the plan, Shoghi Effendi followed up with a July letter that indicated "[t]he forces that have been released though the birth of the Plan must be directed into the most effective channels, the spirit that has been kindled must be continually nourished, the facilities at the disposal of its organizers must be fully utilized, each and every barrier that may obstruct its expansion must be determinedly removed."[19]

Additional cables and letters sent in October and December of 1946, and January and March of 1947, indicate a subtle change in Shoghi Effendi's communications. These letters made even stronger, although still indirect, references to the need to launch the plan more successfully. An October communication, only six months into the plan, indicated that the opening phase was drawing "inexorably to a close" tasked community members to "redouble their efforts, evince a nobler spirit of self-sacrifice, display greater resourcefulness, unity, initiative, steadfastness and enterprise, rise to loftier heights of heroism and self-abnegation, and establish, more convincingly than ever, their right to be regarded as the worthy champions of a glorious Cause...."Their duty, in this light, was to "scatter more widely and as far as the extremities of both the North and South American continents, to cross the ocean in ever-increasing numbers."[20]

> There is no time to lose. The task, though prodigious, is not beyond the capacity of those, who, in so short a time, in such distant fields, over so wide an area, and in the midst of a people so alien

in temperament, language and custom, have won such conspicuous victories for their beloved Faith.[21]

Two days later, yet another cable to the national spiritual assembly called for "[a]n immediate notable increase in the number of pioneers, particularly for the newly-opened transatlantic field of service."[22] Something must have gone well after this, because a December cable was full of praise, although it also asked that nine more pioneers go to Europe. A January communication allowed the Guardian to "[a]cclaim with grateful heart evidences of steadily accelerating movement of pioneers, multiplication of conferences, consolidation of activities of national committees, progress in preliminaries of internal ornamentation of Temple, and formulation of teaching policy in southern states," just before he asked for additional efforts.[23] A March cable indicated that he was "[o]verjoyed, grateful, proud of notable expansion of manifold activities in three continents," but, true to form, asked for even more "[i]ntense, sustained, self-sacrificing efforts."[24]

This is a remarkable series of communications that gives one the overall impression of relentless focus on the part of Shoghi Effendi in making sure that the plan began well. This is in marked contrast to the more typical approach to a multiyear plan. Most people, if they had seven years to do something, would give themselves a grace period at the beginning. They would not continuously communicate the urgency of the tasks one month, and then two and three, or five and six months after the beginning of the plan. Shoghi Effendi, however, operated as if, truly, "there is no time to lose." His communications set up high expectations at the very beginning of the plan.

Shoghi Effendi followed much the same course of action with the beginning of the Ten Year Plan. Announced at simultaneous conventions throughout the world, this plan involved twenty-four "tasks" or objectives for the United States. Again he first sent the objectives and then wrote more fully about their implications later. The fuller explanation for the United States's role came three months later, in July. This long letter also repeated and summarized the tasks and emphasized their importance.[25]

Shoghi Effendi used two additional "mechanisms" at the beginning of these last two plans. Early in the plan, he listed the victories already won through previous efforts. This provided an extra push, since it offered proof that capacities were indeed high. In the following example, he notes that the Bahá'ís were successful in spite of war and suggests that they should be at least as successful in times of peace:

> The first Seven Year Plan, ushered in on the eve of the greatest conflict that has ever shaken the human race, has, despite six years of chaos and tribulation, been crowned with a success far exceeding the most sanguine hopes of its ardent promoters. . . . The exterior ornamentation of the House of Worship was completed sixteen months before the appointed time . . . the number of Spiritual Assemblies in the United States and Canada was almost doubled. No less than fourteen Republics of Latin America were provided with such Assemblies. Active groups began to function in the remaining Republics. . . . The second Seven Year Plan, set in motion on the morrow of that universal and cataclysmic upheaval, must, despite the great confusion that still prevails, the spiritual torpor, the disillusionment, the embitterment . . . meet, as it gathers momentum . . . with a success no less startling and complete.[26]

The second method that he used, which was quite simple but of great importance, was to help establish priorities by indicating which objective was the most important to focus on first, such as international settlement.[27] This is in marked contrast to the circumstances that many people face with complex plans or tasks. Often it is not clear where to start. In the case of plans overseen by Shoghi Effendi, however, it was always clear where it was most important to begin.

THE MIDDLE PHASE OF THE PLAN

In the middle of the two Seven Year Plans, Shoghi Effendi wrote most of his plan-related communications to the North American community. Our definition of "the middle of the plan period" is that phase of the plan which began after the first year's implementation and continued until approximately one year before the end of the plan. For the first of the two Seven Year Plans, that portion of the "middle" correspondence (1938-1943) which is published in the compilation Messages to America required most of fifty-one pages of typeset copy; even more is available in the archives. The extensive letter *The Advent of Divine Justice* is a special case, since it served many fundamental purposes beyond direct guidance in the first Seven Year Plan, but it too was written in the beginning of this middle period, completed in December, 1938, and comprising seventy-seven typeset pages.[28] For the second Seven Year Plan, the various forms of "middle" correspondence that are reprinted in *Citadel of Faith* took up most of one hundred and four pages of text. By the time of his death, four years into the Ten Year Crusade, Shoghi Effendi had written at least thirty-seven text pages of "middle" correspondence, in letters and cables addressed to the Bahá'ís resident in the United States of America and focused largely upon their responsibilities for the plan.[29]

It is important to consider how Shoghi Effendi's communications encouraged sustained action over several years, which was surely a difficult feat, given the enormous scope of the tasks involved and the considerable handicaps of distance and typically slow communication between North America and the Middle East. Looking at this body of "middle" plan correspondence reveals several major approaches that Shoghi Effendi used to help ensure that the North Americans' actions remained sustained and focused. The first and most important, perhaps, was simply his habit of writing frequently; a second was his indication of what should be done first.

In addition, Shoghi Effendi divided the longer periods of time—seven or ten years—into phases of one or two years and then urged specific actions by phase. This was not a fixed process, according to Rúḥíyyih Rabbani: "[He] did not have the period of these phases fixed in his mind at the inception of the Plan; they were a result of the natural growth of the forces released by the Crusade and the nature of the victories won."[30]

This approach of using shorter, more manageable portions gave the multi-year plan several "beginnings and ends" and allowed certain portions of the plan to be accomplished in the first two years, others in the second, and so on. The practical benefits of such phasing are many: for one, they helped release the final phase of the multi-year plan from frantic, last-minute attempts to meet goals which, if addressed at a more leisurely pace, would have been much more attainable.

His communications during this middle phase were typically characterized by several types of comments about the structural progress of the plan. These were not unlike his communications at the beginning of the plan. Shoghi Effendi was usually careful to describe, in tones suitably illumined by praise and other lofty references, the accomplishments that had been won thus far. He usually stated as well which objectives remained yet to be accomplished or what work remained to be done, sometimes in very specific terms that in essence refined the strategies needed. Finally, he also typically asked for increased endeavors in order to carry out the remaining objectives of the plans.

Except in the shortest of cables, postscripts, and letters, Shoghi Effendi often assessed what had been accomplished thus far before giving additional directions or feedback, either within a letter itself or in a letter or cable that immediately preceded it. This is, perhaps, a planner's version of common courtesy. His fellow believers could trust that Shoghi Effendi noticed the accomplishments they had already achieved.

In April 1939, for example, he sent the North American convention a cable that began: "Brilliant conclusion of second year in Seven Year Plan evokes universal admiration of the Bahá'í world. . . . Closing phase of Temple . . . ornamentation already entered" and then went on to list several major tasks completed during the first two years of the current plan. Then he listed objectives yet to be won: "Guatemala, Honduras, Salvador, Nicaragua, Costa Rica, Panama, Cuba, Dominica and Haiti immediate objectives. . . . These unexplored territories hold forth inestimable prizes for audacious adventures in the path of Bahá'í service." Shoghi Effendi's habit of pushing for additional effort to accomplish even more is apparent in the same cable: "Task admittedly laborious, hour laden with fate, privilege incomparable, precious divinely-promised aid unfailing, reward predestined immeasurable. Appeal to all believers, white and Negro alike, to arise and assume rightful responsibilities. Urge prolongation of sessions of Convention."[31]

Here is another example of this three-themed approach. In his address to the 1940 North American convention, Shoghi Effendi happily noted yet another round of victories:

> Overjoyed, elated that dynamic energy, invincible valor of American believers impelled them far outstrip the goal fixed for third year of Seven Year Plan. Temple ornamentation has been uninterruptedly pursued. The theatre of operation of the teaching campaign is already embracing entire Central America and every South American Republic excepting Paraguay and Colombia. Number of countries within the orbit of the Faith is now exceeding sixty. Intercontinental crusade, through path broken by Martha Root and seal set by May Maxwell's death yielding destined fruit. Galvanized, permanently safeguarded. Together with Keith they

forged through sacrifice a triple cord indissolubly knitting the community of North American believers to cradle of Faith in every continent of Old World and Latin America.[32]

In this passage, Shoghi Effendi skillfully wove stirring praise of the "dynamic energy, invincible valor" of the implementers of the plan with a very practical listing of several major accomplishments the community had won. In a letter written to the National Spiritual Assembly of the Bahá'ís of the United States ten days before, he had listed these successes in more detail; this convention letter served to reiterate his points, more publicly transmit his joy concerning these accomplishments, and simultaneously mention three heroines of the plan, recently deceased women who in their lifetimes had travelled to foreign lands to help fulfill the goals of the plan.[33]

Then Shoghi Effendi's convention cable continued, indicating tasks remaining to be done, in language that was bound to cause increased effort:

Unperturbed by gathering gloom of tottering civilization without, contemptuous of the assault of the perfidious enemies within, the executors of 'Abdu'l-Bahá's mandate must and will strain every nerve in the course of the ensuing year to multiply the number of enrolled pioneers to consolidate work achieved in newly opened North American States and Provinces, to insure prompt settlement of remaining Republics, to prosecute unremittingly ornamentation of last unit of Mashriqu'l-Adhkár [House of Worship], to expedite formation in isolated centers of nuclei capable of the establishment of local Assemblies.[34]

Shoghi Effendi did not hesitate to tell the Bahá'ís, promptly and in no uncertain terms, when they were not carrying out the tasks necessary for the success of the plan. In July of 1947, for example, he sent a communication that indicated progress and asked for additional resources: "rejoice at evidences of continued vigorous activity. Renew plea to believers possessing independent means to volunteer for European pioneer field, both settlers and itinerant teachers."[35] An October message was similarly complimentary. In January of 1948, however, he said that he was "deeply concerned at critical stage of task confronting North American Teaching Committee," and noting the upcoming due date for the interim goal of 175 assemblies, he warned that "emergency measures carefully, promptly devised by national representatives of the community and wholeheartedly supported by entire mass of the believers of the North American continent, designed to safeguard the existing assemblies and rapidly multiply their number, are imperative." Making it clear that the goal of increasing the number of assemblies must prevail, he asked that actions related to the House of Worship, the reinforcement of the Canadian community, the consolidations in Latin America, and "even the multiplication of pioneers in the European field, should be unhesitatingly subordinated to demands of the one disconcerting aspect of an otherwise successfully conducted Plan."[36]

That letter was sent on January 10th. On February 1st, he sent another letter, stern in tone and moving in pathos. The last part of this letter was cited when discussing Shoghi Effendi's personal commitment to the success of plans (see page 105, above). This fuller quotation demonstrates that the imminent failure of one objective of the plan is what caused Shoghi Effendi such grievous sadness:

> The gravity of the emergency facing the North American believers is unprecedented since the initiation of the Divine Plan and unparalleled in the history of the American Bahá'í Community since 'Abdu'l-Bahá's passing. No obstacle is insuperable, no sacrifice too great for attainment of supremely important objective. The eyes of her sister communities in every continent of the globe and of her daughter communities of Latin America, handicapped by a variety of adverse circumstances, are fixed upon the community of followers of Bahá'u'lláh in North American continent. . . . The three months' interval is swiftly running out. My heart aches at contemplation of the possibility of failure of the stalwart community to rise to the heights of the occasion. I refuse to believe that its members, invested with unique apostolic mission of 'Abdu'l-Bahá, will shrink from meeting the most challenging requirement of the present hour.[37]

This was surely a devastating letter; but the heartfelt appeal apparently produced results. After another anxious communication in February, Shoghi Effendi was able to write on April 6th that he was "[g]reatly encouraged by the splendid progress of the tremendous

112 Planning Progress

drive initiated in response to my appeal. The zero hour is inexorably approaching. Nineteen additional settlers can and must be provided. Praying with increasing fervor for total success, complete victory."[38] By the 1948 convention, his April 26th message acclaimed the "heroic feat of raising to almost two hundred the number of spiritual assemblies in the North American continent," far exceeding the target number.[39] This was still only two years into the plan. In similar fashion, Shoghi Effendi coaxed and coached the North Americans through each objective and each phase, until they finished the Seven Year Plan triumphantly.

The End Phase of the Plan

The ends of plans supervised by Shoghi Effendi were, ironically, less fastpaced than the beginnings. By the time the last year of the first Seven Year Plan approached, Shoghi Effendi was able to write letters filled with praise for objectives already won and focused largely on the few remaining tasks at hand. This is surely a sign of good planning: the ability to carry out, near the end of the plan, what little had not already been done, in a fairly leisurely fashion. With the second Seven Year Plan, the record was even better. Shoghi Effendi indicated seventeen months before the end of that plan that the objectives of the plan had "been in the main, attained."[40] He listed a few tasks that remained but then talked about the next multiyear plan.[41] The first plan was due to end in April of 1944, but by the previous August Shoghi Effendi could write that the "seven year enterprise" was coming to a victorious end and that America's "sister communities of Persia, British Isles, Egypt, 'Iraq, India, Syria, Australia and New Zealand marvel at the scale of the prodigious labors of the American Bahá'í community . . . and are galvanized into action, inspired to emulate its example."[42]

Listing the specifics of that example to the world, he noted that they had accomplished

> [t]he multiplication of Bahá'í centers in recent years in both East and West, the erection of administrative headquarters, the purchase of historic sites, the settlement of virgin areas, the migration into neighboring territories The initial stages of the momentous plan have been brilliantly executed. The most formidable

obstacles impeding its progress have been courageously faced and progressively swept away. Its first fruits, exemplified by the completion of the exterior ornamentation of the Temple and the formation of a nucleus of the Faith in every Republic of Latin America, have been triumphantly gathered.[43]

True to form, Shoghi Effendi then indicated that "[t]he range of its unfinished tasks is swiftly diminishing," but that these were in fact evident, upon closer examination:

Total victory is within sight but the six remaining virgin areas of Alaska, Saskatchewan, Prince Edward Island, South Carolina, North Dakota and South Dakota, as well as the inadequately reinforced Republics of Nicaragua, San Domingo, Paraguay, Bolivia, Venezuela, and Peru still demand the concentrated and sustained attention of the National representatives.[44]

Similar letters followed thereafter. In each communication, he either indicated how important it was to carry out the remaining tasks, or he repeated accomplishments won and simultaneously expressed the certainty that more would be won, or he encouraged individuals to arise, with such stirring language as the following:

Whoever will rush forth, at this eleventh hour, and cast his weight into the scales, and contribute his decisive share to so gigantic, so sacred and historic an undertaking, will have not only helped seal the triumph of the Plan itself but will also have notably participated in the fulfillment of what may be regarded as the crowning act of an entire century. The opportunity that presents itself at this crucial hour is precious beyond expression.[45]

Finally, as a reward for all of this effort, the Bahá'ís received a warm and laudatory letter in April, at the end of the Plan and the end of the first century of their religion's history. This 1944 letter, here set in clusters for ease of reading, opened by addressing the three major tasks of the plan and how they had been won:

The one remaining and indeed the most challenging task confronting the American Bahá'í Community has at long last been brilliantly accomplished. The structural basis of the Administrative Order of the Faith of Bahá'u'lláh has, through this superb victory, ... been firmly laid by the champion-builders of His World Order in every state of the Great Republic of the West and in every Province of the Dominion of Canada.

In each of the Republics of Central and South America, moreover, the banner of His undefeatable Faith has been implanted by the members of that same community, while in no less than thirteen Republics of Latin America as well as in two Dependencies in the West Indies, Spiritual Assemblies have been established and are already functioning—a feat that has outstripped the goal originally fixed....

The exterior ornamentation of the first Mashriqu'l-Adhkár of the West ... has been successfully completed, more than a year in advance of the time set for its termination.

The triple task undertaken with such courage, confidence, zeal and determination ... is now finally accomplished and crowned with total victory.[46]

Shoghi Effendi was pleased with the success of this plan, as he was with the success of the next, and he let his co-workers know this, with extensive expressions of gratitude and thanksgiving.

He did, however, offer one more set of challenges. Even though another major plan was not given to the North Americans until two years after the first, in 1946, when the war was finally over, Shoghi Effendi expected them to continue working. He asked, in fact, for specific goals to be won for the 1944-45 year, which was a supposedly "interim" period. Well over a year before the end of the second Seven Year Plan, Shoghi Effendi began talking about the third plan. Shoghi Effendi was careful to assess overall accomplishments in the context of efforts yet to be made. The lesson here is that the end point of the plan was not the occasion for ceasing action, but rather the occasion for a short pause before renewing action. In like manner, those wishing to carry out a process of continuous planning would be advised to spend the end of one plan in preparation for the beginning of the next.

Shoghi Effendi used a key method to help prepare for the next plan and celebrate accomplishments. He created or sponsored reports that tallied the various victories that had been won. These made real the fact that the Bahá'í Faith was in the midst of evolution and growth, and gave Bahá'ís around the world a compendium of useful facts by which they could measure that growth. Much information was issued in *The Bahá'í World: A Biennial International Record*, a series that covered various global accomplishments for several years at a time. In the 1940s, the North Americans published these volumes under the sponsorship and review of Shoghi Effendi.[47] In a separately published statistical compilation that covered the period from 1844 to 1952, Shoghi Effendi listed the countries in which Bahá'ís lived, the languages into which Bahá'í literature had been translated and published, the minority groups and races "with which contact has been established by Bahá'ís," and—a point of particular pride for him—the number of African tribes represented in the religion. He listed the existing national spiritual assemblies, along with the dates of their establishment, and the number and names of local spiritual assemblies in the United States, India, Pakistan, Burma, Central America, South America, and Canada. Even the places where Bahá'ís resided in the United States and in Persia he deemed fit to publish. In specific confirmation of the successes of the second Seven Year Plan, he also listed the "Bahá'í Centers in the Ten European Countries Opened to the Faith by the American Bahá'í Community Under the Second Seven-Year Plan."[48]

The total effect was to confirm that the Bahá'í Faith had indeed become a global religion. These facts were also a useful way to tally the effects of all of those planning efforts. Combined with Shoghi Effendi's habit of mapping territories and nations to which Bahá'ís had traveled, offering a visual record of global spread, the end-of-the-plan compendia of accomplishments won surely had a wonderfully confirming effect.[49]

TABLE 5.3
MONITORING ACTION: STAGES OF THE PLANS

OVERALL CATEGORY	SHOGHI EFFENDI'S APPROACH
Beginning Phase of the Plan	• Clarified and adjusted objectives/strategies as needed • Wrote frequent, focused communications about the need to get started early and effectively • Indicated the most important goal or objective with which to start
Middle Phase of the Plan	• Wrote frequent letters and cables elaborating on key themes, mandates, and requirements • Used phases to pace activity; indicated most important objective for each • Carefully described and praised, on a regular basis, accomplishments and tasks completed thus far • Indicated frankly which objectives and tasks needed more work; revised suggested strategies as needed • Continued to issue inspiring "calls to action" and to encourage endeavors
Ending Phase of the Plan	• Praised highly accomplishments won • Indicated exactly which tasks remained to be done • Developed complete, factual reports concerning global accomplishments during the life of the plan • Prepared communities for post-plan activity

SUMMARY

Sometimes leadership requires attention to details, to the nuts and bolts of implementation. Where plans are concerned, this means paying attention to whether or not the plan is working and to what has to be adjusted to make it work better. Unfortunately, such "monitoring" has proved difficult for many people and organizations. Although in some cases programs have included a "feedback loop" to receive information and make adjustments, in other cases this does not happen, yet the professional planning and evaluation literature clearly indicates the importance of such oversight.

As Hofferbert suggested, this process is not the exclusive domain of professional researchers or evaluators. He argued for "monitoring" as a natural part of program management, to help those who are carrying out programs—or, in similar fashion, carrying out plans—determine what needs to change in the field. He suggested that the relationship between those who monitor and those who implement, if these are not the same people, should be helpful, nonadversarial, cooperative, and supportive. He also suggested that the evaluator should avoid gratuitous criticism, since the relationship should be one of cooperation and support.[50]

This chapter presented the unique monitoring style of Shoghi Effendi as one example of how it is possible to monitor in a way that combines loving support with rigorous assessment of unmet needs. His particular style of plan oversight was extremely effective, as his written communications about the global plans show, yet he never lost his ability to inspire, encourage, and uplift. Although the workload must have been enormous, Shoghi Effendi greatly valued these plans, gave them high priority, and cared deeply about their success. Lack of success saddened him enormously, and several letters refer to either his deep distress when tasks were not being completed or his joy at their success. This discussion of his personal feelings helped give his letters a sense of genuine immediacy and commitment, and surely helped motivate his fellow believers to even greater action.

It is, however, possible to discern somewhat different patterns of communication for different stages of the plans. In the beginning phase of the plan, Shoghi Effendi was prone to clarify and sometimes amplify plan objectives given to the North American "standard-bearers." These letters and cables impress us with their frequency and power; it is almost as if he singlehandedly pushed the Bahá'ís forward, telling them: You will start this plan immediately and do it well! Notably, he did so with such uplifting language, with such inspiring references to their "world-embracing crusade," which was "unprecedented" and divinely inspired, that perhaps they did not feel unnecessarily pushed. He quite often used two other means of encouragement early in the plan. One method was to refer frequently to past accomplishments, which must have made people feel that they could indeed tackle a new plan successfully. Another method was to tell the community which objectives were most important to focus upon first, eliminating any confusion about which actions should be started, even if others had to wait.

In the middle phase of the plan, a period that produced the bulk of the communications, we see these techniques repeated and amplified. As before, Shoghi Effendi continued to send a stream of communication about the specific objectives and what needed to be done. He also kept a running tally of accomplishments won so far, offering praise as appropriate; assessed tasks that needed to be accomplished; and explained the spirit in which these should be carried out, including a feeling of unity, love, and cooperation among the Bahá'í communities and spiritual growth and development for individuals. He expressed frank disappointment when activities were not being achieved as planned, but leavened critical commentaries with praise of accomplishments won and with uplifting reassurances that they could indeed succeed.

By the time of the ending phase of the plan, Shoghi Effendi could focus largely on praising accomplishments won and indicating what few things still needed to be done. He continued to offer inspiring feedback until most of the objectives were won, and he wrote complete reports that summarized worldwide accomplishments of the plans. These were part of his efforts to end plans with preparation for follow-up activities or subsequent plans.

One would think that the constant flow of letters and cables must have been reassuring on the one hand, since they indicated exactly how well or how poorly the North American Bahá'ís were doing, while simultaneously suggesting measures needed to amplify successes or to rectify failures. On the other hand, some of these communications, cited in this chapter, must have been difficult to absorb. Shoghi Effendi's less than positive responses, to "true believers," could have potentially paralyzed action. As indicated in the last chapter, however, praise lightened many a load. A rereading of these passages also reveals the loving encouragement that underlies all exhortations to try harder.

Here are lessons learned from this chapter for those who would aim to improve the implementation of plans by improving the process of monitoring:

- Indicate which people, or groups of people, are responsible for monitoring. In this case, the responsibility lay jointly with a widely recognized leader and an elected national spiritual assembly; but in other cases a committee, group, or other party

may be able to play the same role. Make sure that the monitors understand the importance of their role.
- Those responsible should prepare for active involvement, on a regular basis, in the monitoring process ranging over almost the entire time frame of the plan. To increase the effectiveness of plans, someone needs to be involved in an ongoing process of assessing accomplishments of the objectives, refining strategies as necessary, and encouraging participants to complete the goals of the plan.
- Ensure that there is a means of collecting information about the progress of the plan on a frequent basis. In the case of Shoghi Effendi, information flowed via letters and reports sent between him and national spiritual assemblies and committees, local communities, and individuals in the field. In other cases, the flow of information will have to be tailored to the circumstances.
- Demonstrate personal commitment and investment in the success of the plan. Communication about progress of the plans without "life" may have no effect at all. Whether the leader is an individual or a group, leadership's attitude toward the plan and its success can make a world of difference in the spirit with which everyone else considers his or her role in the successful completion of the plan.
- Start plans with a high energy level, tackling high priority objectives soon and successfully. Do not assume that most of the tasks can be done later. If many of the most important tasks are successfully tackled early in the process, it may become possible at a later time to relax the pace of activity.
- Consider giving continual feedback about accomplishments won and tasks yet to be undertaken. It is important to give praise for those tasks that have been carried out successfully, so as to create a sense of pride and satisfaction. This chapter and previous chapters have suggested several means of encouragement that might prove useful. It is also important to encourage those who are promulgating the plan to complete tasks still undone.
- Give an overall assessment of the accomplishments of the plan in light of the objectives, once the plan period is drawing to a close or at its end. Immediately move into a phase of consolidation or preparation for a new plan and a new set of tasks.

Chapter 6

Leadership and Social Change

Where there is no guidance, the people fall, but in abundance of counselors there is victory.
—Solomon, Proverbs 11:14

Without consultation, plans are frustrated, but with many counselors they succeed.
—Solomon, Proverbs 15:22

The members of the Government should consider the laws of God when they are framing plans for the ruling of the people. The general rights of mankind must be guarded and preserved.
—'Abdu'l-Bahá, *Paris Talks*

MUCH CONTEMPORARY SOCIAL ACTION FALTERS because of an incomplete understanding of the proper role of leadership in the context of broader participation and decision making. On the one hand, visible leadership seems indispensable at times. Examples are Gandhi's campaigns for Indian independence, Mandela's influence for racial equality in South Africa, and Martin Luther King Jr.'s crusade for civil rights. In other settings, many worthy initiatives such as universal health care, literacy, or civil rights have failed without a leader to provide the needed direction, drive, and inspiration. No leadership has yet arisen capable of moving the United States toward meaningful reform of inadequate health care coverage for all citizens, for example, although some have tried.

On the other hand, inappropriate or misguided "leadership" can stifle human progress, and dependence upon charismatic leaders to solve difficult social problems is a recipe for disappointment. Many of the leaders mentioned above arose after widespread dissatisfaction with some situation emerged from groups and individuals in the community at large. African Americans did not wait for Martin Luther King Jr. to appear as a leader before they launched the civil rights movement. They created a context—a series of court cases, protest activities, and liberation writings dating back several decades—which made his emergence natural and his contributions part of a holistic movement.

When people, organizations, or governments try to impose leadership by mandating programs, policies, or plans without widespread consent and participation, those initiatives are doomed to fail. Hundreds of social and economic development programs have failed because international funding agencies or national governments,rather than the people themselves, created them. In contrast, Shoghi Effendi used global plans as a tool for nurturing leadership abilities and distributing leadership tasks rather than concentrating them.

Leadership and Consultation

Rosabeth Moss Kanter, author of several award-winning books on leadership and management, calls leadership "one of the most enduring, universal human responsibilities." Humanity has experienced leadership throughout its history, and history is often an account of the actions and events surrounding leaders. Kanter notes that certain traits characterize a wide range of historical leaders, whether from religion, politics, or the arts:

> Thus, in most important ways, leaders of the future will need the traits and capabilities of leaders throughout history: an eye for change and a steadying hand to provide both vision and reassurance that change can be mastered, a voice that articulates the will of the group and shapes it to constructive ends, and an ability to inspire by force of personality while making others feel empowered to increase and use their own abilities.[1]

These qualities—of vision, change, assurance, articulation, inspiration—make leadership a central component of human organizations. In the corporate world, chief executive officers are paid well for their supposed ability to "make or break" the organization. In the world of government service, typically leaders are not well paid, but their importance is recognized; highly placed political leaders may gain in fame what they lose in salary.

Human society has experienced many bad or repressive leaders. As people have learned to their lasting sorrow, strong leaders can arise for amoral or immoral, reprehensible, even hideous purposes, yet gain followers and stay in power long enough to do grievous harm. The archetypal example is Germany's Adolf Hitler, but he is not alone; one need only attend to the daily news in order to hear accounts of negative or unprincipled political leadership, in eastern Europe, in central Africa, in North and South America, or elsewhere in the world. Stephen Covey is one of several popular authors who call on leaders of the future to have and to hold fast to principles, to be known as men and women of integrity. His work in this sphere is important because it acknowledges that being a good leader is not unconnected to being a good person. He states forthrightly that a good leader of the future must be both humble and courageous, and must have integrity, which he defines as "integrating ourselves with principles."[2]

Covey identifies three basic functions for leadership. The first, pathfinding, is the process of tying together values, vision, and needs to chart a strategic plan of action for the future. The second function is aligning, which consists of ensuring that the organization and its activities contribute to achieving its vision and mission. Previous chapters have shown that Shoghi Effendi carried out these functions of pathfinding and aligning extremely well. He also excelled at Covey's third function, empowering. Covey says that a good leader should help to ignite a "fire . . . within people that unleashes their latent talent, ingenuity, and creativity to do whatever is necessary and consistent with the principles agreed upon to accomplish their common values, vision, and mission."[3]

Historically, one of the great flaws of some leadership was its failure to develop a decentralized decision-making process characterized by inclusion rather than exclusion. Traditionally, the leader at the top decided what should be done and how it should be done. A persistent focus on the person at the top, the "lead horse," has many flaws, however. It can be demoralizing, according to corporate management consultant Sally Helgesen, "because the relentless aggrandizement of those at the top leads organizations to fall prey to a heroes-and-drones syndrome, exalting the value of those in powerful positions while implicitly demeaning the contributions of those who fail to achieve top rank." Most people will in fact never become the top leader of their organization, because the number of such positions is too limited. "Thus the equation of leadership skills with [top] position must by its nature breed frustration and cynicism among those in the ranks, denying them a feeling of ownership in the enterprise in which they are engaged and discouraging their full-hearted participation."[4] She recommends that effective leaders give autonomy and support to people in the ranks of their organizations, encouraging "grass-roots leadership" to flourish, where such leadership is linked not to an individual's rank but rather to other personal attributes.[5]

This is very similar to what another popular author, Gifford Pinchot, calls creating organizations with "many leaders." In Pinchot's vision, organizations will become more effective if they move away from rigid hierarchy and toward a radical decentralization of work and incentive systems, allowing not only "participation" or "consultation" but also self-determination by various units within the organization, particularly concerning their unit's future plans.[6]

The general direction of this leadership literature confirms what planning and development experts have known for some time: It does little good to create development projects or plans from the top down, with little participation, involvement, or self-determination by the people involved. It was in development projects, in fact, that the strong importance of participatory planning for social progress first became evident. David Korten, one of the co-editors of *People-Centered Development*, suggests that experience has shown that it is most effective to support and build upon the efforts of poor people to address their own needs. For economic development, for example, this might involve building upon the strengths of people's own economic structures rather than imposing completely new ones.[7] Grace Goodell criticizes the policy of simply giving to low-income people "the amenities we know they need, instructing them in how to use these improvements correctly: pumps, new seeds, clinics, electricity." Experts in more economically developed nations do this "without so much as a nod" of the low-income communities' assent, making decisions for people because of some misguided exercise of paternalism. She postulates that "[t]he main purpose of involving the poor in their own development is to strengthen their initiative and critical abilities, and to help them build their own reliable channels for expression as well as for accountability. To achieve these goals, they and we must take their initiatives seriously." This can only happen, she suggests, if development helps local people acquire material gains "in the process of achieving economic benefits, indispensable political skills and institutions."[8]

Such a participatory approach would actually help formal leaders. Alvin Toffler, futurist and global thinker, indicates that demands now face leaders, particularly political ones, from a bewildering array of sources. Many of these demands are competing, contradictory, and impossible to respond to within current societal structures. The pressure for accurate decision making rises just as the environment in which decisions must be made grows more complex:

> The result is that our political decision-makers swing wildly back and forth between doing nothing about a problem until it explodes into crisis and, alternatively, racing in with ill-conceived, poorly pre-assessed crash programs.
>
> Any decision system is ultimately capable of handling only a given "decision load." The load gets heavier as needed decisions multiply, grow in complexity, or speed up. At some point the decision load is greater than the system can handle. At this point the fuses blow. . . .
>
> What we are witnessing is crushing decisional overload—in short, political future shock.[9]

Toffler counsels that two contrasting approaches could deal with such decisional overload, or "future shock." The first is to try to strengthen centralized decision-making, "adding more and yet more politicians, bureaucrats, experts, and computers," in what will probably be a futile attempt to out run complexity. Another is to reduce the decision load by "sharing it with more people, allowing more decisions to be made 'down below' or at the 'periphery'" instead of concentrating power, authority, and initiative at the overstressed center.[10]

All of this leads to the heart of the matter: The process of making decisions—whether about government or any other category of social improvement—should have some element of decentralization. This allows for wide participation in the planning process and for an interactive relationship of shared responsibility between the "ruler" or "planner" and the people at large. John Friedmann, planning theorist, indicates that not only responsibility but also learning should be shared. Then the planner can learn from the people benefiting from the plan, and they in turn can learn from the planner, in a mutually beneficial cycle. Action should go hand in hand with a "dialogue" or a process of communication focused on the action experience. This dialogue would, in turn, fertilize action, which is continually evolving and improving.[11]

Collectively, these authors offer fascinating insights into the process of planned action. It appears that capable leadership must become more decentralized and more keenly focused on empowering those who are led. Theorists about the process of decision making are increasingly recognizing the importance of relinquishing centralized authority and enabling dialogue to inform action.

A Bahá'í Concept of Leadership

These theories offer an interesting prologue to a further consideration of spiritual concepts of leadership and governance, a topic first introduced in chapter two. Bahá'í concepts about how to lead and how to govern have many of the positive characteristics identified as important in the professional literature cited above, and they avoid many of the pitfalls.

'Abdu'l-Bahá's 1875 book, *The Secret of Divine Civilization*, made many references to the responsibilities of leaders to become people worthy to guide society. If 'Abdu'l-Baha were alive today, he would likely be pleased with Stephen Covey's call for leadership with "principles," for this is very close to what 'Abdu'l-Bahá called for in *The Secret of Divine Civilization*. Specifically, 'Abdu'l-Bahá noted that good leaders of government should be "righteous, God-fearing, high-minded, incorruptible," as well as fully aware of "the laws of God" and "the highest principles of law."[12] 'Abdu'l-Bahá addressed many of his comments to "the spiritually learned," who he felt were the "lamps of guidance among nations," and whose station was not dependent upon rank or office, as suggested in Helgesen's call for grassroots leadership. Although, as a religious leader, 'Abdu'l-Bahá was obviously more focused on the spiritual life than those authors quoted above, he also felt that good "principles" were key for the spiritually learned:

> The spiritually learned must be characterized by both inward and outward perfections; they must possess a good character, an enlightened nature, a pure intent, as well as intellectual power, brilliance and discernment, intuition, discretion and foresight, temperance, reverence, and a heartfelt fear of God.[13]

He described many attributes of the spiritually learned, including the need to attain "learning and the cultural attainments of the mind," and the need to oppose "passions" by not allowing oneself to fall into moral excesses.[14] In this view, the leader is a person of influence in the community, of learning and high character, spiritually mature, and in control of his or her own baser temptations and inclinations.

Bahá'u'lláh set up a system of governance for the Bahá'í Faith that was explicitly decentralized and based on a new concept of leadership. Each locality was to be governed by a council (now known as a local spiritual assembly) composed of nine people elected each year without any campaigning or nominations. He also indicated that nine people, elected "in similar manner, should make up the worldwide governing board, the Universal House of Justice. 'Abdu'l-Bahá further explained the necessity of what are now known as national or regional spiritual assemblies, also elected without campaigns.

What was the process of decision making like for these new bodies? At all levels of society, the process of decision making was consultation—that is, the way that people were encouraged to interact with one another was to consult in ways consistent with spiritual principles. Consultation is a system of communication that would contribute greatly to resolving the problems with participation, dialogue, and mutual learning identified as necessary by the writers cited earlier. The concept itself is old; the epigraph for this chapter cited King Solomon's proverbial statement that "without consultation, plans are frustrated, but with many counselors they succeed." The context of such consultation, as indicated in chapter two, should be one of love, support, and tolerance for the views of others.

In addition to providing for a democratic selection system for governance and dialogue-based decision making, Bahá'u'lláh encouraged individual initiative in spiritual development and prohibited a professional Bahá'í clergy. He established instead two arms of administration, the spiritual assemblies referred to above, and another advisory branch called the counsellors, collectively referred to as "the learned." People would be appointed to serve in this advisory auxiliary branch, but they would simply provide inspiration and support, without legislative authority. On the contrary, all administrative decision-making would be centered in the body of nine elected believers, at the local, national (or regional), or international level.[15] 'Abdu'l-Bahá's will and testament specifically created the institution of the Guardianship and appointed

Shoghi Effendi as world leader, known by the title of Guardian. In the future, the Guardian was to work in conjunction with the Universal House of Justice in a closely defined relationship of mutual support, checks, and balances.[16]

Consequently, the Bahá'í governance structure was to provide not only for global leadership but also for massive decentralization of leadership based upon a highly interactive system of decision making. Because of circumstances, it is true that Shoghi Effendi served as sole "head" of the worldwide community, since he predated his twin institution of the elected Universal House of Justice, and he left no successors eligible to become Guardian. However, much of Shoghi Effendi's lifetime work involved preparation for the day when Bahá'í institutions would function as envisioned, with a decentralized, worldwide governance system.[17]

Moreover, Shoghi Effendi painstakingly educated his fellow believers about the fundamental requirements necessary for them to establish local and national activities in keeping with spiritually informed principles. He did this in part by translating relevant materials from Persian and Arabic into English, but also by explaining the applicability of the principles to specific situations. To explore further this building up of what Shoghi Effendi called the Administrative Order, the interested reader can peruse, among other sources, his book *Bahá'í Administration: Selected Letters 1922-1932*, which reprints several key foundational letters and documents that continue to guide Bahá'í communities throughout the world.[18]

Consequently, in the context of the Bahá'í ethos, Shoghi Effendi served in a peculiar, interim position. To him alone was left the responsibility of ensuring that the Bahá'ís of the future would depend on no one person. The reader might ask about the global plans he helped initiate. In what sense were they decentralized and participatory?

The plans were both participatory and decentralized, but in ways bound by the limitations of circumstance. One person operating in one corner of the world was responsible for helping to spur activity in a wide variety of locations, using institutions that were just beginning to learn the fundamentals of their own administrative principles, much less their planning principles. Nevertheless, as far as possible, Shoghi Effendi carried out a consultative process with national and local spiritual assemblies and with individuals, largely via constant correspondence. At the same time, he encouraged elected bodies themselves to create a context of consultation. As he explained, "the keynote of the Cause of God is not dictatorial authority but humble fellowship, not arbitrary power, but the spirit of frank and loving consultation." He noted that the duties of elected representatives were "not to dictate, but to consult, and consult not only among themselves, but as much as possible with the friends whom they represent. . . . They should never be led to suppose that they are the central ornaments of the body of the Cause, intrinsically superior to others in capacity or merit."[19]

As for decentralization of leadership, this was the very essence of what he was trying to accomplish, as the next section will show.

Shoghi Effendi's Use of Plans as a Tool for Maturation

Shoghi Effendi was faced with the task of building up, for a widely scattered yet numerically small global community, the infrastructure necessary to allow decentralized governance and planning to take place. Rather than viewing the global plans as a manifestation of that future state, he instead used them as a tool to reach it. He did this in two ways. First was the more obvious way of using the plans to expand community membership, disperse Bahá'ís around the world, and multiply the number of established local and national communities. Second, he used the planning process to help national and local communities mature into more capable institutions. Among its many benefits, such an endeavor would obviously have relieved him of the burdens of centralized supervision and decision making, lest he suffer from what Alvin Toffler referred to earlier as an unmanageable "decision load."

The evolutionary role of the plans becomes clear by referring to Shoghi Effendi's work with the North American Bahá'ís. After summarizing the effects of these plans on the maturation of the North American Bahá'í communities, it should prove instructive to broaden our perspective by considering the impact of these endeavors upon another national community, the Bahá'ís of Australia and New Zealand.

The Maturation of the North American Bahá'í Community

Significant accomplishments in the internal growth and development of North American Bahá'í communities came about because of the plans. These benefits included the winning of the goals and objectives of the three global plans for the United States and for Canada, but other benefits emerged as well. Shoghi Effendi made it clear that the process of carrying out such goals as settling the states and provinces would contribute to the organizational capacity necessary to fulfill other, more ambitious goals.[20]

Shoghi Effendi's letter of May 22, 1939, written during the first Seven Year Plan, contains one of the best examples of his careful tutoring about the relationship between prosecuting plans and expanding the capacity of the North American Bahá'í community. He noted that the North Americans would have to learn how to continue to carry out their geographic expansion goals and yet not lose the gains they had already made. He characterized two categories of action. The first

> aims at the safeguarding and consolidation of the work already achieved . . . [and] depends chiefly for its success upon the capacity, the experience and loyalty of wise, resourceful and judicious administrators, who, impelled by the very nature of their task, will be increasingly called upon to exercise the utmost care and vigilance in protecting the interests of the Faith, in resolving its problems, in regulating its life . . . in preserving the pristine purity of its precepts.

The second category of action, he noted, was designed to enlarge the sphere of operation, and it related more to individuals than to institutions. It "is essentially pioneer in nature, demanding first and foremost those qualities of renunciation, tenacity, dauntlessness and passionate fervor." To those who were carrying out the administration of all of these plan-related affairs, he said:

> they are steadily and indefatigably perfecting the structural machinery of their Faith, are multiplying its administrative agencies, and are legalizing the status of the newly established institutions. . . . They are exploiting its potentialities, broadcasting its message, publicizing its literature, fostering the aspirations of its youth, devising ways and means for the training of its children, guarding the integrity of its teachings, and paving the way for the ultimate codification of its laws.[21]

In sum, all of this activity was "promoting the growth and consolidation of that pioneer movement for which the entire machinery of their

Administrative Order has been primarily designed and erected." He went on to state, with no hesitation, that the North Americans were thereby laying the foundation of the "edifice of this New World Order" heralded by the Báb, Bahá'u'lláh, and 'Abdu'l-Bahá.[22]

One of the earliest evidences of the likely link, in Shoghi Effendi's mind, between successfully carrying out the plan and becoming adept at administrative development is his expectation that the North Americans not only give birth to other national communities but also teach those communities how to develop their own national capacity. As any schoolteacher knows, if a school administrator assigns a person to teach a certain subject, it is perhaps an indication of the teacher's knowledge about that subject, but this is not necessarily the case. In the process of teaching, however, the teacher will almost certainly become much more knowledgeable about that subject. This analogy allows us to see the wisdom behind Shoghi Effendi's exhortation that the North Americans teach other national groups how to grow and consolidate. A December 3, 1940, letter urged them to provide "the necessary support, guidance, recognition and material assistance" needed "to enable these newly-fledged groups and Assemblies to function in strict accordance with both the spiritual and administrative principles of the Faith of Bahá'u'lláh." To do this, he indicated, would require them to "nurse these tender plants of the Vineyard of God, to foster their growth, to direct their development, to accord them the necessary recognition, to help resolve their problems, to familiarize them with gentleness, patience and fidelity with the processes of the Administrative Order."[23] Thus emerges the effective image of the loving parent or teacher or gardener helping other national communities to grow and mature, a process that would have helped the institutions grow as well.

Earlier, in *The Advent of Divine Justice*, Shoghi Effendi said much the same thing. There, he indicated that the end of the first plan should witness the establishment of new communities throughout Central and South America in which a foundation had been laid for future growth. The responsibility of the North American Bahá'ís would not end with the launching of these new communities:

> Theirs will be the task, in the course of successive decades, to extend and rein force those foundations, and to supply the necessary guidance, assistance, and encouragement that will enable the widely scattered groups of believers in those countries to establish

independent and properly constituted local Assemblies, and thereby erect the framework of the Administrative Order of their Faith. The erection of such a framework is primarily the responsibility of those whom the community of the North American believers have converted to the Divine Message. It is a task which must involve, apart from the immediate obligation of enabling every group to evolve into a local Assembly, the setting up of the entire machinery of the Administrative Order in conformity with the spiritual and administrative principles governing the life and activities of every established Bahá'í community throughout the world.[24]

This, then, was to be the proving ground. In previous communications, Shoghi Effendi had praised the North American Bahá'í community's understanding of administrative matters. The necessity of making sure that this understanding translated into fully functional offspring communities would surely have tested them, requiring them to grow and evolve in ways that would not otherwise have been possible.

Although Shoghi Effendi offered goals, objectives, strategies, and timetables for the completion of the global plans, he left major spheres of responsibility in the hands of the national Bahá'í communities themselves. The quotations above make it clear that the North Americans were supposed to train and consolidate the new communities they helped establish. The text thus far, however, could possibly mislead the reader into overemphasizing Shoghi Effendi's role in the execution of all aspects of the national plans. In fact, from the beginning, Shoghi Effendi's wish was for the North Americans themselves to build the institutional capacity necessary to create and execute plans.

Hence, in 1936, one year before the launch of the first Seven Year Plan, when Shoghi Effendi noted that a "systematic, carefully conceived, and well-established plan should be devised, rigorously pursued, and continuously extended," he indicated that this plan should be "[i]nitiated by the National representatives of the American believers" "His role was to suggest feasible and inspiring objectives.[25] Shoghi Effendi expanded upon his suggestions in letters and cables preceding the 1937 launch, especially in *The Advent of Divine Justice*, but as one might well imagine, the tasks associated with actually carrying out such a plan extended far beyond even the extraordinary assistance that Shoghi Effendi gave. To carry out the plans required the national spiritual assembly to create committees, give them instructions, create and spend within carefully allocated budgets, communicate with their local spiritual assemblies and institutions, and in other ways carry out the myriad details associated with implementing a plan. Shoghi Effendi provided goals and progressively applicable strategies, and suggested ways of carrying them out, but the nature of these tasks required extensive decentralized decision-making.

Here is one small example. For the first Seven Year Plan, the North American Bahá'ís wrestled at some length with the question of how to proceed with the "teaching" (making direct contact with potential new believers) that was required by the objectives of the plans. Shoghi Effendi had urged them to expand into unopened territories, but how would they do this? They settled upon three approaches, but each required them to stretch old capacities and acquire new ones as they struggled to operate "on a collective basis under the direction of Bahá'í administrative bodies."[26] Their national teaching committee decided one approach was to encourage North American believers to hold introductory meetings in their homes. This approach was explained in publications, but the process was too decentralized to allow tracking of the results.

As a second strategy, they initiated systematic teaching campaigns, dependent upon exceptional Bahá'í lecturers who traveled and could attract and sway large audiences, but this too required thought, preparation, and reassessment. According to researcher Roger Dahl, this strategy was problematic because most of these women (and most of the best lecturers at that time were women) could not work on an ongoing basis with the considerable number of people they attracted to the Bahá'í Faith through their talks and classes. If the national community could not send supplemental teachers able stay for a longer period of time, these newly attracted people drifted away. Furthermore, the strategy faltered in the Deep South, where encouraging open public meetings with racially mixed groups, in accordance with Bahá'í principles, proved difficult. After a period of encouraging stellar teachers, the teaching committee had to consider other routes.

The third strategy proved more useful. It involved the previously untried concept of sending Bahá'í settlers or pioneers to unopened territories within North America as well as abroad. Here, too, work was required at the national level to recruit the volunteer pioneers, to help them find means of employment, and to make sure they stayed in their new places of residence.

This example shows that the goal of opening up new and unsettled territories to the Bahá'í Faith required considerable planning and implementation work by the North American national community rather than by Shoghi Effendi. Development of the Plan was therefore decentralized, requiring considerable time, thought, and testing of alternative strategies. Once these were determined and tested, they were communicated to Shoghi Effendi for further advice, but the trying and the testing had to take place in the field.

On the one hand, the North American Bahá'ís relied heavily upon Shoghi Effendi for guidance in vexing matters of administration. For example, his leadership in helping them see how to promulgate expansion plans in the southern United States, given the poor condition of race relations, was invaluable. To one query, concerning the "problem of teaching among the colored people," he answered that "whatever the plans you may initiate for the extension of the teaching work among the colored sections of the population," they should tolerate "[n]o racial discrimination whatsoever in teaching." In that same 1939 letter, he responded to a question about the relationship between an administrative building and the House of Worship by indicating that this would have to be decided in the future. On the other hand, the national spiritual assembly was taking on leadership of the plans. In the same letter, Shoghi Effendi's secretary noted that he "welcomes the step taken by your Assembly to increasingly devote its meetings to the consideration of major policies and plans, and to dwell less on matters of details and of more secondary administrative character."[27] With such comments, he urged them to take over policy and planning leadership and to make many decisions themselves. In a message written a few months later, the assembly in turn promised that it

> realizes deeply and reverently its greatly increased res[p]onsibility for contributing its utmost to the success of the third year of the Seven Year Plan, inaugurated so gloriously by your Convention message and the fervor of the delegates and friends. The American Bahá'ís have begun to think in inter-continental terms, and their collective response, through the Convention delegates and through the pioneers who have arisen under the inspiration of your appeal, is greatly encouraging. All alike realize that a new spiritual dimension has been created in which the Bahá'í life can and must respond to larger opportunities and more serious discipline.[28]

The same trend was evident in communications during the next year, 1940. The assembly's secretary indicated that "[t]he American believers realize more and more that the extension of the teaching campaign to Central and South America is a formidable task requiring intensive preparation," and that their annual conventions demonstrated the maturation process. "[T]he nature of the annual Convention has been undergoing a change in the direction of capacity to assume mature responsibility. The American believers this year, through their delegates, will be brought closer than ever before into the collective consciousness which your communications invoke."[29]

Two years later, this process still seemed to be in place. Whereas in earlier days letters from the national spiritual assembly appeared to ask detailed administrative questions up front, as the years went by they concentrated, early in the text of the letters, upon discussing the important work related to the plans. Apparently, the nature of meetings had shifted as well. Here is a major example, a letter which indicated that

> [t]he January [national spiritual assembly] meeting concentrated almost entirely upon teaching activities, as was indicated by one of the three cables sent you on January 4, and on the general question of the activities of the friends under present international conditions. The work to be accomplished by the Teaching Committee, the Regional Teaching Committees and the local Assemblies by 1944 is truly enormous, but the rising spirit of the believers is a great augury of success.

Furthermore, they proceeded to explain, they were themselves taking the initiative to tap into their own communications medium (*Bahá'í News*) and turn attention even more widely to the Plan:

> In the January issue of *Bahá'í News*, now on the press, the theme is North America teaching, and the schedule of work, together with our collective instruments and resources, is laid before the believers with strong pleas and most helpful suggestions by the Teaching Committee and the N.S.A. Upon this basis of fact, and in the spirit of ['Abdu'l-Bahá's] Tablets and your communications, the teaching work now seems to be a powerfully moving tide which will soon set the entire Bahá'í community into the exhileration [*sic*] of active service to the Cause.[30]

Hence it appears that Shoghi Effendi was able to inspire North American Bahá'ís to arise on their own to encourage additional decisions about plan implementation. This was only as it should have been, since it was impossible for Shoghi Effendi, many miles away, to cross the ocean every time a decision needed to be made for the promulgation of the plans.

The strongest indication that Shoghi Effendi's careful tutorials in institutional readiness had taken root was that after his death, the North American Bahá'ís nonetheless arose to complete their part of the Ten Year Plan successfully. The true test for the North American Bahá'ís, that is, came with the death of their planning leader in the middle of their most challenging plan.

According to the personal testimony of Paul Pettit, who became a member of the National Teaching Committee in 1960, and later a member of the United States National Spiritual Assembly, many feared that after Shoghi Effendi's death the United States's objectives would not be won.[31] They had already sent many pioneers out to international posts, in keeping with the first phase of the Ten Year Crusade. That left the domestic tasks, particularly the numerical objective of 300 local spiritual assemblies in the United States, needing to be won hard on the heels of a plan (the second) during which they had struggled to get 175 local assemblies. Suddenly and without warning, in November of 1957, Shoghi Effendi died. Now the Hands of the Cause, highly respected members of the "learned" branch appointed by Shoghi Effendi, ably took over global leadership until the Universal House of Justice could be elected in 1963. It was not the same, however. No one would now send urgent cables and letters and postscripts at the pace Shoghi Effendi did, urging victory in the plan. How would they succeed?

A few years before the 1963 deadline for the end of the plan, national leaders of the American Bahá'ís realized that, at the pace they were going, they were not going to succeed. In the summer of 1958, a specially appointed committee wrote the national spiritual assembly a passionate letter calling for "an instantaneous dynamic and decisive plan of action." This plan would focus on the guidance given by Shoghi Effendi in his last major letter to the Americans, urging "spiritual reinvigoration, administrative expansion, and material replenishment." The committee laid out a systematic, three-point plan for galvanizing the American community. This was to combine strong appeals from the national spiritual assembly for a focus by all institutions and individuals upon the Ten Year Plan; publications, visits, and conferences designed for encouragement; and assistance through the preparation of special materials and classes. In concluding its detailed letter and plan of action, the committee recommended that the national spiritual assembly appoint "a continuing committee of its body to follow through on whatever plans are adopted at this meeting . . . so that there will be no slackening of emphasis or assistance in the teaching effort in the four years ahead of us."[32]

The American teaching committee helped carry out many of these suggestions. One of the mechanisms they used graphically illustrates the impact of Shoghi Effendi's planning methods. The "circuit teaching" plan, according to a November, 1958, report from the national teaching committee, stemmed from Shoghi Effendi's suggestion that the Americans "pay particular attention to getting teachers with spiritual capacity and a deep knowledge of the Covenant out to the weaker communities on circuit teaching trips." Accordingly, the national committee compiled a list of suitable teachers for each region and set in place a plan whereby a circuit teacher would visit communities with just under the number (nine) necessary to form a local spiritual assembly. These visits were to take place over a period of four weeks, with two days of each of those weeks spent with each of three communities, and one day of rest for the circuit teacher.[33]

According to Paul Pettit, who served as a circuit teacher for more than five years, from approximately 1959 to 1965, many of these hardy circuit teachers used their own financial resources to work full-time in this service. They traveled as bidden to goal areas and met with different groups every two nights for weeks or months at a time. Velma Sherrill, who was secretary of the national teaching committee during most of this period, trained the circuit teachers how to instruct local communities to plan. The methods she used, Pettit indicates, were basically the same as Shoghi Effendi's: developing easily measurable objectives, working on individual growth and commitment, and monitoring activity. The directions she offered in her letters indicate her translation of Shoghi Effendi's style to suit the pressing needs of completing the Ten Year Plan.

In one letter, for example, Sherrill called on each area teaching committee to meet and consult and "outline a plan for servicing your goal groups for the remaining eight months of the Bahá'í year, advising the American National Teaching Committee of your plan, as well as assistance desired in the form of circuit teachers and settlers." She cited Rúḥíyyih Rabbani's statement that "[w]e should keep our minds on our objectives, decide which are the *most important* things to concentrate our energies on and remember that every single moment that escapes us is not coming back. In this way the work will go forward."[34]

Sherrill centered several of her committee letters and training materials on one particular quotation, from a letter written on behalf of Shoghi Effendi, that emphasized the spiritual underpinnings of their work and the need for action (emphasis in original):

> The beloved Guardian has stressed over and over again that to effectively teach the Faith, the individual must *study deeply* the Divine Word. . . . He should then *meditate* on the import of the Word, and finding its spiritual depths, *pray* for guidance and assistance. But, most important, after prayer is *action*. After one has prayed and meditated, he must arise, relying fully on the guidance and confirmation of Bahá'u'lláh to teach His Faith. *Perseverance* in action is essential, just as wisdom and audacity are necessary for effective teaching. The individual must sacrifice all things to this great goal, and then the victories will be won.[35]

Secretary Sherrill also instructed the circuit teachers to make sure that each of the goal communities they worked with, even if composed of only a few people, had the basics of a plan in place for its own locality. She advised:

> In your consultation with the friends please stress the importance of their having:
> 1. A Plan—and working it!
> 2. "Follow-up" work to augment your efforts.
> 3. Evaluation consultations—wherein the friends periodically "take a look" to determine if their plan is effective, or needs changing.[36]

The intensive action plan worked. The national spiritual assembly held conferences focused on the Plan and rallied its auxiliaries to action. By the 1961 convention, with two years remaining in the Plan, the American National Teaching Committee had assisted 100 groups, sponsored 33 extended circuit teaching visits lasting from four days to six months, and initiated 250 two- to three-day circuit visits. Approximately 65 groups were becoming assemblies within that year, and 72 new ones a year were needed to meet the objective of 300 new assemblies.[37] By the end of the Ten Year Plan, this objective was won.

That the American Bahá'í community was able to accomplish its challenging objectives without the living presence of Shoghi Effendi was remarkable. Doubtless, the pathos evoked by his death helped in no small part, since this surely helped galvanize individuals to action. Simply being galvanized was not enough, however. Also needed was a viable action plan that would allow all energies to focus on the objectives, rally around a sensible strategy, and meet Plan objectives successfully. The Americans were able to do this by creating their own miniplans for the last phase of the Ten Year Plan, as they had been trained to do, very effectively, by their planning mentor Shoghi Effendi.

THE MATURATION OF OTHER NATIONAL COMMUNITIES

Other national Bahá'í communities had multiyear plans as well. For example, in 1946, the combined communities of India, Pakistan, and Burma launched a four-and-a-half-year plan (1946-1950). In 1947, the Iraqi community began a three-year plan composed of internal (domestic) goals only, as was the Australian-New Zealand plan (1947-1953).[38] The stalwart community of the British Isles, reeling from the effects of World War II, nevertheless spontaneously appealed to Shoghi Effendi in 1944 to allow that community to begin a Six Year Plan, which he supported and which they concluded, with great difficulty, in triumph.[39]

Iran (formerly Persia) is another country that received extensive attention from Shoghi Effendi, who helped the Bahá'í community there grow and plan for its own development. That Bahá'í community was special in many ways, not the least of which being that it struggled under the burden of continued, bloody repression even though—or perhaps because—Bahá'u'lláh and the Báb, cofounders of the Bahá'í Faith, were Persians. Persia was the site of one of the first local spiritual assemblies in the world, in Tehran, which was an important forerunner of the Persian National Spiritual Assembly established in 1934. Influenced by Shoghi Effendi's direct instructions, this community succeeded in becoming spiritual leaders among Bahá'ís of the world. They gathered and safeguarded important holy documents, established a firm system of membership statistics, carried out a superb child and youth education program, and sent pioneers and traveling teachers to such wide-ranging places as Iraq, Turkish Kurdistan, and various countries in Europe, Latin America, Asia, Australia, and North America. According to Ali-Akbar Furútan, their steadfastness and sacrifices in the face of continued persecution and martyrdom "were all the result of thirty-six years of divine education and training" under the leadership of Shoghi Effendi.[40]

TABLE 6.1
TEN YEAR CRUSADE: NATIONAL PIONEER GOAL AREAS
ASSIGNED BY SHOGHI EFFENDI (1953)

NATIONAL SPIRITUAL ASSEMBLY	# OF PLACES ASSIGNED	CONTINENTS ASSIGNED
United States of America	29	4: Africa, Asia, Europe, America (plus others as needed)*
India, Pakistan, Burma	16	2: Asia and Africa
Persia	13	2: Asia and Africa
Canada	13	2: America and Asia
British Isles	11	2: Europe and Africa
Germany and Austria	11	1: Europe
South America	9	2: America and Asia
Central America	7	2: America and Asia
Australia and New Zealand	7	1: Asia
Egypt and Sudan	6	1: Africa
Italy and Switzerland	6	1: Europe
Iraq	3	2: Asia and Africa

Source: Shoghi Effendi, *The Bahá'í Faith, 1844-1952: Information Statistical and Comparative, Including Supplement: "Ten Year International Bahá'í Teaching and Consolidation Plan 1953-1963"* (Wilmette, IL: Bahá'í Publishing Committee, 1953) 59-62.
* United States Bahá'ís were asked to go wherever they could, even to areas assigned to other national spiritual assemblies.

The list of communities that participated in the Ten Year Plan is also a good list of national groups existing in 1953, when the plan began. As shown in Table 6.1 above, some communities had more responsibilities assigned to them than others. The more experienced and capable the national or multinational assembly—and the more unfettered by serious religious persecution, which hampered several communities in the Middle East—the more work Shoghi Effendi assigned it to do. Apparently, in this third global plan launched in 1953, Shoghi Effendi still relied upon the Americans to carry out most of the work of expansion throughout the globe.

Also listed in that table, however, are a number of other capable national or multinational spiritual assemblies. These range from Persia and India-Pakistan-Burma to Germany-Austria and South America. Among those who had struggled mightily to appear on this list were the assemblies of Australia-New Zealand, Egypt-Sudan, and Italy-Switzerland. Shoghi Effendi had helped to nurture these communities just as he did the Americans, Persians, and other communities listed. Although this book focuses upon his cultivation of the North American planners (because of their preeminent status as "cradle" of the Administrative Order and because of their extensive responsibilities for Shoghi Effendi's three global plans) the other nations' plans were extremely important as well. It is by considering other nations, in fact, that we can best see how strongly Shoghi Effendi believed that teaching national groups how to plan for their own growth and evolution would make them self-sufficient and fully functioning.

The Bahá'ís of Australia and New Zealand provide one example. As did the North American community, those Bahá'ís collected many of the communications Shoghi Effendi sent them and compiled these in a book, *Letters from the Guardian to Australia and New Zealand*, which covers the period from 1923 to 1957. The Australian and New Zealand community began as a fairly small outpost of a few Bahá'ís. Although they formed a joint national spiritual assembly in 1934, the same year as Persia, their community was far smaller in numbers than the Persian community and not nearly as enriched with a history and culture that was uniquely Bahá'í. Letters in the 1920s, 1930s, and 1940s addressed to them from Shoghi Effendi continually stressed the need to develop local and national communities characterized by excellent spiritual principles. These letters also indicated, however, that Shoghi Effendi held them in high esteem. He wrote in 1938 that the "record of their manifold accomplishments warms my heart and cheers my spirit." Another letter indicated that "I truly admire the manner in which the national representatives of the believers of Australia and New Zealand are discharging their responsibilities and fulfilling their vital and manifold functions."[41]

In 1946, a notable shift occurred in these letters. Those letters written by Shoghi Effendi, as well as those written on his behalf (commonly by his helper and wife Rúḥíyyih Rabbani), began to stress the importance of creating a plan. Although the letters of the Australians and New Zealanders to Shoghi Effendi covered a range of topics, his reply letters always emphasized the need to plan. Often Shoghi Effendi used the example of the efforts of other national communities to spur them on.

For example, Rúḥíyyih Rabbani wrote in May of 1946, on his behalf:

> The Bahá'ís in the United States have just embarked on their second Seven Year Plan; India is working hard on a Four and a half Year Plan; England is straining every nerve to achieve, during the Six Year Plan the friends have chosen for themselves, 19 assemblies. It is only right and proper that such a vast and promising territory as Australia, New Zealand, and Tasmania represent, should likewise win for itself new laurels in the Bahá'í teaching field during the next few years! He therefore suggests you choose, after surveying your own possibilities and soliciting suggestions from the friends, certain immediate objectives, and then work unitedly towards achieving them.[42]

Apparently, the templates being held up here were the plans of North America, India, and Great Britain, with the clear implication that a part of the maturation process for those in Australia and New Zealand was to begin the planning process, first by choosing a few suitable objectives. Evidently Shoghi Effendi did not receive a positive response to this suggestion, however, because two months later Rúḥíyyih Rabbani wrote again to emphasize the point:

> He also feels that, if the N.S.A. [National Spiritual Assembly] considers such a course of action feasible, definite plans should be made for carrying the Cause to certain goal towns; in other words, a real plan with fixed objectives and a time limit is now possible for Australia, and should be speedily set in motion.

She continued this plea for a "real plan with fixed objectives" by noting that Shoghi Effendi "feels that the N.S.A. should meet more often," since apparently that body was meeting only once every few months, carrying out their business by correspondence.[43] Shoghi Effendi added a substantial postscript to this letter that praised what they did do well and more gently indicated that they could, indeed, focus on expansion and prepare for the planning process:

The ever-expanding activities of the Bahá'í communities of Australia and New Zealand, so clearly reflected in the reports and minutes forwarded recently by your Assembly, demonstrate the character of the Faith which so powerfully animates you. . . . The attention of the believers throughout all centres in both communities should now be focused on the steady multiplication and consolidation of these institutions which constitute the bedrock of the Administrative order of which your Assembly is the appointed trustee and chief promoter.

He firmly indicated the connection with plans:

A supreme effort, on the part of all, . . . is absolutely essential in the course of the present year, and as a prelude to the initiation of future plans aiming at a still greater development and further enrichment of the life of both communities. All secondary matters should be subordinated to the primary requirements of the present day.[44]

Thus he offered guidance in the same effective manner that he did with other nations: praising past efforts, indicating the primary needs for the present day, attempting to focus attention away from issues of less importance, and asking for everyone to arise and make a "supreme effort."

They evidently, however, continued to focus on "secondary matters." Another series of letters from the Australians and New Zealanders asked for advice regarding a great variety of concerns. According to his usual practice, Shoghi Effendi allowed several sets of letters from this community to accumulate before answering them. Nevertheless, after almost a year and several letters, Rúḥíyyih Rabbani did respond directly in March of 1947, on behalf of Shoghi Effendi. She pulled them back to the main issue with a straightforward reporting of Shoghi Effendi's advice:

He feels very strongly that the main thing for your Assembly and all the believers of both Australia and New Zealand to concentrate on are teaching plans. The United States, India, Persia, and England are all embarked on ambitious and bold teaching campaigns, and it is a great pity that Australasia, where the Cause is now firmly established and boasts an active National Assembly, should not have a definite plan, with fixed goals, of its own.

When the believers are embarked on a definite teaching schedule there will be less time for them to constantly occupy themselves with purely secondary administrative points of procedure.⁴⁵

Rúḥíyyih Rabbani was (and is) a very plainspoken woman and not shy about transmitting Shoghi Effendi's opinions without qualification or ceremony. Shoghi Effendi read and approved all of the correspondence she and others wrote on his behalf, however, and often composed lengthy addenda, sometimes in his own handwriting. His lengthy note at the end of this particular letter clearly illustrated, more than anything yet cited in this chapter and perhaps in this book, his firm belief in the power of planning. His response appealed to them to arise and lend unprecedented impetus to the growth and consolidation of their religion in their homeland, via a plan:

> The initiation of a Plan, carefully devised, universally supported, and designed to promote effectively the vital interests of the Faith, and attain a definite objective within a specified number of years, would seem, at the present hour, highly desirable and opportune, and will, as a magnet, attract, to an unprecedented degree, the blessings of Bahá'u'lláh on the members of both communities....
>
> I fully realize how small are your numbers, how circumscribed are your means, how vast the distances that separate the centres already established. But I firmly believe that the initiation of a Plan to remedy the very deficiencies from which the infant Administrative Order is now suffering, and a firm resolve to carry out its provisions, as well as a sustained effort to make the necessary sacrifices for its consummation, will set in motion forces of such magnitude, and draw upon both communities blessings of such potency, as shall excite the wonder of the believers themselves, and cause their Faith to enter an era of unprecedented expansion and marvellous and fruitful development.⁴⁶

Thus in a few short sentences, backed by over ten years of experience helping guide national plans in countries around the world, Shoghi Effendi once again urged, cajoled, and encouraged the believers of Australia and New Zealand to adopt a plan, promising them innumerable benefits.

Finally, they did create such a plan, and a letter Shoghi Effendi sent four months later lauded this important step and advised that the "attention of the members of both communities must henceforth be focused on the Plan, its progress, its requirements, its significance and immediate objectives."[47] Letters sent in the following year praised their plan-related efforts. Rúḥíyyih Rabbani indicated that the "devotion and perseverance of the believers in seeking to meet the requirements of their Plan pleases and touches [Shoghi Effendi] immensely" and Shoghi Effendi himself added that the "Plan launched by the small yet highly promising community of devoted believers in Australia and New Zealand constitutes a landmark of unusual significance in the history of the evolution of the Faith in that far-off continent."[48] Shoghi Effendi also asked to receive complete reports about the progress of teaching efforts and copies of national spiritual assembly minutes. His letters in 1950 were few, but consistently offered feedback concerning the prosecution of their plan, sometimes reminding them of its importance and of the stirring example of other national communities. Finally, in 1953, this apt bi-national pupil received a June letter from Shoghi Effendi that must have provoked pride and celebration:

> The victorious conclusion of the Plan formulated by your Assembly . . . has filled my heart with joy and thanksgiving, has evoked profound admiration in the hearts of the followers of the Faith in both Hemispheres, and fully qualified the Bahá'í Communities in Australia, New Zealand and Tasmania to embark upon their Ten-Year Plan, which constitutes so important and vital a phase of the global Crusade.[49]

To confirm that this community had matured to a considerable degree, they received many subsequent letters from Shoghi Effendi filled with praise. His last letter, written in 1957, is especially poignant:

> The progress achieved in recent years, rapid and extraordinary as it has been ... has been highly gratifying and has served to deepen my confidence in their ability to achieve their high destiny, and to evoke sentiments of ever increasing admiration for the manner in which they have acquitted themselves of their task in the face of varied and almost insurmountable obstacles.[50]

He particularly congratulated the Australian community members for helping the New Zealand community to make rapid strides, so that it might form its own national spiritual assembly, "as a distinct and separate member of the world-wide family of Bahá'í national and regional Spiritual Assemblies."[51]

This short summary of Shoghi Effendi's plan-related letters to one national spiritual assembly highlights how closely connected in his mind were the processes of institutional development and planning. These communications indicate his wish for the various national communities to grow and develop their own institutions. Recall the image that Shoghi Effendi himself held up to the North Americans when he urged them to look after the institutional maturation of their charges in South and Central America. His requests that they nurture these "tender plants" were in fact exhortations for the North Americans to treat their charges as he treated them, and as he treated other national spiritual assemblies, by supplying "the necessary guidance, assistance, and encouragement that will enable the widely-scattered groups of believers in those countries to establish independent and properly constituted local Assemblies, and thereby erect the framework of the Administrative Order of their Faith."[52]

Summary

Although it has historically been good to have exemplary leaders, their role is changing in the organizational culture and in the world at large. It is becoming increasingly important for leaders to demonstrate different kinds of skills than they have in the past. Timeless elements of good leadership include capable vision for change and the ability to articulate group needs and to inspire, yet to enable people to direct change for themselves. Increasingly, leaders will also have to exhibit utmost integrity, yet still be able to envision, align resources, and empower native capacity. Leaders will no longer be protected by unquestioned hierarchy; they will have to learn how to share power and influence.

The leadership literature dovetails with the literature that focuses on "people-centered development." According to the latter, efforts to bring about social and economic progress in the past failed miserably when development experts neglected to engage supposed beneficiaries as willing and capable partners. This approach is proving futile at any rate as society and organizations increase in complexity. Decisions threaten to bury top administrators, forcing them to consider the benefits of sharing decision making throughout the organization. Doing so in an environment that encourages dialogue and interactive experience generates a greater probability of success. The Bahá'í Faith greatly honors the station of leaders. However, the writings cited were indicative of a careful balance of encouraging leadership while also encouraging more broadly based decision making. Bahá'u'lláh indicated that political rulers held a great station in the world, but they also had great responsibilities to govern in a judicious, principled manner. 'Abdu'l-Bahá offered extensive guidance to leaders, not only those of high secular, political rank but also those who are "spiritually learned." Both Bahá'u'lláh and 'Abdu'l-Bahá laid the groundwork for an administrative structure in their own religion that combined the best of leadership with the best of grassroots participation. The glue holding this combination together was to be the process of consultation, by which people brought together their opinions in a context of spiritual insight, tolerance, and detachment.

One of the most important tools Shoghi Effendi used to build up decentralized capacity was the preparation and execution of global plans. In the case of the North American Bahá'ís, global plans encouraged them to perfect the machinery of administration, as well as to gain a greater insight into the spiritual attributes of true leadership. Their responsibility was not only to improve their own leadership and administration but also to assist other national groups to be born, to expand, and then to establish their own leadership and administrative skills. As they executed these plans, they exercised a great amount of decentralized decision-making, as Shoghi Effendi only gave them the broad framework and periodic feedback, necessitating their working through of the day-to-day problems of developing and refining specific strategies.

In the case of other national communities, plans also served to build capacity and facilitate decentralization of decision making. Australia and New Zealand, a fledgling bi-national community repeatedly urged to plan, rose to the occasion and promulgated a plan with such success that they became one of the select planning communities charged with carrying out the Ten Year Plan.

This chapter has offered numerous suggestions that the reader might productively apply to a wide range of planning circumstances. Below is a summary:

- Treasure the power of leadership, which has been important throughout human history and will be for the foreseeable future. Implicit throughout this book has been the observation that having a principled, capable leader was a great benefit to the Bahá'í community. Good leaders also exist in other walks of life and in other contexts, and these leaders have the potential to activate human progress in numerous ways.
- Understand, however, that the best leadership rests on widespread consensus and participation in the activities of the organization. This will become even truer in the future. Using such means as ongoing communication and consultative dialogue can help ensure consensus and unified effort.
- Be aware that groups of leaders will need to develop the same style of capable planning leadership, as a whole, that Shoghi Effendi did as an individual. Just as he offered capable vision and bold yet achievable objectives, and just as he effectively helped motivate individuals to move from goals to action, today's more decentralized leadership structures will have to do the same.
- Aim, therefore, to develop purposefully decentralized leadership capacity and activity. For plans, one way to do this would be to form smaller groups charged with the responsibility of carrying out focused components of a larger set of tasks, just as Shoghi Effendi divided global initiatives into manage able portions for each of several nations.
- Use the process of planning as a means for organizational growth and development, but maintain sensitivity to human nature. One way to do this is to learn from Shoghi Effendi's analogy of the gardener (see page 132 above); he suggested that our organizations are like new plants, needing focused encouragement and care.

Chapter 7

Planning Progress

> He presented another parable to them, saying, "The kingdom of heaven is like a mustard seed, which a man took and sowed in his field; and this is smaller than all other seeds; but when it is full grown, it is larger than the garden plants, and becomes a tree, so that the birds of the air come and nest in its branches."
> —Matthew 13:31-32

> It is, therefore, evident and proved that an effort must be put forward to complete the purpose and plan of the teachings of God in order that in this great Day of days the world may be reformed, souls resuscitated, a new spirit of life found, hearts become illumined, mankind rescued from the bondage of nature, saved from the baseness of materialism and attain spirituality and radiance in attraction toward the divine Kingdom.
> —'Abdu'l-Bahá, *Promulgation of Universal Peace*

THIS BOOK BEGAN BY DESCRIBING the importance of human progress and the role of planning in reaching increasingly higher stages of human progress. For many reasons, people do not always have faith in the potential for social progress. Instead, it seems we as a human species are finding it more and more difficult to cooperate, to develop a cohesive vision of the future, and to move deliberately toward that vision.

Shoghi Effendi believed in the power of human progress and was able to lead his community in new and creative ways toward a vision of a better society. The approach used in this book to describe Shoghi Effendi offered examples of his leadership of global plans. Drawing on a mere fraction of his writings, this author tried to discern patterns of thought that could prove useful.

In some ways this was a futile task, very much like listing the colors apparent in an iridescent butterfly's fluttering wings as a way of describing its beauty: very difficult and very incomplete. The main problem is that the complexity of this individual and his natural lack of self-conscious technique makes any description inadequate. Furthermore, as indicated at several points, Shoghi Effendi's work was essentially focused upon spiritual upliftment and what he saw as a divinely inspired mandate. Attempting to relate this particular mission in secular language, using conventional methods of verbal description, cannot fully succeed. It is indeed true of his plans, as Rúḥíyyih Rabbani indicated, that

> [i]t would be hard indeed to find a comparable figure in history who, in a little over a third of a century, set so many different operations in motion, who found the time to devote his attention to minute details on one hand and on the other to cover the range of an entire planet with his plans, his instructions, his guidance and his leadership.[1]

In many ways, Shoghi Effendi's approach was timeless, in keeping with the approach of many other great leaders. Again, in the words of Rúḥíyyih Rabbani:

> There are not so many ways of doing things on this planet. Right methods are right when applied to different fields. Shoghi Effendi was a spiritual general leading a spiritual army to win spiritual prizes—but the campaign method was immemorial: organize your forces, conceive your strategy, attack your goal, occupy the position, keep your communications open to your base, bring up reinforcements, establish garrisons in the conquered territory, muster your forces and start the next campaign. As the armies of brilliant leaders get more and more experience the lull between campaigns diminishes. This was equally true of Shoghi Effendi's Plans.[2]

Since Shoghi Effendi was so accomplished in planning leadership, the question has arisen concerning how well his planning work applies to the challenges facing more ordinary planning and planners in the world at large. This last chapter summarizes some key aspects of the overall picture drawn thus far and points out a few additional parallels between Shoghi Effendi's methods and those of others.

INSTITUTIONS AND INFORMATION

One of the most important undertakings by Shoghi Effendi was to help build capacity in the institutions that he advised. This was the fresco wall that Rúḥíyyih Rabbani referred to when she explained Shoghi Effendi's overall method (described on page 41 above), which was first to draw the broad outlines of the picture that was to appear in the fresco and then to fill in the details. The broad outline and the proper preparation of the "canvas" were absolutely essential elements of Shoghi Effendi's approach to plans. He did not propose that national groups develop plans until he was fairly sure that they could carry them out. It sometimes took years to build capacity sufficient for these communities to absorb the responsibilities associated with planning. This is a warning to those readers who would glean inappropriately from the lessons gained from this book and rush out to impose some form of the planning process on all manner of organization; this is a sure path to keen disappointment. Even though the capacity to plan is a human attribute, this does not mean it should be used without constraint in all circumstances. It is a distinct sign of maturity and capacity for any group, organization, or even individual to be able to plan effectively for anything more complex than a simple meeting. The preparation necessary for even that level of maturity may be extensive and challenging. If groups are not careful, in fact, such preparation may be all-consuming, and they may never progress beyond this stage.

Gathering information was also an area to which Shoghi Effendi gave extensive attention. He found it absolutely essential to receive a huge amount of information about the communities he helped lead, and he kept receiving and responding to such data throughout his lifetime. This allowed him to coordinate a range of activities even though he was not on site and did not have the benefit of being able to see with his own eyes how plans were progressing in the field. Having a rich store of information also helped with various stages of the plans, such as setting objectives, counseling strategies, monitoring action, and summarizing accomplishments.

These particular characteristics of Shoghi Effendi's planning style are widely accepted as necessary parameters for organizational progress. Except in the youngest and most immature of organizations, most people recognize that it is not possible for a group to carry out effective plans for action unless it has an organizational base in place. Likewise, organizational, city, national, and other planners firmly believe in the power of gathering appropriate information. Particularly since the advent of computers, this function has indeed taken on too much importance in some contexts. If urban planners are not careful, for example, they can spend all of their time gathering information about the demographics, land use, physical environment, economy, and history of a place without ever getting around to creating and implementing a plan. Information-gathering technology now allows planners easily to create colorful, analytical maps of geographic information systems, but the hard choices remain about what to do with all of this attractive information.

Shoghi Effendi's contribution to these areas of thought and inquiry are subtle but important. In terms of institution building, he obviously would counsel that it is essential to build institutional capacity before attempting to carry out complex functions. However, the example of his leadership also suggests that the administration and institution building should not be ends in themselves, but rather means to create new, progressive initiatives. Particularly in many Western nations, the national character often tends to be very attuned to mastering the complexities of administration. Shoghi Effendi did not help build up institutions merely for the love of institutions or administration for its own sake, but for the love of what such increased capacity could accomplish. Therefore, to build a community, city, or company that functions well but is without direction is an exercise in futility.

The same is true for gathering information, an activity which can become too intensive. The information is only a means to an end. That end is the focused movement toward a vision of change, such as progressive improvement in the state of humankind. What was unique about Shoghi Effendi's approach is that he fully absorbed and integrated the information he received, but put it to the service of the respective plans' goals, which remained all-important in his mind.

Vision

Vision has also become a popular concept, widely accepted among a range of people. It was not so popular in the days of Shoghi Effendi as it is today, the extensive literature on the subject suggests, but the idea of vision has deep roots dating back to prehistoric times. What was particularly special about Shoghi Effendi's vision was its content, its consistency, and its power to help shape all of his community's efforts to move forward.

The overall vision under which he and his fellow believers operated was one of a progressively spiritually mature population that understood its relationship to divine power and that worked for the deliberate betterment of humanity. Shoghi Effendi's major contribution was to illustrate graphically how important the overarching vision of a better society in a distant future was to everyday life in the here and now. The magnificent letters in which he stated and restated the vision offered constant renewal of the vision as a source of inspiration. The way he used statements of vision to remind people constantly of the purpose of their activities and to connect them with their unique and priceless mandate was nothing short of masterful. Reminding the North American Bahá'ís of their special mission and station vested all their activities with grave importance and granted them noble associations with valor, sacrifice, and heroism. References to the over all context of the world, which was in many cases quite literally falling down around them, safeguarded community members from the skepticism and uncertainty that must surely have haunted those who lived through the horrors of war and political strife. Indicating their place in the context of time heightened their sense of mission and helped give meaning to efforts that could have otherwise seemed small and futile. Offering an inspiring context, in the form of the construction of the holy buildings on Mt. Carmel, provided visible connection to the great mission upon which they had embarked. Referring to smaller or more immediate visions, of a completed House of Worship or of the end of their plan, gave them hope that they might see proof of the success of their efforts. These simple but inspirational references had power.

While there has been a flood of books, articles, and exhortations about the concept of vision in contemporary society, this does not mean that people have nothing more to learn about vision. As indicated in chapter three, cultivating a sense of vision allows organizations and people to create a more positive environment for their lives and their activities. Aiming toward a desired end state is an important source of motivation and has been used in a wide variety of circumstances to rally change. "Visioning" the future is an essential part of the planning process for everyone ranging from national leaders to individuals trying to direct their personal lives.

Again turning to the example of urban planning, "visioning" is so popular that in the United States the federal government has demanded it as part of municipal planning for certain functions. Those communities applying for federal Empowerment Zone or Enterprise Community designation in the mid-1990s, for example, were required to include within their strategic plan a clear statement of their vision for their economically distressed city or rural area. As those who participated in these challenging application processes can testify, however, in many cases this exercise high lighted the futility of mandating vision.

Simply used as a technique, the process of visioning has limited power. At its worst, vision building can be simply a perfunctory step, carried out and then ignored. While it is possible to state that one's vision for a city is one of livable communities, viable businesses, and attractive public facilities, merely stating this for the record has little effect. Even if someone actually believes in this vision—perhaps the mayor, or the chief planner, or even the council—it does not mean that anyone else does or that the vision has the power to produce change. Change is even less likely if the vision was created to fulfill a requirement for an application or a report.

This is an obvious dilemma, but so is whether or not the vision is widely supported. If the vision belongs only to a few people, it loses power, and several authors have discussed at some length the need to ensure that every one is committed to the vision. A third dilemma is even more serious, however. Sometimes the problem is the vision's content. Suppose the vision is indeed widely supported and widely believed, but exclusionary. This is of particular concern in the case of competing organizations or corporations. Each one can develop its own vision, but if each vision substantially aims to triumph over everyone else, then all the competing visions are of little use to the industry as a whole. As another example, what if a neighborhood or city develops a vision of a community that is peaceful and productive for its members, but implicitly or explicitly keeps out all of those who do not fit? This situation is also of little use to the betterment of society as a whole. Yet affluent communities in multiracial societies often hold fast to visions of peaceful tranquillity and community life that somehow manage to exclude racial minorities or low-income people.

It may not be worth the effort if the vision toward which one is moving is not worthy of inspiration. Worthy visions cannot be narrow, selfish, materialistic, or pecuniary, for thereby they lose power. When human beings attach their energies to noble causes, causes that assist them to do their best to serve and elevate humanity, they can harness great power.

Given these caveats, Shoghi Effendi's use of vision requires a second look. His tireless promotion of the vision of Bahá'u'lláh is one of the few recorded cases of a leader in modern times actively supporting a vision that is global in scope yet not repressive or exclusionary. In the power of his cause, Shoghi Effendi found endless reservoirs of strength, as his religion's sacred writings had promised, and he drew from as worthy a set of visions as one could ever hope to find. Shoghi Effendi gave visions primacy by evoking their beauty, exploring their manifestations, and constantly referring to them in many ways and in many different contexts.

The Universal House of Justice, which has taken up the challenge of carrying forth Shoghi Effendi's global leadership, has issued several letters and statements that can help orient society as it grapples with contemporary issues near the beginning of the twenty-first century. In *The Prosperity of Humankind*, widely distributed among international leaders, the Universal House of Justice calls for humanity to aim for a vision that is one of global peace and prosperity, indicating:

> Everywhere the signs multiply that the earth's peoples yearn for an end to conflict and to the suffering and ruin from which no land is any longer immune. . . . The effort of will required for such a task cannot be summoned up merely by appeals for action against the countless ills afflicting society. It must be galvanized by a vision of human prosperity in the fullest sense of the term—an awakening to the possibilities of the spiritual and material well-being now brought within grasp. Its beneficiaries must be all of the planet's inhabitants, without distinction.[3]

This is the kind of vision that is worthy of effort and attention by every thinking human being. The challenge is not so much to develop a vision, as to develop an appropriate vision that has the potential to help create a better world for all peoples.

Goals and Action

About that most common and yet difficult set of planning tasks—choosing appropriate goals and effectively linking them with action—Shoghi Effendi also offered new insights. All but forsaking more general goals for the firmer ground of specific objectives or tasks that could be measured, Shoghi Effendi excelled in helping his religious community move purposefully toward their collective vision. Informed as he was by a ceaseless stream of correspondence that told him very well the capacities and limitations of the groups with which he corresponded and gifted as he was with a keen understanding of human nature and of his fellow believers, Shoghi Effendi chose objectives extremely well. These were simple, clear, few in number, but powerful in impact. They meshed perfectly with the overall vision and mission, which was to create a globally based religion characterized by a diversity of peoples and nations. They allowed the community charged with carrying them out to take incremental steps toward this vision, in this case by spreading progressively outward from one nation to one continent, another continent, and then the world.

For carrying out these objectives, Shoghi Effendi suggested a remarkable set of strategies, broad in scope yet detailed in direction, which simultaneously counseled effective action and tutored the community in how to treat people with sensitivity, warmth, and respect. He offered lessons in character building by making it clear that only through good character, defined in nontraditional terms such as freedom from racial prejudice as well as more traditional terms such as chastity and moral rectitude, would their plans succeed. He continued the process of institution building by noting that only through scrupulously fair, just, and humane processes and decisions would those institutions be able to carry out the strategies necessary for the triumph of their plan.

To this basic framework for action he added structural ornaments that were as important as the concrete panels sheathing the outside of the American House of Worship. These included absolute reliance upon the power of prayer and divine assistance, as taught by 'Abdu'l-Bahá, and faith in the connection of their plan with a greater purpose for humanity. References to heroes and heroines who had gone before them personalized the struggle and reminded community members of their spiritual forebears. Calls to action allowed Shoghi Effendi to state forthrightly that all should arise and do their part in the great campaign. Also, Shoghi Effendi used all manner of praise, in a wonderful variety of creative ways, ranging from pure words of gratitude filled with heartfelt compliments, to sincere expressions of his personal pleasure with their accomplishments, to special mention of outstanding individuals.

Each of these approaches could greatly benefit both religious and secular efforts to plan. Although they may seem tailored to religious contexts, his approaches would in fact resolve several of the dilemmas now facing other planners as well.

Developing goals, objectives, and strategies is a common exercise. More popular now that personal time and career management has risen to the fore, goal setting and strategy setting are tools that have been used for many years in national economic development plans, urban and regional plans, and corporate plans. As you read this page, thousands of present and future organizational leaders are probably receiving lessons, somewhere, in the importance and techniques of creating goals, objectives, and strategies. Sometimes presented in the context of strategic planning, such techniques are popular because in many cases they work.

These efforts can sometimes be of enormous benefit. One small community-based organization in Detroit, Michigan, for example, has been using such devices ever since its main officers received training in strategic planning. They have embraced this manifestation of the planning process with zeal and use it to identify likely areas of endeavor and to organize their energies on a yearly basis. Their objectives give them clear ideas about what they are trying to accomplish and whether they have done so.

For groups such as this or for bigger organizations such as cities or nations, it remains a challenge to create simple, clear, appropriate goals and strategies. In part, the problem is one previously identified as lack of widespread agreement about goals. But, in part, the problem is also knowing what to do. Knowing what to do takes sophisticated understanding and analysis of the environment, like that capacity gained by Shoghi Effendi through information gathering, but it also takes knowledge about the character and nature of the people involved in making the plan succeed.

An additional problem facing planners is not so much technique as tone. At some point, many people stall in this whole process of setting goals, objectives, and strategies because they see it as rigid, mechanical, or dehumanizing. While some personality types revel in the attention to detail that all of this could entail, others bridle at the perceived tendency of organizational planners to attempt to channel or direct behavior.

For some reason, very little professional literature exists about these problematic areas of individual commitment to plan-making. In classical urban planning theory, some scholars deal with the whole issue by proposing alternative models of planning, based largely on interactive dialogue or muddling through. These approaches get them around the dilemma of setting up objectives and strategies ahead of time, when information is imperfect and human behavior individualistic, unpredictable, and resistant to being channeled. Strategic planner John Bryson has dealt with this subject to some extent. He would counsel setting up a politically informed process, when key stakeholders are talking together at one table in a few focused sessions and thrashing out processes to be followed. When this works, it is one viable solution, although the potential for conflict must be enormous. Only in the personal planning literature, such as that which supports time-management and personal-improvement seminars, can one find some insight into the importance of emotions and commitment to the success of plans. For some reason, this literature has not spurred the growth of a comparable literature concerning motivating people to support plans for groups.[4]

Shoghi Effendi's approach of setting up the framework for action and yet allowing broad areas of self-determination seems sensible and worthy of further attention. One way around the resentment that could accompany rigid plan-making is simply to let decentralized groups or individuals develop their own plans and their own ways of meeting the goals of broader plans. In that manner, strategies become their own, not someone else's. This gives new importance to Shoghi Effendi's extensive writings concerning the role of individuals in contributing to the success of community plans. Although he helped identify institutional responsibilities, one of his unique contributions was his focused attention upon individuals, whose commitment is absolutely essential to the advancement of any larger group.

Another good idea with universal applicability is his approach of reminding his comrades of principles and standards for strategies. Even though he provided, in great detail, specific suggestions for strategies, he seemed most interested in the standards governing their activities, and these standards stood the test of time, while more specific strategies became outmoded. The standards he urged most forcefully included steady adherence to moral principle; sensitive encouragement and support for those involved in the plan; active involvement for native populations rather than outsiders; freedom from personal, racial, or national prejudice; and gradual empowerment and decentralization through grassroots institution-building.

Planning informed by such examples would focus less on specifying strategies and more on specifying overall policies or building individual or institutional capacities that can adjust to a wide range of circumstances with flexibility and grace. Although in many situations it would be difficult to emulate the power of his call for upright personal behavior, in other situations it might not be. It is not unusual, for example, for service and retail operations that are trying to improve their relationships with clients and customers to train their representatives to be courteous, patient, and sympathetic. An organization that is planning for other kinds of improvement would do well to consider the potential effect of encouraging personal virtues among its visible representatives.

Of additional interest is the dilemma of how to inspire ourselves and our organizations to act. In the case of Shoghi Effendi's global plans, references to the Tablets of the Divine Plan, the heroes and heroines, as well as the construction projects in the Holy Land were powerful motivating forces. The reader's task, however, is to find his or her own means of spurring motivation, or to help a group or organization to do so.

Such means for motivating vary for every circumstance, but praise and encouragement are universal tools, particularly when these are based upon close attention to actual accomplishments. An immediate way to encourage successful completion of a plan is to make sure that people working for the plan's advancement are properly nourished with expressions of appreciation for the work they have done and with encouragement to finish the work they have yet to tackle. Another essential lesson is the need to make "calls to action," continually reminding coplanners of the plan, not allowing it to fade from memory. This could be done by constantly calling attention to the vision. In terms of symbolism, one powerful image for most people is the need to create a better environment for the children and the grandchildren who are yet to come. Another image is the sacrifice that others in the organization (heroes and heroines) made years before, and the present challenge such sacrifice offers.

It is indeed curious that the literature on planning seldom mentions such considerations. For example, urban and regional planners, as a profession, still have a lot to learn about motivating people to support urban plans. Although some prominent examples of widespread enthusiasm for urban or regional plans or projects exist, in most cases these projects have relied heavily on "patrons"—political or business leaders with clout—or have enjoyed little support from anyone. For urban planners, the prospect of generating widespread and heartfelt enthusiasm for an improved urban society, with even a fraction of the effectiveness of Shoghi Effendi, should be enormously attractive.

Monitoring

Monitoring is another area in which technical expertise is important, but it should not outstrip application that is both people-sensitive and effective. Shoghi Effendi excelled in this area and did not hesitate to mix praise with forceful reminders of tasks remaining to be done, or to watch week in and week out for the kinds of results that were needed for success to be assured. This is the characteristic that is perhaps hardest for other people to emulate. How many people have, or deserve, such self-assurance? How is it possible to watch so carefully, and to assess so unflinchingly, the progress of others?

Again, Shoghi Effendi was not evidently conscious of a common evaluation approach or technique. Rather, it appears that he watched so carefully because he was genuinely attached to the origins, purpose, and the out comes of the plans. The national communities carrying them out were his proteges. The flood of ideas that translated into objectives and strategies, the anxious feelings which prompted numerous cables, the heartfelt attachment to success or lack thereof, were apparently natural and spontaneous. Such actions stemmed from a level of commitment that is hard to fake.

It is difficult to find enough documented examples of energetic oversight of plans so as to make even the most perfunctory comparison with that which Shoghi Effendi offered. Little seems to be recorded about such situations. Somewhat comparable circumstances might be the drive felt by a corporate executive about a great initiative designed to bring about revolutionary change in the corporation, or the attachment that ancient rulers must have felt toward huge construction projects such as the building of the Pyramids. To match Shoghi Effendi's style, however, the executive or pharaoh would have had to be highly committed—personally involved in clarifying the overall goals and vision, actively enthusiastic about laying out different strategies for action, and constantly watching and giving feedback about progress or lack thereof. In particular, the monitoring would require sustained, relentless focus over a period of many years.

In the world at large, two approaches are either to become too focused on the technical research aspects of evaluation and monitoring, or to do nothing at all. As indicated in chapter five, some researchers seized upon evaluation studies as a sphere of expertise that would allow them to reshape social change. They defined their role as assessing whether people were carrying out programs which produced results that the researchers could measure. It is not surprising that this approach suffered in popularity. Many program managers do not want to be evaluated solely on the basis of program "success" or "failure." Even if they do, the attractiveness of receiving this information in a supportive and constructive manner while there is still time to adjust the program and make it successful, is obvious. This is why the work of people such as Richard Hofferbert is important, because it brings a higher degree of humanity into the dialogue about how to evaluate and monitor social action in a way that is responsible yet humane.

Although many professional evaluators are beginning to learn from these experiences, the more typical situation in the world of implementation is probably lack of noticeable monitoring of any kind. Only a few articles have appeared in the past several years about the possibility of monitoring whether or not urban plans have succeeded; the more typical approach is simply to implement them or not.[5] Arguably, if all types of plans were tallied in the world at large, it would become obvious that only a small percentage receive even a fraction of the kind of focused attention to successful implementation that Shoghi Effendi offered.

After reading Shoghi Effendi's letters, it is hard not to be inspired to begin to pay more attention to smaller, more modest plans. Surely if he was able to lead, inspire, and monitor plans under such difficult situations, more common circumstances lend themselves to possible refinement.

The most important lesson one could learn from Shoghi Effendi's letters is to pay attention and to develop a genuine commitment to the success of the plan. By extension, of course, this means one must care about the people who are carrying out the plan. When Shoghi Effendi was explaining to his fellow believers that he had confidence in their abilities and that his heart ached to contemplate the possibility of their failure, he was offering a level of commitment that gave all of his subsequent comments impact. Paying attention also means noting what the priorities are, starting with those, and then dividing the workload into manageable portions, such as phases. Paying attention means noticing on a regular basis which objectives are not being won, and then making a special push to make sure they are won. It also means celebrating accomplishments and moving on to additional tasks. This was a feature of Shoghi Effendi's approach.

Since few comparable leaders exist and since leadership is becoming more decentralized, it is important to begin to apply such focused attention to our own plans. Rather than await the leader who can apply such rigor to evaluating the progress—or lack of progress—of our plans, it is important instead to build institutions that exemplify the fine balance between self-determination and leadership.

Another task is to become more systematic in our individual plan-related efforts. This last concept was suggested by the Universal House of Justice as it wrote the worldwide Bahá'í community about its Four Year Plan, extending from 1996 to 2000. A 1998 letter counseled an approach far more modest and personalized than would be necessary to follow in Shoghi Effendi's footsteps. The Universal House of Justice again called attention to the fact that individuals are the building block for the success of all plans and asked for an "orderliness of approach," pointing out that it is important to allow for individual initiative and spontaneity, yet "be clear-headed, methodical, efficient, constant, balanced and harmonious." In the tradition of Shoghi Effendi, the Universal House of Justice directly connected the need to act for the advancement of plans with the need to monitor personal action:

> the Plan, among other things, gives direction, identifies goals, stimulates effort, provides a variety of needed facilities and materials to benefit the work of teachers and administrators. This is of course necessary for the proper functioning of the community, but is of no consequence unless its individual members respond through active participation. In so responding, each individual, too, must make a conscious decision as to what he or she will do to serve the Plan, and as to how, where and when to do it. This determination enables

the individual to check the progress of his actions and, if necessary, to modify the steps being taken. Becoming accustomed to such a procedure of systematic striving lends meaning and fulfilment to ... [life].[6]

It is really not necessary to be as successful as Shoghi Effendi at leading and monitoring plans. It would suffice to focus on doing the best job possible within one's own sphere of action. Institutions and groups will have to create improved capacity in these areas, but this too is simply a broader version of the kind of activity suggested in the above quotation.

LEADERSHIP

This book offers both a strong endorsement of the power of leadership and a strong argument for changing it. The endorsement came at the very beginning, in chapter two, when among the spiritual principles of good planning was listed leadership, albeit "enlightened leadership." Implicit as well in the whole premise of this book has been the idea that Shoghi Effendi was a good leader worthy of emulation. This might seem in contrast with the professional literature and the development literature cited, which seems to diminish the importance of individual leaders. It seems that leadership must be tempered with constraints and decentralized, according to some. According to others, the process of social decision-making should be almost entirely democratic, based upon self-determination and consultation.

At one stage of its history, human civilization depended upon leaders at every level, especially at the national level. Monarchs ruled the day. Most modern nations have moved away from governance by one individual alone, opting for systems of shared power and rotating leadership. Unfortunately, the pendulum may have swung too far in some cases. Whereas it was important to moderate the extraordinary power that kings and rulers wielded, it is also important to recognize that such systems were not all bad. If nothing else, they sometimes supplied nations with stable and predictable leadership, at least for a while. In contrast, in many modern countries, it seems as if national leaders have become national punching bags, frequently blamed for all woes and rarely credited for any accomplishments.

Leaders can be very important to human society in general and to a wide range of groups and organizations in particular. The key is to reform abuses of the past but still recognize that good leadership can be a very helpful tool for social progress. The benefits that Shoghi Effendi was able to bring to his community are indicative of the best qualities of leadership. In the world at large, leaders and members of leadership bodies need to reflect these qualities, which include outstanding personal character, commitment, compassion, and enthusiasm. Leadership qualities also include vision, the ability to help lay a path to the future, and ability to rally the "troops" to accomplish the seemingly impossible.

Fortunately, the need to create a more humane leadership is becoming more apparent in the professional literature, particularly in business circles. It is no longer impossible to find books that talk about "principled" or "visionary" leadership, or leadership with "soul." In one remarkable example, it is now even possible to find discussions of "love" and "virtue" and leadership, in a popular mainstream book that directly draws upon the spiritual writings of the world's great religions.[7] This would have been unimaginable even twenty years ago.

The key concept is "leadership," not "the leader." The era of Shoghi Effendi was one that passed this way but once. As he well knew, his role in history was to link one generation with another, to be a forceful, singular leader so that in the future no such singular leader would be necessary. As evident in the last chapter, the whole purpose of his activities was to set in place a global system characterized by decentralized decision-making and self-determination, all within the framework of global cooperation and governance. As the last of his line to lead alone, Shoghi Effendi must have worked frantically to prepare his fellow believers for his absence and the absence of any future such Guardian as leader.

The lessons to be learned from this extraordinary individual must some how become translated into a group consciousness, into a system of shared decision-making and decentralized leadership. Using such tools as consultation, encouraged by such principles as the basic equality of humankind, inspired by such leadership as this, our charge is to take these lessons and apply them in entirely different contexts. It is such challenges that make life interesting.

Appendix

A Basic Primer on Planning

Would you like to know how to create and carry out a plan that works? Of course, no single way to plan exists, as chapter three indicates in its brief overview of several different theories about the planning process. However, this appendix offers a few ideas about how to proceed with plans, ranging from the very simple to the more elaborate. These suggestions are based largely on the popular "rational" model, but the section on "alternative process frameworks" suggests other possible approaches.

Unfortunately, many people and organizations shy away from planning activities because they see them as too complicated. As this appendix will demonstrate, it is not necessary to create a complex plan in order to create an effective one. First, the basic components of an exemplary planning process will be considered. Then guidance is offered for creating "a very simple plan" and "a simple plan," and for using other process frameworks.

AN EXEMPLARY PLANNING PROCESS

An exemplary planning process creates a plan that is successful in its results and is simultaneously supported by all affected parties. Several ways exist to create such a plan, which is why several forms of the "planning process" exist. This section will focus on the most important components of exemplary plans, in particular, successful results and active support by all affected parties. This means that the first two elements listed below are especially important. An exemplary planning process is one characterized by:

- Knowledge
- Participation
- Collaboration
- Vision, Upliftment
- A Strong Implementation and Evaluation Model
- Readiness

KNOWLEDGE

One of the requirements for effective planning is that it be based on knowledge. This knowledge may be of several types. Sometimes people have innate knowledge of a situation, particularly if they are planning for themselves or their communities and are therefore intimately aware of their own conditions, strengths, and weaknesses. The need to tap innate knowledge is one reason it is important to ensure participation. In many cases, however, it is necessary to gather new information in order to plan well. This can include gathering related facts and figures, assessing the needs of the population, or inquiring into the conditions affecting the immediate environment. Another important kind of knowledge concerns the group's purpose, direction, and mission. Gaining this knowledge might require studying recent letters or directives from authoritative sources, or examining previous or related plans and policies. Shoghi Effendi acquired in-depth knowledge of the conditions facing his comrades through constant correspondence and study of reports, but he also urged them to gain knowledge for themselves by assessing their situation, studying their history and sacred texts, and immersing themselves in their mandate documents, such as *The Tablets of the Divine Plan*. In addition, he and his forebears counseled tapping into spiritual powers as a source of knowledge and "potency" (see quotation on page 22).

PARTICIPATION

The best way to ensure that the plan and its implementation are supported by all is to involve people in the creation of the plan and in its implementation. Such involvement should exemplify the best principles of consultation, which include respect for the opinions of others, harmonious exchange of frankly expressed opinions, and willingness by all to submit to—and support—the final decision of the group. Consultation also implies more involvement than "advising" leaders of an organization, since such advice is sometimes perfunctory or barely heeded. In contrast, a consultative process would solicit active input from those who would be expected to help carry out the plan.

In some cases, such involvement is difficult. For example, when a board or council is planning an initiative that involves a large territory and great numbers of people, mechanisms such as a broad "town" or community meeting could be geographically impossible, poorly attended, or culturally nonviable. In those cases, some accepted approaches are to select a representative advisory group, to carry out surveys or other formal means of collecting opinions, or to hold several consultative meetings about the plan in various places over a period of time. A steady stream of correspondence and dialogue with the population in question could also help improve the participatory nature of the process.

COLLABORATION

A collaborative process involves cooperation with affiliated organizations and institutions. This concept is different from mere participation because it assumes that some people and institutions are more important to involve in the planning process than others. John Bryson, well-known strategic planner cited in chapter three, referred to these people and institutions as "stakeholders," and declared their involvement absolutely necessary for successful planning. A city council that is planning to improve housing in a subsector of its inner city not only should involve that area's citizens at large (in a participatory process, as explained above) but also should consider seeking collaboration with key institutions such as the state or provincial government, local offices of federal agencies, nearby and surrounding area community-based organizations, the regional planning agency, neighborhood businesses, and local organizations of real-estate owners, landlords, tenants, or corporate leaders. Such institutional linkages help to avoid overlap, gain new ideas, and extend the resources of the council by soliciting active support of other partners. Religious communities also have important parties with whom they should collaborate. A church board might find that the bishop, supervising minister (e.g., "district superintendent"), and congregational committees are key planning partners. Local Bahá'í communities might choose to plan collaboratively with other nearby assemblies or groups, regional training or teaching institutes, or members of the Auxiliary Board and their assistants.

VISION, UPLIFTMENT

An effective planning process is also one that is vision driven. This point would seem obvious, but it often is not. As explained in chapter three, vision gives us hope and an image of the future toward which we can move. Several key ways of promoting vision-driven action include creating a verbal (or visual) picture of the vision and then using that vision to guide more mundane actions, making sure that everyone involved understands and becomes committed to the vision. Another approach is to focus on developing (and then acting in accordance with) an agreed-upon mission for the organization or group. Appropriate goals and objectives are also part of becoming vision driven, because these can help move us out of our comfort range—the way things are always done, on a day-to-day basis-and aim for something better in the future. Focusing on this better future is central to planning for human progress. That this vision of the future should be progressive, worthy, and uplifting is one of the lessons learned from the world's best leaders.

A STRONG IMPLEMENTATION AND EVALUATION MODEL

A strong implementation and evaluation model means that these good intentions for the future, put in concrete terms through a decision-making process guided by the principles of participation and collaboration, must be implemented. This is where many plans fail. Part of the way to ensure implementation is to make certain everyone involved is committed to the plan, which is helped by their participation in creating it. The key idea is that those involved in the plan should set up means for helping to ensure that anticipated activities are actually carried out. In some cases, it is necessary to create institutional structures, policies, or programs to help carry out the plan. This book has also suggested pairing implementation with monitoring, a form of evaluation, to make sure that planning leads to action.

The simple planning model explained in the section below is to select a few objectives, associated strategies, and a monitoring system designed to assess and guide action. When the monitor is a widely respected leader with active commitment to the success of the plan, as Shoghi Effendi was, the results can be spectacular. Plans are weakened when no one pays attention to whether or not they are being carried out. While monitoring should take place throughout the plan, that phase near the beginning is of particular importance, because this is the period of time during which data collection or feedback systems can be set up, key objectives to be focused on first identified, and plan adjustments made as action begins. It is also important to assess the results of the plan when its time frame has elapsed, so as to better inform future action.

Readiness

Another concept of importance is that of readiness, which can have several meanings. In the plans led by Shoghi Effendi, the concept meant that those national communities which Shoghi Effendi asked to participate in a formal planning process were expected to have mastered at least the basics of administrative procedures. In those cases, this meant the national governing bodies had to meet fairly frequently, exemplify key principles in their work, and be capable of carrying out such tasks as were necessary for the plan's successful administration. Previous chapters also defined readiness in other ways, such as access to sufficient resources (financial, human, or spiritual), or access to information about current conditions so as to choose objectives and carry out activities with confidence. One challenge is to acknowledge the importance of readiness and yet not to let perceived lack of readiness stymie action. In some cases, people or groups wait until they are "ready," failing to do anything at all.

A Very Simple Plan

One of the least complex approaches to planning is the classic style exemplified by the *Tablets of the Divine Plan*, a book that contains a series of plan-related letters that were simple in construction although far-reaching in foresight, implications, and scope (see chapter two). 'Abdu'l-Bahá's concept or vision of the future was that Bahá'í communities would thrive in all the regions of the world. Revealed during the era of World War I, *Tablets of the Divine Plan* established an overall goal of dispersing the Bahá'ís of North America throughout the continent and the globe. He urged those few Bahá'ís who lived in North America at that time to work toward this goal, and he identified their key mission or overriding purpose as taking the tenets of their religion to the peoples of the world, a feat which he promised would bring them everlasting honor.

He suggested one key strategy: they should travel to other places, particularly as speakers and teachers, and "shine" as resplendent examples of human beings, thus attracting new members to their ranks. In most cases, he was clear about who should go where: in the central states region of the United States, for example, 'Abdu'l-Bahá urged those members of the religious community living in Illinois, Wisconsin, Ohio, Michigan, and Minnesota to arise and travel to Indiana, Iowa, Missouri, North Dakota, South Dakota, Nebraska, and Kansas. He laid out such directions for residents of a series of regions, and also for residents of the North American continent as a whole, and he named specific countries in other parts of the world as destinations. 'Abdu'l-Bahá was particularly skillful in addressing the issues of motivation and principled action. He counseled his readers to exemplify outstanding spiritual growth and urged them to emphasize such good community qualities as fellowship, love, and unity. He also indicated that travelers should exemplify such key personal attributes as detachment from material comforts, and he created beautiful prayers specifically designed to help with these initiatives. These directions and suggestions were all supportive means for implementing the key strategy, which was very straightforward: travel.

Such a simple but potentially powerful approach to planning is possible in those cases when group cohesion is strong, one goal is all-important, some knowledge about the situation exists, and the mission is clear. In such cases, it may be possible to try the steps indicated in Chart A-1. This very simple approach of choosing one worthy objective, selecting an effective strategy, and then conscientiously acting includes some of the most basic components of planning. For many situations, no more complex formula is needed. If you choose the desired goal or objective well and the strategy or set of strategies is reasonable, it becomes easy to succeed if you act upon this desire with enthusiasm, focus, consistency, cohesion, and support.

CHART A-1

A PROCESS FOR A VERY SIMPLE PLAN

- Start from the basis of "knowledge." Using a consultative process, focus upon one key and worthy accomplishment—that is, goal or objective[1]— for the future, for yourself, or for your group or community. Usually this

accomplishment should specify a "changed state," that is, some future improvement over current conditions.
- Taking into account your situation and your potential, decide upon at least one potentially effective strategy for reaching your goal or objective, and be clear about who should act or how this should be carried out.
- Act. The key to making such a simple construction work is to act upon it, and in some sense to monitor action on a regular basis, which means to check frequently to see if progress is taking place and to adjust action as necessary.

A Simple Plan

Plans led by Shoghi Effendi were in many ways simple and elegant in construction, even though their implementation and monitoring were often quite elaborate. These plans were most certainly visionary; in fact, Shoghi Effendi evoked several levels of *visions of the future*, ranging from the long-term transformation of human society to the near-term vision of a larger and more capable Bahá'í community at the end of each plan. He also clarified the role of the plans within the overall *mission* of the North American Bahá'ís, which was to carry their religion to the world, and thereby to help provide the pattern for a new world order.

The elegance of these plans is particularly evident in their ambitious and yet attainable *objectives*. Although Shoghi Effendi sometimes used the words "goals," "objectives," and even "tasks" interchangeably, usually the accomplishments he suggested had the clear ring of well-chosen objectives, since at the end of the plan it was easy to see if they were met or not. For example, for the first Seven Year Plan promoted for the North American Bahá'ís, he suggested that North American Bahá'ís should settle in every state of the United States and in every republic of the continent. He also suggested that by 1944 they should complete the exterior ornamentation of their ambitious and uniquely constructed House of Worship. For each of these two clearly measurable objectives, he suggested *strategies*, and he elaborated upon these strategies in a series of long and short letters. He also clearly explained who was *responsible* at each of several levels, ranging from individuals to national organizations, and he offered special ways to feel encouraged and motivated. Particularly exemplary was his diligent *monitoring* of the success of each national plan, along with his continual suggestions about how to make it more effective. Another special contribution Shoghi Effendi made was to offer thorough assessments of the *results* of plans as they ended and to help make preparations for future initiatives.

Typically, a group, organization, or community needs to reach more than one accomplishment for its plan. One simple way to include some of the unique qualities of Shoghi Effendi's approach is to create a variation of the above-described "very simple plan." Again, carrying this out is easiest if widespread agreement exists about the mission of the group and the direction in which the group is headed. An exemplary planning process, discussed previously, can help bring about such agreement. Ensuring a firm base of knowledge is also important (see page 165). This may mean studying mandate documents or other key sources of current guidance, gathering relevant facts, assessing conditions, or drawing on spiritual sources of insight and wisdom, such as prayer. Then a series of appropriate steps, which need not be sequential, are indicated in Chart A-2.

Note that the "simple plan" is merely an elaboration of a "very simple plan." Both aim toward carrying out a few, easily identifiable accomplishments. More complex plans arise when more objectives are needed and when no widespread organizational vision exists, but also when more organizations and people are involved in the process. As noted above, planning is simpler in those situations characterized by a great deal of group cohesion, innate knowledge, and a strong sense of mission. When these do not exist, it becomes even more important to carry out an exemplary planning process, described previously. Such an exemplary process is always useful, however, since a good planning process helps create a good plan.

CHART A-2

A PROCESS FOR A SIMPLE PLAN

- Start from the basis of knowledge. Using a consultative process, choose a few objectives, perhaps no more than three or four unless your organization is very experienced with plans or has extensive human and material resources available and readily accessible.
- Taking into account your situation, resources, and potential, and using consultation as appropriate for your circumstances, decide upon at least one potentially effective strategy (or line of action) for reaching each of your objectives.

- For each strategy, be clear about who should act or how this strategy should be carried out. This means clarifying levels of responsibility, as well as indicating who is expected to help carry out each objective, and what standards are desired (see sample chart at the end of this appendix). Be sure that each strategy has the potential to contribute to the desired results. Revise strategies throughout the life of the plan, as necessary.
- Decide on the most important objective or strategy for the first phase of your plan and begin action there.
- As you begin action—which need not wait for the above steps to be completed—do not hesitate to adjust your plan as the nature of the tasks becomes clearer through action. Pay special attention to encouraging motivated effort, using such means as making inspiring calls to action, providing emotional support for individual actors, using frequent references to the overarching vision and mission, educating participants about the nature of the plan, and creating focused work teams to carry forth action steps.
- As you begin action, set up a way to monitor activities, using a system that is supportive rather than adversarial. Check on a regular basis to see that action is taking place and to make adjustments as necessary. Assess the plan's ending results—if the plan has an ending point—as well as a final stage of monitoring before preparing for future action.

ALTERNATIVE PROCESS FRAMEWORKS

Most of the discussion in this book has assumed that a simple form of the "rational" planning model should guide action. Such a model assumes that information is available and that it is logically possible to go through the steps of choosing courses of action (goals, objectives, strategies) and then carrying them out. Several other models of the planning process, however, are possible as well, and various places in this book have mentioned some of them in passing. Here is more detail about two such models: strategic planning as promoted by John Bryson, and transactive planning as promoted by John Friedmann. Both of these authors were cited in chapter three.

STRATEGIC PLANNING MODEL

The strategic planning model, briefly mentioned on page 37, has the benefit of suggesting a process that solicits the cooperation of stakeholders and gathers critical information. Some readers might find this approach helpful for complex planning situations, where no clear mission or organizational unity exists, or when objectives and strategies are not apparent upon first examination. Strategic planning, once mastered, is also an excellent way to get a group of people to focus on a set of achievable strategies that can be accomplished in a short period of time.

Strategic planning as described by Bryson[2] places strong emphasis upon involving all stakeholders and upon assessing the environment in which planning takes place. His first suggested step is for key decision-makers to agree that a strategic planning process should take place and to agree upon its steps and upon the people asked to collaborate in the process. For his second step, he counsels identifying organizational mandates, and then, for a third step, clarifying the organizational mission and values, in a process that involves the organization's key stakeholders such as clients, affiliated agencies or institutions, or key leaders. The second step has great value because it recognizes that the organization may operate in the context of charters, contracts, or other materials that offer guidance in terms of the direction in which it should move. Knowing the mission and values of the organization is important for the same reason; this can eliminate a great deal of potential disagreement or conflict, according to Bryson, as well as provide inspiration for those involved in the planning process.

The fourth step he suggests is to assess the organization's external and internal environments. This can be done in one or more sessions when the participants in the planning process tally resources, challenges, and opportunities. Such information can help stakeholders identify the key strategic issues facing the organization, the fifth step. He then suggests that it is time to formulate strategies and plans to manage the issues (sixth step), and then review and adopt those strategies and plans (seventh step)—two separate activities designed to ensure that all parties involved approve of the approach. Only then does he counsel carrying out the last three steps of establishing an effective organizational vision of success, developing an action plan for implementation, and reassessing strategies and the strategic planning process as a form of evaluation.

Bryson's model contains all the elements identified as part of "an exemplary planning process"—it is extremely participatory and collaborative, and also includes a strong implementation and evaluation component, as well as outstanding assessment of readiness. This process does not require clear agreement upon goals, objectives, or strategies at the beginning of the process. In many cases, the only difficulty that has arisen is that the steps suggested for strategic planning can be very time consuming, if organizations attempt to move through all the steps without guidance as to how to carry out such activities with a minimum of time involved. Even so, many groups have successfully used this approach or variations of this approach.

TRANSACTIVE PLANNING MODEL

Transactive planning is a model proposed by theorist John Friedmann that harmonizes well with the concept of people-centered development.[3] That model does not have a series of clearly identifiable steps, as the strategic planning model does. However, its benefit is that, again, it does not require the selection of goals and objectives required by the rational model. It also does not assume that agreement has been reached, but rather focuses upon self-determination and mutual learning.

In the transactive approach, the assumption is that someone serves as "planner" but may be an outsider, and someone else serves as "client" or "population served." The main principle for the planning process is that it involves mutual learning between the planner and the population served. Friedmann suggests that, except in situations where technical expertise is strongly resident in the planner, the planner (or planning body or board) merely provides the concepts and theory, perhaps some analysis of the situation, and help in searching for new ideas and strategies. The "client" or population served, however, knows the context intimately, has a firm grasp of realistic alternatives, knows its own priorities, and can provide operational details. The planning process is, in essence, a process of dialogue between these two parties that leads to action plans. The "clients" then help carry out these plans, or take them over completely.

This approach has some limitations. It may appear to apply largely to professional planning situations, for one, and to be fairly loose in structure, for another. However, it also has certain advantages. Building on the basis of assuming no outside expertise except in narrow technical problems and of encouraging continued interaction between "planner" and "client," some people have been able to create extraordinary planning successes in planning contexts throughout the world, such as low-income neighborhoods. In such situations, the issues of power and control are key, and the critical need is to help people learn how to solve their own problems, whether or not they take more standard approaches to planning. One particularly successful variation of the transactive approach, which is actually a merger of the rational and transactive theories, is the "action planning for cities" practiced by authors Hamdi and Goerthert in countries ranging from Sri Lanka to South Africa. A book by these authors describes how they serve as planning consultants, becoming catalysts for an intensive planning process that lasts only a few weeks but involves participants in collecting data, analyzing that data, developing strategies, and then finalizing an effective work plan.[4]

A SIMPLE PLAN FOR A STEERING COMMITTEE OF A COMMUNITY CENTER

Now that we have reviewed the basic elements of an exemplary planning process, key components of a very simple plan and of a simple plan, and two alternative process frameworks, it might be useful to provide a hypothetical example and a companion blank worksheet for the reader to copy and use as needed. The example is a summary of a simple plan for improving the operations of a community center.

FINAL SUMMARY/WORKSHEET

Vision: Our Brownsville Community Center will be a vibrant and attractive center of gravity for the neighborhood in which we are located and for the community at large. It will be an attractive and welcoming destination for community functions, educational programs, and informal gatherings. Day after day and night after night, its rooms will be filled with people of all races, ages, and creeds.

Process: This plan was created under the leadership of the Steering Committee after extensive consultation with community members. This dialogue yielded three main objectives and strategies for each objective, which we will attempt to accomplish with the help of the community as partners.

Time Frame/Priorities: Within the next three years, we will make significant movement toward our vision by achieving these three objectives.

Our first priority is to enhance the center's physical attractiveness, and so for the first year we will concentrate on the first objective listed. During that first phase, we will also poll the community and begin to train center staff.

CHART A-3
SAMPLE WORKSHEET OF A SIMPLE PLAN FOR A STEERING COMMITTEE OF A COMMUNITY CENTER

OBJECTIVES	STRATEGIES, ACTIONS	KEY IMPLEMENTERS
1. Greatly enhancing the physical attractiveness of the community center *(first priority; phase one)*	A. Obtain new furnishings and refurbish the old B. Plant surrounding garden and set up maintenance system for them C. Find sources of funding for future building expansion	A./B. Center Upkeep Committee C. Fundraising Committee
2. Doubling the number of high-quality program offerings held at the center	A. Poll community for suggestions of highly desirable programs that could prove popular B. Approach people known in the community to offer new programs C. Begin new program on a phased basis, making sure to maintain high quality	A. Steering Committee secretary B./C. Center program director
3. Tripling the number of attendees at center functions, maintaining high satisfaction with the atmosphere of the center and with its program offerings	A. Train all center staff, program managers, and officers in enhanced human relations and community-building skills B. Secure cosponsorship of center activities by exemplary local partners C. Launch a public relations campaign in the neighborhood and larger community, aiming especially for diversity D. Make sure that satisfaction remains high, as measured with a simple questionnaire administered every few months to participants	A. Volunteer communications expert (Mattie White) B. Steering Committee as a whole C. Volunteer skilled in human relations (Matthew Black) D. Steering Committee

178 Planning Progress

CHART A-4
BLANK SAMPLE WORKSHEET OF A SIMPLE PLAN

Vision or Mission:
Process:
Time Frame/Priorities:

OBJECTIVES	HAS OBJECTIVE BEEN IMPLEMENTED*	STRATEGIES, ACTIONS	KEY IMPLEMENTERS
1.			
2.			
3.			

*Add a check mark, date, or other mark to this column when objective (or when each strategy) has been reached

Bibliography

'Abdu'l-Bahá. *Paris Talks: Addresses Given by 'Abdu'l-Bahá in Paris in 1911.* 11th ed. London: Bahá'í Publishing Trust, 1969.

———. *The Promulgation of Universal Peace: Talks Delivered by 'Abdu'l-Bahá during His Visit to the United States and Canada in 1912.* Comp. Howard MacNutt. 2d ed. Wilmette, IL: Bahá'í Publishing Trust, 1982.

———. *The Secret of Divine Civilization.* Trans. Marzieh Gail with Ali-Kuli Khan. Rev. ed. Wilmette, IL: Bahá'í Publishing Trust, 1975.

———. *Selections from the Writings of 'Abdu'l-Bahá.* Trans. Marzieh Gail et al. Comp. Research Dept. of the Universal House of Justice. Haifa: Bahá'í World Centre, 1978.

———. *Tablets of the Divine Plan: Revealed by 'Abdu'l-Bahá to the North American Bahá'ís.* 2d ed. Wilmette, IL: Bahá'í Publishing Trust, 1993.

Baer, William C. "General Plan Evaluation Criteria: An Approach to Making Better Plans." *Journal of the American Planning Association* 63.3 (1997): 329–44.

Bahá'í International Community. *The Prosperity of Humankind.* Wilmette, IL: Bahá'í Publishing Trust, c. 1995.

Bahá'í World: A Biennial International Record Vol. 2. 1926-1928. New York: Bahá'í Publishing Committee, 1928.

Bahá'í World: A Biennial International Record. Vol. 8. 1938-1940. Wilmette, IL: Bahá'í Publishing Committee, 1942.

Bahá'u'lláh. *Gleanings from the Writings of Bahá'u'lláh.* Trans. Shoghi Effendi. 2d ed. Wilmette, IL: Bahá'í Publishing Trust, 1976.

———. *Kitáb-i-Aqdas: The Most Holy Book.* Haifa: Bahá'í World Centre, 1992.

Bahá'u'lláh. *Writings of Bahá'u'lláh*. Rev. ed. Delhi: Bahá'í Publishing Trust, 1994.

Bond, J. Jameson. "The Vision of Shoghi Effendi and the Unfoldment of the Tablets of the Divine Plan." In *The Vision of Shoghi Effendi: Proceedings of the Association for Bahá'í Studies Ninth Annual Conference*. Ottawa: Bahá'í Studies Publications, 1993. 1–7.

Branch, Melville C. *Planning: Universal Process*. New York: Praeger, 1990.

Bryson, John M. *Strategic Planning for Public and Nonprofit Organizations: A Guide to Strengthening and Sustaining Organizational Achievement*. Rev. ed. San Francisco: Jossey Bass, 1995.

Cameron, Glenn, with Wendi Momen. *A Basic Bahá'í Chronology*. Oxford: George Ronald Publishers, 1996.

Chakravarty, Sukhamoy. *Development Planning: The Indian Experience*. Oxford: Clarendon Press, 1987.

Chatterjee, Partha. "Development Planning and the Indian State." In *The State and Development Planning in India*. Ed. Terence J. Byres. Delhi: Oxford University Press, 1994. 51–72.

Compilation of Compilations Prepared by the Universal House of Justice 1963-1990. Vol. 1. Comp. Research Dept. of the Universal House of Justice. Maryborough: Bahá'í Publications Australia, 1991.

Covey, Stephen R. "Three Roles of the Leader in the New Paradigm." In *The Leader of the Future: New Visions, Strategies, and Practices for the Next Era*. Ed. Frances Hesselbein, Marshall Goldsmith, Richard Beckhard. San Francisco: Jossey-Bass, 1996. 149–60.

Dahl, Roger M. "Three Teaching Methods Used during North America's First Seven-Year Plan." *Journal of Bahá'í Studies* 5.3 (1993): 1–15.

Friedmann, John. "Planning as Social Learning." In *People-Centered Development: Contributions toward Theory and Planning Frameworks*. Ed. David C. Korten and Rudi Klauss. West Hartford, Conn.: Kumarian Press, 1984. 189–94.

———. *Planning in the Public Domain: From Knowledge to Action*. Princeton, N.J.: Princeton University Press, 1987.

———. *Retracking America: A Theory of Transactive Planning*. Garden City, N.Y.: Anchor Press/Doubleday, 1973.

Furután, Ali-Akbar. "The Guardian and the East." In *The Vision of Shoghi Effendi: Proceedings of the Association for Bahá'í Studies Ninth Annual Conference.* Ottawa: Bahá'í Studies Publications, 1993. 69–72.

Giachery, Ugo. *Shoghi Effendi: Recollections.* Oxford: George Ronald Publishers, 1973.

Goodell, Grace. "Political Development and Social Welfare: A Conservative Perspective." In *People-Centered Development: Contributions toward Theory and Planning Frameworks.* Ed. David C. Korten and Rudi Klauss. West Hartford, Conn.: Kumarian Press, 1984. 273–79.

Hamdi, Nabeel, and Reinhard Goerthert. *Action Planning for Cities: A Guide to Community Practice.* West Sussex, U.K.: John Wiley and Sons, 1997.

Hatcher, William S. "An Analysis of The Dispensation of Bahá'u'lláh." In *The Vision of Shoghi Effendi: Proceedings of the Association for Bahá'í Studies Ninth Annual Conference.* Ottawa: Bahá'í Studies Publications, 1993. 73–90.

Hatcher, William S., and J. Douglas Martin. *The Bahá'í Faith: The Emerging Global Religion.* Rev. ed. Wilmette, IL: Bahá'í Publishing Trust, 1998.

Helgesen, Sally. "Leading from the Grass Roots." In *The Leader of the Future: New Visions, Strategies, and Practices for the Next Era.* Ed. Frances Hesselbein, Marshall Goldsmith, Richard Beckhard. San Francisco: Jossey-Bass, 1996. 19–24.

Hofferbert, Richard I. *The Reach and Grasp of Policy Analysis: Comparative Views of the Craft.* Tuscaloosa: University of Alabama Press, 1990.

Huddleston, John. *The Search for a Just Society.* Oxford: George Ronald Publishers, 1989.

Jordan, Daniel C. "Knowledge, Volition, and Action: Three Steps to Spiritual Transformation." *World Order* 7.2 (1972-73): 43–48.

Kanter, Rosabeth Moss. "World-Class Leaders: The Power of Partnering." In *The Leader of the Future: New Visions, Strategies, and Practices for the Next Era.* Ed. Frances Hesselbein, Marshall Goldsmith, Richard Beckhard. San Francisco: Jossey-Bass, 1996. 89–98.

Korten, David C., and George Carner. "Planning Frameworks for People-Centered Development." In *People-Centered Development:*

Contributions toward Theory and Planning Frameworks. Ed. David C. Konen and Rudi Klauss. West Hartford, Conn.: Kumarian Press, 1984. 201–9.

Laszlo, Ervin. *Vision 2020: Reordering Chaos for Global Survival*. Yverdon, Switzerland: Gordon and Breach, 1994.

Locke, Alain. "Impressions of Haifa." *Bahá'í World: A Biennial International Record. Vol. 2. 1926-1928*. New York: Bahá'í Publishing Committee, 1928. 125–27.

The Ministry of the Custodians 1957-1963: An Account of the Stewardship of the Hands of the Cause. Haifa: Bahá'í World Centre, 1992.

Marcic, Dorothy. *Managing with the Wisdom of Love: Uncovering Virtue in People and Organizations*. San Francisco: Jossey-Bass, 1997.

Nanus, Burt. *Visionary Leadership: Creating a Compelling Sense of Direction for Your Organization*. San Francisco: Jossey-Bass, 1992.

New American Standard Bible. Reference edition. Philadelphia: A. J. Holman Company, 1973.

Nyi Nyi. "Planning, Implementation and Monitoring of Literacy Programmes: The Burmese Experience." *Assignment Children* 63164.2 (1983): 87–99.

Peattie, Lisa. *Planning: Rethinking Ciudad Guayana*. Ann Arbor: University of Michigan Press, 1987.

Pinchot, Gifford. "Creating Organizations with Many Leaders." In *The Leader of the Future: New Visions, Strategies, and Practices for the Next Era*. Ed. Frances Hesselbein, Marshall Goldsmith, Richard Beckhard. San Francisco: Jossey-Bass, 1996. 25–39.

Roberts, Peter. "Managing the Strategic Planning and Development of Regions: Lessons from a European Perspective." *Regional Studies* 27.8 (1993): 759–68.

Rossi, Peter H., and Howard E. Freeman. *Evaluation: A Systematic Approach*. 5th ed. Newbury Park, Calif.: Sage, 1993.

"Rúḥíyyih Khanum Addresses Over 200 British Bahá'ís During London Visit." *Bahá'í News* 337 (March 1959): 2–3.

Rúḥíyyih Rabbani. *The Priceless Pearl*. London: Bahá'í Publishing Trust, 1969.

Sala, Emeric. "Shoghi Effendi's Question." In *The Vision of Shoghi Effendi: Proceedings of the Association far Bahá'í Studies Ninth*

Annual Conference. Ottawa: Bahá'í Studies Publications, 1993. 189–93.

Senge, Peter M. *The Fifth Discipline: The Art & Practice of the Learning Organization*. New York: Doubleday/Currency, 1990.

Shoghi Effendi. *The Advent of Divine Justice*. 4th ed. Wilmette, IL: Bahá'í Publishing Trust, 1984.

———. *Bahá'í Administration: Selected Letters 1922-1932*. Rev. ed. Wilmette, IL: Bahá'í Publishing Trust, 1974.

———. *The Bahá'í Faith, 1844-1952: Information Statistical and Comparative. Including Supplement: "Ten Year International Bahá'í Teaching and Consolidation Plan 1953-1963*. Wilmette, IL: Bahá'í Publishing Committee, 1953.

———. *Citadel of Faith: Messages to America, 1947-1957*. Wilmette, IL: Bahá'í Publishing Trust, 1965.

———. *God Passes By*. Rev. ed. Wilmette, IL: Bahá'í Publishing Trust, 1974.

———. *Letters from the Guardian to Australia and New Zealand 1923-1957*. Sydney: National Spiritual Assembly of the Bahá'ís of Australia, 1970.

———. *Messages to America: Selected Letters and Cablegrams Addressed to the Bahá'ís of North America 1932-1946*. Wilmette, IL: Bahá'í Publishing Committee, 1947.

———. *Messages to the Bahá'í World 1950-1957*. 2d ed. Wilmette, IL: Bahá'í Publishing Trust, 1971.

———. *Unfolding Destiny: Messages from the Guardian of the Bahá'í Faith to the Bahá'ís of the British Isles*. London: Bahá'í Publishing Trust, 1981.

———. *The World Order of Bahá'u'lláh: Selected Letters*. Rev. ed. Wilmette, IL: Bahá'í Publishing Trust, 1974.

Smith, Melanie, and Paul Lample. *The Spiritual Conquest of the Planet: Our Response to Plans*. Riviera Beach, Fla.: Palabra Publications, 1993.

Talen, Emily. "After the Plans: Methods to Evaluate the Implementation Success of Plans." *Journal of Planning Education and Research* 16.2 (1996): 79–92.

Thomas, John W., and Merilee S. Grindle. "After the Decision: Implementing Policy Reforms in Developing Countries." *World Development* 18.8 (1990): 1163–81.

Toffler, Alvin. "The Crisis of Democratic Governance." In *People-*

Centered Development: Contributions toward Theory and Planning Frameworks. Ed. David C. Konen and Rudi Klauss. West Hartford, Conn.: Kumarian Press, 1984. 243–49.

United States Bahá'í National Archives. National Teaching Committee Files. Bahá'í National Center. Wilmette, IL.

United States Bahá'í National Archives. Office of the Secretary: Shoghi Effendi Files. Bahá'í National Center. Wilmette, IL.

Universal House of Justice. Letter to the Bahá'ís of the World. Riḍván 155 B.E. (1998).

Vision of Shoghi Effendi: Proceedings of the Association for Bahá'í Studies Ninth Annual Conference. Ottawa: Bahá'í Studies Publications, 1993.

World Almanac and Book of Facts 1995. Mahwah, N.J.: Funk & Wagnalls, 1994.

Notes

Foreward to 2024 Edition

1   Letter dated 28 November 2023 to the Bahá'ís of the World. Unless otherwise indicated, all subsequent references are to letters written by or on behalf of the Universal House of Justice.

2   Ibid.

3   Ibid.

4   Ibid.

5   Ibid.

6   Ibid.

7   Riḍván 2024 message to the Bahá'ís of the World.

8   For example, many would agree with Calhoun et al that "[p]olitical parties are broken, functioning as little more than ideologically polarized fundraising machines" (216), and that society, more generally, is now characterized by "declining citizen efficacy, weakening local communities, fraying intergenerational bonds, evaporating small-scale economic opportunity, and eroding social ties that had once knit citizens together across lines of difference and fostered solidarity" (209). Craig Calhoun, Dilip Parameshwar Gaonkar, and Charles Taylor, *Degenerations of Democracy* (Cambridge: Harvard University Press, 2022). See also the following references for similar analyses of democratic decline: Anne Applebaum, *Twilight of Democracy: The Seductive Lure of Authoritarianism* (New York: Doubleday, 2020); Steven Levitsky and Daniel Ziblatt, *How Democracies Die* (New York: Penguin Random House, 2019); Todd Smith and Benjamin W. Kelly, "Public Discourse and Wilful Incommensurability: A Case for Attentive Free Speech," *Frontiers of Sociology* 9 (2024) 1–16. doi: 10.3389/fsoc.2024.1178525.

9   Letter dated 28 November 2023 to the Bahá'ís of the World.

10   Letter dated 18 January 2019 to the Bahá'ís of the World.

11   It might be added that perpetuating these trends is the increasing entrenchment of deleterious proclivities, such as the penchants to fragment reality, quash alternative perspectives, and dismiss seemingly inconvenient information while fabricating and purveying disinformation in its place. These

inclinations are, in turn, incessantly fortified by traditional allegiances, much of mainstream and social media, and the unreflective embrace of consumerism and other forms of escapism.

12 Letter dated 18 January 2019 to the Bahá'ís of the World.

13 Ibid.

14 This section is informed by my paper "Crisis and the Power of an Inclusive Historical Consciousness: Progressing from Delusional Habits to Dynamic Freedom," *Journal of Bahá'í Studies* 30 no. 1–2 (2020): 47–113.

15 Letter dated 28 December 2010 to the Conference of the Continental Boards of Counsellors.

16 Letter dated 18 December 2014 to the Bahá'ís in Iran.

17 Letter dated 2 March 2013 to the Bahá'ís in Iran.

18 Ibid.

19 Ibid.

20 Office of Social and Economic Development at the Bahá'í World Centre, 26 November 2012.

21 Letter dated 28 December 2010 to the Conference of the Continental Boards of Counsellors.

22 These themes are addressed in more detail in Smith and Kelly, "Public Discourse and Wilful Incommensurability."

23 In its letter of 19 April 2007 to a National Spiritual Assembly, the House of Justice states: "In every cluster the institutions and agencies guiding the process—the Auxiliary Board members and the institute, together with the Area Teaching Committee—need to examine the dynamics of growth on a regular basis and analyze the way in which these elements are working together, in order to identify gaps and determine what adjustments should be made."

24 Letter dated 30 December 2021 to the Conference of the Continental Boards of Counsellors.

25 For fuller discussions of this theme, see pages 55–61 of Michael Karlberg's book *Constructing Social Reality: An Inquiry into the Normative Foundations of Social Change* (Ottawa: Association for Bahá'í Studies, 2020) and Chapter 6 of Paul Lample's book *Revelation and Social Reality: Learning How to Translate What Is Written into Reality* (Riviera Beach, FL: Palabra Publications, 2009).

26 Letter dated 2 March 2013 to the Bahá'ís in Iran.

27 June Manning Thomas, *Planning Progress: Lessons from Shoghi Effendi* (Ottawa, Association for Bahá'í Studies, 2024), 32.

28 'Abdu'l-Bahá, *The Secret of Divine Civilization* (Wilmette: Bahá'í Publishing Trust, 1990), 23–24.

29 Thomas, *Planning Progress* 127.

30 *Light of the World*, Section 76.

31 Letter dated 28 December 2010 to the Conference of the Continental

Boards of Counsellors.

32   Letter dated 28 November 2023 to the Bahá'ís of the World.

33   Letter dated 30 December 2021 to the Conference of the Continental Boards of Counsellors.

34   Ibid.

35   It is worth noting that this mindset similarly differs from current conceptions of freedom, specifically those informed by the philosophy of individualism. There are some merits to this philosophy. It has, for example, been a fundamental impetus behind the widespread acceptance and codification of universal rights and freedoms, emphasized freedom of conscience and the independent investigation of truth, led to many beneficial innovations, and helped to spur on the rise of democratic government. But, carried too far, it leads to a me-centrism, or cult of individualism, that often entails a posture of entitlement. Such atomistic freedom results in a dissipation of standards, fuels identity politics, and so undermines the integrity of the collective. In so doing—if we accept the premise that we are all essentially interconnected—it ironically undermines the individual him- or herself. This theme is explored in more depth in Smith, "Crisis." Among other related themes, in this paper it is explained that individualism today essentially values three freedoms: 1) the freedom to do what I want when I want; 2) the freedom to access the necessary resources to carry out the first freedom; and 3) the freedom to take the first two freedoms for granted, which, again, amounts to a sense of entitlement.

36   For an in-depth investigation into the merits of each position, and particularly that of Rousseau's, see Rutger Bregman's book *Humankind: A Hopeful History* (New York: Little, Brown and Company, 2019).

37   Ironically, we also seek recognition for our advancements in the eyes of others.

38   Riḍván 2012 message to the Bahá'ís of the World.

39   Letter dated 29 December 2015 to the Conference of the Continental Boards of Counsellors.

40   Michael Karlberg, *Beyond the Culture of Contest* (Oxford: George Ronald, 2004).

41   Letter dated 19 May 1994 to the National Spiritual Assembly of the United States.

42   Letter dated 1 December 2019 to all National Spiritual Assemblies.

43   Letter dated 22 July 2020 to the Bahá'ís of the United States.

Preface

1   Full name, Shoghi Effendi Rabbani. The honorific Effendi (sir, mister) and surname Rabbani (one who longs) were conferred by his grandfather 'Abdu'l-Bahá.

2   Books first analyzed were *Citadel of Faith: Messages to America, 1947–1957* and *Messages to America: Selected Letters and Cablegrams Addressed to the Bahá'ís of North America, 1932–1946*. The second book is currently out of print. *The Advent of Divine Justice* was also examined.

Chapter I

1   Bahá'u'lláh, *Gleanings from the Writings of Bahá'u'lláh*, trans. Shoghi Effendi, 2d ed. (Wilmette, IL: Bahá'í Publishing Trust, 1988) 215.

2   Ervin Laszlo, *Vision 2020: Reordering Chaos for Global Survival* (Yverdon, Switzerland: Gordon and Breach, 1994) 56.

3   Melville C. Branch, *Planning: Universal Process* (New York: Praeger, 1990) 12, 29–30.

4   Ibid. 30.

5   Ibid. 12.

6   Ibid. 26.

7   Ibid. 26.

8   Ibid. 173.

9   Peter Roberts, "Managing the Strategic Planning and Development of Regions: Lessons from a European Perspective," *Regional Studies* 27 no. 8 (1993) 763–64.

10   Partha Chatterjee, "Development Planning and the Indian State," in *The State and Development Planning in India*, ed. Terence J. Byres (Delhi: Oxford University Press, 1994) 52–53.

11   Sukhamoy Chakravarty, *Development Planning: The Indian Experience* (Oxford: Clarendon Press, 1987) 3, 81.

12   Ibid. 18.

13   Ibid. 8–9.

14   Chatterjee, "Development Planning and the Indian State" 57.

15   Chakravarty, *Development Planning* 83–84.

16   William S. Hatcher and J. Douglas Martin, *The Bahá'í Faith: The Emerging Global Religion*, rev. ed. (Wilmette, IL: Bahá'í Publishing Trust, 1998) 23.

17   Rúḥíyyih Rabbani [née Mary Maxwell, also known as Rúḥíyyih Khanum], *The Priceless Pearl* (London: Bahá'í Publishing Trust, 1969) 391–92.

18   Ibid. 396–99.

19   *The Vision of Shoghi Effendi: Proceedings of the Association for Bahá'í Studies, Ninth Annual Conference* (Ottawa: Bahá'í Studies Publications, 1993).

20   Ugo Giachery, *Shoghi Effendi: Recollections* (Oxford: George Ronald, Publishers, 1973).

21   Melanie Smith and Paul Lample, *The Spiritual Conquest of the Planet: Our Response to Plans* (Riviera Beach, FL: Palabra Publications, 1993).

22   *The Advent of Divine Justice*, 4th ed. (Wilmette, IL: Bahá'í Publishing Trust, 1984).

23   *Citadel of Faith: Messages to America, 1947-1957* (Wilmette, IL: Bahá'í Publishing Trust, 1965) and *Messages to America: Selected Letters and Cablegrams Addressed to the Bahá'ís of North America, 1932-1946* (Wilmette, IL: Bahá'í Publishing Committee, 1947), unfortunately, contain only selected portions of many letters. These books are in large part comosed of the cables and postscripts that Shoghi Effendi wrote as attachments to letters written on his behalf by his secretary. Although this still yields a considerable amount of material, not all parts of all communications are included in these published versions. The author supplemented this material by reviewing the records of the United States Bahá'í Archives, Office of the Secretary, Shoghi Effendi Files. This archive contains a more complete collection of letters and cables between Shoghi Effendi and the United States National Spiritual Assembly, and the author was able to gain access to files dating up to 1947.

Chapter 2

1   The Báb is the forerunner of Bahá'u'lláh. Both are known as the "Twin Manifestations" of God in the Bahá'í ethos. This chapter does not reference the Báb's writings, which are not as abundant in English translation as those of Bahá'u'lláh, but in concept these support the ideas presented here. Bahá'u'lláh was at first an adherent of the Báb, who, before his death, exhorted his followers to look for "He Whom God will make manifest," later revealed to be Bahá'u'lláh (qtd. in Shoghi Effendi, *God Passes By*, rev. ed. [Wilmette, IL: Bahá'í Publishing Trust, 1974] 94). Shoghi Effendi was related to the Báb through paternal lineage, and descended from Bahá'u'lláh and 'Abdu'l-Bahá through maternal lineage. For a more thorough background on these issues, refer to a basic introductory text such as William S. Hatcher and J. Douglas Martin, *The Bahá'í Faith: The Emerging Global Religion*, rev. ed. (Wilmette, IL: Bahá'í Publishing Trust, 1998).

2   In this context, "spiritual principles" refer to such qualities as personal morality, altruism, devotion, courtesy, honesty, trustworthiness, justice, equity, and humility.

3   'Abdu'l-Bahá, *Tablets of the Divine Plan*.

4   Shoghi Effendi, *The World Order of Bahá'u'lláh: Selected Letters*, rev. ed. (Wilmette, IL: Bahá'í Publishing Trust, 1974) 203–4.

5   Bahá'u'lláh, "Tablet of Maqṣúd" 298–99.

6   Ibid. 298.

7   Ibid. 300.

8   Bahá'u'lláh, The Ninth Ishráq, "Splendours," *Writings of Bahá'u'lláh* 273.

9   Bahá'u'lláh, Eighth Leaf, "Words of Paradise," *Writings of Bahá'u'lláh* 235.
10   Bahá'u'lláh, The Sixth Ishráq, "Splendours," 271.
11   Bahá'u'lláh, Ninth Leaf, "Words of Paradise," 235.
12   Bahá'u'lláh, "Tablet of Maqṣúd" 294.
13   Ibid. 298.
14   Ibid. 296.
15   Ibid. 295.
16   Bahá'u'lláh, The Fifth Ishráq, "Splendours," 271.
17   Ibid. 273.
18   "Consultation: A Compilation," in *The Compilation of Compilations Prepared by The Universal House of Justice 1963-1990*, vol. I (Maryborough: Bahá'í Publications Australia, 1991) 93.
19   Bahá'u'lláh, "Tablet of Maqṣúd," 296.
20   Ibid. 294.
21   Bahá'u'lláh, "Words of Paradise," 228.
22   'Abdu'l-Bahá, *The Secret of Divine Civilization*, trans. Marzieh Gail with Ali-Kuli Khan, 3d ed. (Wilmette, IL: Bahá'í Publishing Trust, 1975) 35.
23   "Consultation," in *The Compilation of Compilations* 96, 97, 98.
24   Ibid. 96–97.
25   Ibid. 98.
26   Ibid. 95.
27   'Abdu'l-Bahá, *Selections from the Writings of 'Abdu'l-Bahá* (Haifa: Bahá'í World
Centre, 1978) 110–11.
28   'Abdu'l-Bahá, *Paris Talks: Addresses Given by 'Abdu'l-Bahá in Paris in 1911* (London: Bahá'í Publishing Trust, 1969) 16.
29   Ibid. 18.
30   'Abdu'l-Bahá, *Promulgation of Universal Peace: Talks Delivered by 'Abdu'l-Bahá during His Visit to the United States and Canada in 1912*, comp. Howard MacNutt, 2d ed. (Wilmette, IL: Bahá'í Publishing Trust, 1982) 249.
31   Daniel C. Jordan, "Knowledge, Volition, and Action-The Steps to Spiritual Transformation," *World Order* 7 no. 2 (Winter 1972-73): 43–48.
32   'Abdu'l-Bahá, *Promulgation* 250.
33   'Abdu'l-Bahá, *Selections* 64.
34   Ibid. 306–7.
35   'Abdu'l-Bahá, *Tablets of the Divine Plan* 5.
36   Ibid. 12, 16, 22, 27.
37   Ibid. 15-16.
38   The "covenant," a term in use since the time of Abraham in the Old Testament, refers on one level to the agreement or contract between God and

humanity. At another level, it refers to a believer's promise to obey the guidance of the Manifestation of God, in this case Bahá'u'lláh, and the institutions set up by that Manifestation. Although more complex than the term "faith," that latter term, used in Table 2.1 below, will be more familiar to many readers.
39 'Abdu'l-Bahá, *Tablets of the Divine Plan* 49.
40 Ibid. 52.

CHAPTER 3

1 Burt Nanus, *Visionary Leadership: Creating a Compelling Direction for Your Organization* (San Francisco: Jossey-Bass, 1992) 3.

2 The full text of the proverb suggests that another possible meaning of this passage is that without the Revelation of God people do not bother to keep the law and are unrestrained. Note that "revelation" is an alternative meaning of the word often translated as "vision."

3 In Friedmann's book, the four general schemes, each explained with its own chapter, are: (1) policy analysis, particularly systems analysis, public administration, and the work of policy scientists such as Aaron Wildavsky; (2) social learning, involving the concepts of scientific management and organizational development, recently elaborated upon by Donald Schon; (3) social reform, as presented by sociologists such as Max Weber, institutional economists such as John Galbraith, pragmatists such as John Dewey, and recent writers such as Amitai Etzioni; and (4) social mobilization, including the historical materialism of Karl Marx and Mao Tse-tung, the neo-Marxists such as Manuel Castells, the Frankfurt School thinkers such as Habermas, and the utopians, social anarchists, and radicals represented by Robert Owen, Lewis Mumford, Saul Alinsky, and many others. See John Friedmann, *Planning in the Public Domain: From Knowledge to Action* (Princeton: Princeton University Press, 1987).

4 Friedmann, *Planning in the Public Domain* 37.
5 Melville C. Branch, *Planning: Universal Process* 35–39.
6 John M. Bryson, *Strategic Planning for Public and Nonprofit Organizations*, rev. ed. (San Francisco: Jossey-Bass, 1995) 23.
7 Ervin Laszlo, *Vision 2020* 64–77.
8 Ibid. 87.
9 Lisa Peattie, *Planning: Rethinking Ciudad Guayana* (Ann Arbor: The University of Michigan Press, 1987) 60–61.
10 Peter M. Senge, *The Fifth Discipline: The Art & Practice of the Learning Organization* (New York: Doubleday/Currency, 1990) 205–6. For another account of the Spartacus incident, see John Huddleston, *The Search for a Just Society* (Oxford: George Ronald, Publishers, 1989) 41.
11 Rabbani, *Priceless Pearl* 38.

12   Alain Locke, "From 'Impressions of Haifa,'" cited in Ugo Giachery, *Shoghi Effendi* 191. Originally published in *Bahá'í World* 2 no. 127.
13   Giachery, *Shoghi Effendi* 127–28.
14   Rabbani, *Priceless Pearl* 373.
15   Ibid. 381.
16   Ibid. 381.
17   Ibid. 382, 375.
18   Shoghi Effendi, *The Bahá'í Faith, 1844-1952: Information Statistical and Comparative* (Haifa: Bahá'í World Centre, 1952) 27–28.
19   Rabbani, *Priceless Pearl* 342.
20   Shoghi Effendi, *The Bahá'í Faith, 1844-1952* 12.
21   Ibid. 6; Rabbani, *Priceless Pearl* 392.
22   'Abdu'l-Bahá, *Tablets of the Divine Plan* 62.
23   Shoghi Effendi, *Advent* 6.
24   Ibid. 8–9.
25   Ibid. 16–20.
26   Rabbani, *Priceless Pearl* 388.
27   Ibid. 383–84.
28   Shoghi Effendi, *Messages to America 1932-1946* 7.
29   Shoghi Effendi, *The Bahá'í Faith, 1844-1952*, passim. See also Supplement, "Ten Year International Bahá'í Teaching and Consolidation Plan, 1953-1963," 7, 8, 24.
30   For an explanation of this transition process, see *The Ministry of the Custodians 1957-1963* (Haifa: Bahá'í World Centre, 1992), particularly 28–31, 433.
31   Vital support for the plans come from people known as Counsellors (widely respected teachers) and their assistant Auxiliary Board members, all of whom consider themselves partially responsible for the successful prosecution of the current plans.
32   Shoghi Effendi, *World Order* 203.
33   Shoghi Effendi, *Advent* 14.
34   Shoghi Effendi, cable to Bahá'í offices, July 30, 1936, in United States Bahá'í National Archives, Office of the Secretary, Shoghi Effendi Files [referred to hereafter as Archives Shoghi Effendi], Box 2.
35   Shoghi Effendi, *Advent* 7.
36   Shoghi Effendi, *Advent* 8.
37   Cable from Shoghi Effendi to Bahá'í offices, April 5, 1937, Archives Shoghi Effendi, Box 2.
38   Shoghi Effendi, *Messages to America* 13.
39   Ibid. 26.
40   Ibid. 14.
41   Ibid. 42–43.

42   Shoghi Effendi, *Citadel of Faith* 32–33.
43   This theme pervades Shoghi Effendi's writings. For a summary overview of his treatment of the subject, see Smith and Lample, *The Spiritual Conquest of the Planet*.
44   Shoghi Effendi, *Citadel of Faith* 6.
45   Extensive discussion of his enthusiasm for the construction projects is available in Giachery, *Shoghi Effendi*.
46   Shoghi Effendi, *Citadel of Faith* 44.
47   Ibid. 78.
48   Shoghi Effendi, *Messages to America* 18.
49   Giachery, *Shoghi Effendi* 16–28.

Chapter 4

1   Bryson, *Strategic Planning* 112.
2   See in particular Friedmann's discussion of "social learning," *Planning in the Public Domain* 196. For an example, his discussion links the concepts of practice-based learning propounded by Mao Tse-tung with those of John Dewey.
3   Throughout this book, the term *goals* will be used to mean broad indications of desired achievement, and *objectives* will be used to refer to more specific declarations of measurable accomplishments.
4   Bryson, *Strategic Planning* 131.
5   Ibid. 137.
6   Peter Roberts, "Managing the Strategic Planning and Development of Regions: Lessons from a European Perspective," *Regional Studies* 27 no. 8 (1993) 761, 762, 760.
7   John W. Thomas and Merilee S. Grindle, "After the Decision: Implementing Policy Reforms in Developing Countries," *World Development* 18 no. 8 (1990) 1165, 1179.
8   Sukhamoy Chakravarty, *Development Planning* 39, 40–41.
9   According to May Bolles Maxwell's 1924 notes, "Shoghi Effendi discusses the affairs and conditions of the Cause with astonishing openness and frankness; he does not like secrecy and told us many times that this openness, frankness and truthfulness among the friends constitutes one of the great remedies for many of our difficulties, and he sets us the example of free and open consultation, with a modesty and simplicity which one must see in order to appreciate; he invites suggestions and consultation from the visiting friends and from those around him" (quoted in Ugo Giachery, *Shoghi Effendi* 190–91).
10   Rabbani, *Priceless Pearl* 346.
11   J. Jameson Bond, "The Vision of Shoghi Effendi and the Unfoldment of the Tablets of the Divine Plan," in *The Vision of Shoghi Effendi:*

Proceedings of the Association for Bahá'í Studies Ninth Annual Conference (Ottawa: Bahá'í Studies Publications, 1993) 4.

12   Shoghi Effendi sometimes used the terms "goals" and "objectives" interchangeably, but he most frequently used the more conceptually precise term "objectives," or referred to "tasks." Typically, objectives are more precisely stated than goals. Goals indicate general end-states desired; objectives describe those desired ends in language clear enough for someone to tell whether the objective has been met or not.

13   Shoghi Effendi, *Messages to America 1932-1946* 6. The cable text published in this book has an asterisk that indicates "century" refers to "The First Century of the Bahá'í Era, ending May 22, 1944." It is unlikely this asterisked footnote appeared on the original cable, although Shoghi Effendi had in previous communications indicated what he meant by the first century of the Bahá'í Era.

14   Letter from secretary of national spiritual assembly to Shoghi Effendi, June 22, 1936, Archives Shoghi Effendi, Box 2.

15   Shoghi Effendi, *Messages to America* 7.

16   Letter from Shoghi Effendi to a member of the National Spiritual Assembly of the Bahá'ís of the United States and Canada, June 4, 1937. Archives Shoghi Effendi, Box 2. Only a part of the postscript of this letter is included in the published book *Messages to America*. Second reference is to a cable in the same box, dated August 4, 1937.

17   Letter from secretary of national spiritual assembly to Shoghi Effendi, May 11, 1938, Archives Shoghi Effendi, Box 2.

18   Shoghi Effendi, *Messages to America* 88.

19   Ibid. 90.

20   Shoghi Effendi, *Messages to the Bahá'í World 1950-1957*, 2d ed. (Wilmette, IL: Bahá'í Publishing Trust, 1971) 42.

21   Shoghi Effendi, *Citadel of Faith* 115–16.

22   Summarized by Bond, "The Vision of Shoghi Effendi" 6.

23   Shoghi Effendi, *Messages to America* 20.

24   Ibid. 95–96.

25   Shoghi Effendi, *Citadel of Faith* 8–9.

26   Ibid. 22.

27   Shoghi Effendi, *Advent* 26–27.

28   Shoghi Effendi, *Messages to America* 11–12.

29   Shoghi Effendi, *Advent* 29.

30   Ibid. 36.

31   Shoghi Effendi, *Messages to America* 15.

32   Ibid. 28.

33   Shoghi Effendi, *Citadel of Faith* 130–31.

34   Shoghi Effendi, *Messages to America* 17.

35 Ibid. 18.
36 Shoghi Effendi, *Citadel of Faith* 19.
37 Ibid. 45.
38 Ibid. 66.
39 Ibid. 83.
40 Shoghi Effendi, *Messages to America* 10–11.
41 Ibid. 105.
42 Shoghi Effendi, *Citadel of Faith* 119–20.
43 Ibid. 120.
44 Ibid. 74.
45 Shoghi Effendi, *Messages to America* 59–60.
46 Ibid. 44.
47 Ibid. 59.
48 Shoghi Effendi, *Citadel of Faith* 48.
49 'Abdu'l-Bahá, *Tablets of the Divine Plan* 42.
50 Shoghi Effendi, *Messages to the Bahá'í World* 49.
51 Shoghi Effendi, Ibid. 51, 52, 53.
52 Shoghi Effendi, *Messages to America* 20.

Chapter 5

1 Friedmann, *Planning in the Public Domain* 37; Branch, *Planning: Universal Process* 39.
2 Nyi Nyi, "Planning, Implementation and Monitoring of Literacy Programmes: The Burmese Experience," *Assignment Children* 63164.2 (1983) 91.
3 Ibid. 91; for entire case study, see 87–99. Funk & Wagnalls Corporation, via its *World Almanac and Book of Facts 1995*, indicates that the literacy rate in 1990 was 81 percent for the nation as a whole. This source also indicates that military governments ruled Myanmar during much of the period from 1962 to the early 1990s.
4 Peter H. Rossi and Howard E. Freeman, *Evaluation: A Systematic Approach*, 5th ed. (Newbury, CA: Sage Publications, 1993) 5.
5 Ibid. 8.
6 Ibid. 29. The "social experiment" model has been most forcefully promoted by researcher Donald Campbell, cited in this source.
7 Richard I. Hofferbert, *The Reach and Grasp of Policy Analysis: Comparative Views of the Craft* (Tuscaloosa: The University of Alabama Press, 1990) 4–6.
8 Rossi and Freeman, *Evaluation* 35–36.
9 Hofferbert, *Reach and Grasp* 12.
10 Ibid. 19.
11 Rabbani, *Priceless Pearl* 301.

12 Shoghi Effendi, *Messages to America 1932-1946* 43.
13 Shoghi Effendi, *Citadel of Faith* 45.
14 Shoghi Effendi, *Messages to America* 7.
15 Cable from Shoghi Effendi to National Bahá'í Center, May 5, 1946, in Archives, United States Bahá'í National Center, microfilm labeled "Shoghi Effendi's Correspondence 1922-1951."
16 Shoghi Effendi, *Messages to America* 89, 90.
17 Ibid. 90.
18 Ibid. 93.
19 Ibid. 105.
20 Ibid. 106.
21 Ibid. 107.
22 Ibid. 108.
23 Shoghi Effendi, *Citadel of Faith* 1.
24 Ibid. 2.
25 The number of follow-up communications for this third global plan, apparently, was not nearly as large as in the second plan. One possible explanation is Shoghi Effendi's increasing attention to the global context. Another is fatigue. See, for example, the text of a letter written by his wife, Rúḥíyyih Rabbani, to the Bahá'ís of Australia. As she indicates on June 23, 1953, Shoghi Effendi had not been able to answer "any N.S.A. letters from any country for almost a year. He regrets this but unfortunately it was unavoidable," because of the "extreme pressure of work here, which is getting worse all the time" (Shoghi Effendi, *Letters from the Guardian to Australia and New Zealand: 1923-1957* [Sydney: National Spiritual Assembly of the Bahá'ís of Australia, Inc., 1970] 113).
26 Shoghi Effendi, *Messages to America* 97.
27 This focus on pioneering has been mentioned in chapter four. In the case of the Ten Year Plan: "Of all the objectives enumerated in my message to the representatives of this community . . . the most vital, urgent and meritorious, in this the opening year of the initial phase of this world-embracing enterprise, is, without doubt, the settlement of pioneers in all the virgin territories and islands assigned to this community in all the continents of the globe" (Shoghi Effendi, *Citadel of Faith* 117–18).
28 The following discussion focuses largely upon the shorter letters, rather than on an examination of the themes and structure of *The Advent of Divine Justice*, which would require a book's worth of commentary.
29 Additional plan-related letters, addressed to the world at large, were available in *Messages to the Bahá'í World*.
30 Rabbani, *Priceless Pearl* 424.
31 Shoghi Effendi, *Messages to America* 20–21.
32 Ibid. 40-41.

33   Shoghi Effendi offered several tributes to these heroic and devoted women, including the following comments, from a letter dated April 15, 1940: To Keith Ransom-Kehler, whose dust sleeps in far-off Iṣfahan; to Martha Root, fallen in her tracks on an island in the midmost heart of the ocean; to May Maxwell, lying in solitary glory in the southern outpost of the Western Hemisphere—to these three heroines of the Formative Age of the Faith of Bahá'u'lláh, they who now labor so assiduously for its expansion and establishment, owe a debt of gratitude which future generations will not fail to adequately recognize. (*Messages to America* 40)

34   Ibid. 41.
35   Shoghi Effendi, *Citadel of Faith* 38.
36   Ibid. 44.
37   Ibid. 45.
38   Ibid. 46.
39   Ibid. 49.
40   Ibid. 102.
41   Shoghi Effendi sent the Americans only one short letter, about one year before the end of the plan, and then nothing until the plan's completion, according to published compilations. Other material may be available in those portions of the archives that were not open to this author. As cited in footnote 25 above, a letter to the Australian Bahá'í community dated June 23, 1953, indicated that the pressure of work had put a halt to all communication to national spiritual assemblies; a June 14th letter indicated that the Australians should send reports to the International Bahá'í Council during the new Ten Year Crusade (letters signed by secretaries on behalf of Shoghi Effendi, *Letters from the Guardian* 113; 110–13). Shoghi Effendi had brought into being such a council, mentioned on pages 90 and 103 of *Citadel of Faith*, to help him with his tremendous workload and to prepare for the eventual formation of the Universal House of Justice, but he still communicated frequently about the Ten Year Crusade until his death in 1957, four and a half years into that plan.

42   Shoghi Effendi, *Messages to America* 64.
43   Ibid. 64.
44   Ibid. 64–65.
45   Ibid. 67.
46   Ibid. 69.
47   For examples of communications about publication of these volumes, see letter from Shoghi Effendi to the secretary of the National Spiritual Assembly of the Bahá'ís of the United States and Canada, January 28, 1939, in Archives Shoghi Effendi, Box 2, and letter from that assembly to Shoghi Effendi, January 13, 1942, Box 3.

48   Shoghi Effendi, *The Bahá'í Faith 1844-1952* 11, passim; European centers are listed on pages 36–37.

49   For examples of maps, see *The Bahá'í World, 1938-40*, vol. 8: 1036–39; maps in other volumes of *The Bahá'í World* published during Shoghi Effendi's lifetime; and the impressive global map attached to some editions of *The Bahá'í Faith 1844-1963: Information Statistical and Comparative*. That map is reproduced at the back of this book.

50   Hofferbert, *Reach and Grasp*.

Chapter 6

1   Rosabeth Moss Kanter, "World-Class Leaders: The Power of Partnering," in *The Leader of the Future: New Visions, Strategies, and Practices for the Next Era*, ed. Frances Hesselbein, Marshall Goldsmith, and Richard Beckhard (San Francisco: Jossey-Bass, 1996) 89–90.

2   Stephen R. Covey, "Three Roles of the Leader in the New Paradigm," in *The Leader of the Future: New Visions, Strategies, and Practices for the Next Era* 157.

3   Ibid. 153.

4   Sally Helgesen, "Leading from the Grass Roots," in *The Leader of the Future* 20.

5   Ibid. 22, 23.

6   Gifford Pinchot, "Creating Organizations with Many Leaders," *The Leader of the Future* 25–39.

7   David C. Korten and George Carner, "Planning Frameworks for People-Centered Development," in *People-Centered Development: Contributions toward Theory and Planning Frameworks*, ed. David C. Konen and Rudi Klauss (West Hartford, CT: Kumarian Press, 1984) 205.

8   Grace Goodell, "Political Development and Social Welfare: A Conservative Perspective," in *People-Centered Development* 273–74.

9   Alvin Toffler, "The Crisis of Democratic Governance," in *People-Centered Development* 247.

10   Ibid. 247.

11   John Friedmann, "Planning as Social Learning," in *People-Centered Development* 189–94.

12   'Abdu'l-Bahá, *Secret of Divine Civilization* 17.

13   Ibid. 33–34.

14   Ibid. 35, 59.

15   Shoghi Effendi, *World Order* 152.

16   Ibid. 147–50. See also, for an account of a personal conversation with Shoghi Effendi about the twin institutions, Emeric Sala, "Shoghi Effendi's Question," in *The Vision of Shoghi Effendi* 189–93.

17   He also began to establish an international forerunner of the Universal House of Justice, which he called the International Bahá'í Council and

brought into being in 1951, to assist with construction of sacred properties at the Bahá'í World Centre and negotiations with civil authorities, and later to assist with global plans (Shoghi Effendi, *Messages to the Bahá'í World 1950-1957* 7–9). Footnote 41, chapter five, cited a letter to the Australians that noted they should send news of their plan's activities to the council (Shoghi Effendi, *Letters from the Guardian to Australia and New Zealand* 112).

18   Shoghi Effendi, *Bahá'í Administration: Selected Letters 1922-1932*, rev. ed. (Wilmette, IL: Bahá'í Publishing Trust, 1974); William S. Hatcher, "An Analysis of The Dispensation of Bahá'u'lláh," in *The Vision of Shoghi Effendi* 73–90.

19   Shoghi Effendi, *Bahá'í Administration* 63–64.

20   Shoghi Effendi, *Messages to America* 16.

21   Ibid. 21–22.

22   Ibid. 21–22.

23   Ibid. 44–45.

24   Shoghi Effendi, *Advent* 62–63.

25   Shoghi Effendi, *Messages to America* 7.

26   Roger M. Dahl, "Three Teaching Methods Used during North America's First Seven-Year Plan," *Journal of Bahá'í Studies* 5 no. 3 (September-December 1993) 2.

27   Letter written on behalf of Shoghi Effendi to the secretary of National Spiritual Assembly of the Bahá'ís of the United States and Canada, January 28, 1939, Archives Shoghi Effendi, Box 2.

28   Letter from the secretary, National Spiritual Assembly of the Bahá'ís of the United States and Canada to Shoghi Effendi, May 19, 1939, Archives Shoghi Effendi, Box 2.

29   Letter from the secretary, National Spiritual Assembly of the Bahá'ís of the United States and Canada to Shoghi Effendi, May 20, 1940, Archives Shoghi Effendi, Box 3.

30   Letter from the secretary, National Spiritual Assembly of the Bahá'ís of the United States and Canada to Shoghi Effendi, January 13, 1942, Archives Shoghi Effendi, Box 3.

31   Paul Pettit, personal interview with author, July 29, 1997.

32   Letter from Katherine True, Edna True, Charlotte Linfoot to the National Spiritual Assembly of the Bahá'ís of the United States, June 10, 1958, United States Bahá'í Archives, Office of the Secretary Records, National Teaching Committee files [hereafter referred to as Archives N.T.C.], Box 13.

33   Shoghi Effendi, cited on page 7 of the report, which also describes the plan. Untitled mimeographed document, Archives N.T.C., Box 13, November, 1958. Jeopardized assemblies were those which were in danger of falling below the minimum number of Bahá'ís for an assembly to be maintained, which was nine. The report refers only to "weak" assemblies.

34   Letter from the American National Teaching Committee to all area teaching committees, August 19, 1959, Archives N.T.C., Box 13. Quotation from Rúḥíyyih Rabbani comes from March, 1959, issue of *Bahá'í News*.

35   Quotation within a letter signed by Corinne True, Horace Holley, and Paul E. Haney. Printed in "American Hands of the Cause Address Bahá'ís at State Conventions," *Bahá'í News* 311 (January 1957) 1–2.

36   Letter (mimeographed) from American National Teaching Committee (Velma Sherrill, Secretary) to Circuit Teachers, n.d. (c. October, 1959), Archives N.T.C., Box 13.

37   National Spiritual Assembly of the Bahá'ís of the United States, "Bahá'í Annual Reports, 1961-1962" 9–11.

38   Glenn Cameron, with Wendi Momen, *A Basic Bahá'í Chronology* (Oxford: George Ronald, Publishers, 1996) 273–74.

39   Shoghi Effendi, *Unfolding Destiny: The Messages from the Guardian of the Bahá'í Faith to the Bahá'í Community of the British Isles* (London: Bahá'í Publishing Trust, 1981) 169.

40   Ali-Akbar Furútan, "The Guardian and the East," in *The Vision of Shoghi Effendi* 72.

41   *Letters from the Guardian to Australia and New Zealand* 26, 27–28.

42   Ibid. 61–62.

43   Ibid. 63.

44   Ibid. 64.

45   Ibid. 66.

46   Ibid. 67.

47   Ibid. 70.

48   Ibid. 70–71.

49   Ibid. 114.

50   Ibid. 137.

51   Ibid. 138.

52   Shoghi Effendi, *Advent* 62–63.

Chapter 7

1   Rabbani, *Priceless Pearl* 436.

2   Ibid. 401.

3   Bahá'í International Community, Office of Public Information, *The Prosperity of Humankind* (Wilmette, IL: Bahá'í Publishing Trust, c. 1995) 1.

4   An early reader of this book manuscript asked if planning is the same as development. This is a good question. The development literature certainly addresses the problem of commitment, and some of this literature was cited in chapter six. The development literature would suggest that the appropriate way to motivate people to support plans is to make those plans their own, through

consultation. The management literature, partially cited in the same chapter, would frame this as a problem of team building or, more directly, motivation, and several management books on leadership do address this concern.

5   Emily Talen, "After the Plans: Methods to Evaluate the Implementation Success of Plans," *Journal of Planning Education and Research* 16 no.2 (1996) 79–92. William C. Baer, "General Plan Evaluation Criteria: An Approach to Making Better Plans," *Journal of the American Planning Association* 63 no. 3 (1997) 329–44.

6   The Universal House of Justice, letter to the Bahá'ís of the World, Riḍván 155 B.E. (1998).

7   Dorothy Marcic, *Managing with the Wisdom of Love: Uncovering Virtue in People and Organizations* (San Francisco: Jossey-Bass, 1997).

Appendix

1   More general statements of accomplishments are often called "goals," and more specific and measurable goals are called "objectives."

2   Bryson, *Strategic Planning* 23–37.

3   Friedmann, *Retracking America: A Theory of Transactive Planning* (Garden City, NY: Anchor Press/Doubleday, 1973) especially 187.

4   Nabeel Hamdi and Reinhard Goerthert, *Action Planning for Cities: A Guide to Community Practice* (West Sussex, UK: John Wiley and Sons, 1997).

Index

'Abdu'l-Bahá, 8–9
  and action, 21–24
  and consultation, 20–21
  and development, 19
  and focus, 21–22, 169–70
  and geographic targeting, 26
  and goals, 21–22, 168
  and governance, 126
  inspiration and encouragement, 28–30
  and leadership, 18–19, 126–27, 146–47
  and planning, 13, 21–29, 30–31, 169–70
  role in the Bahá'í Faith, 8–9
The Advent of Divine Justice, 10, 49, 75–76, 131, 132
Africa *see* North American Plans
Asia *see* North American Plans
Australia, 86, 129, 141, ch.5 n. 41
  Plans, 141–46, 148

Báb, The, 11
Baer, William C., ch.7 n.5
Bahá'í Faith
  and governance, 126–27
  and leadership, 126–27, 148
  teachings, 8
Bahá'í International Community (BIC), ch.7 n.3
Bahá' u'lláh, 8, 9

Bahá' u'lláh *(continued)*
  and action, 20–21
  and consultation, 21
  and development, 12–17, 60
  and goals, 18–19
  and governance, 12, 15
  and planning, 12, 18–19, 30
  spiritual teachings summarized, 13–14
  view of leadership, 18, 148
  vision of the future, 12–16, 48–49, 56
Bond, J. Jameson, 66, 70
Branch, Melville C., 3–4, 34–35, 94
Bryson, John M., 36, 88, 173–74
  and goals, 61

Cameron, Glenn, ch.6 n.38
Carner, George, ch. 5 n.7
Chakravarty, Sukhamoy, 6-7
Chatterjee, Partha, 6, 7
Chastity, role in plans, 76
Ciudad Guayana, Venezuela, 5, 7, 37
Consultation, 16–18, 20–21
  and governance, 127
  and leadership, 127, 164
Covey, Stephen R., 123, 126

Dahl, Roger M., 133

Development
  Baha'u'llah's concept of, 12–16

Empowerment Zone, xii, 154
Encouragement, 71–72, 117
  as motivation, 81–82, 159
Europe *see* North American Plans
Evaluation (or monitoring)
  and leadership commitment, 160
  models, 96–99
  of plans, 94, 110, 116–19
  of programs, 96
  reports, 115

Freeman, Howard E., 96, 97, 99
Friedmann, John, 34, 62, 94, 175
  and leadership, 126
Furútan, A. A. ('Alí Akbar), 140

Gandhi, Mahatma, 60
Giachery, Ugo, 9, 39–40, 54
Global Plans listed, 45–46
Goals
  and action, 19–20, 59–83
  difficulty within organizations, 61
  implementation of, 62–63
  and information gathering, 157
  and leadership, 61
  noble, 8, 38, 82
  strategies to achieve, 62–63
Goerthert, Reinhard, 176
Goodell, Grace, 124
Governance
  Bahá'í concepts of, 126–29
  decentralized, 129-30
Griffin, Walter B., xiii
Grindle, Merilee S., 63

Hamdi, Nabeel, 176
Hatcher, William S., ch.1 n.16, ch.6 n.18
Helgesen, Sally, 123
Hofferbert, Richard I., 97–99, 118, 161
House of Worship, Bahá'í (Wilmette, Illinois), 67, 69, 80, 85, 89, 10, 113, 114, 134
Howard, Ebenezer, 6
Huddleston, John, ch.3 n.10

Indian plans, 6, 7
Institutional/ organizational development, 151–52
Iran's plans, Bahá'í, 139–40

Jacobs, Allan B., xiii
Jordan, Daniel C., 23

Kanter, Rosabeth Moss, 122
King, Martin Luther, Jr., 34, 121–22
Korten, David C., 124
Krumholz, Norman, xiii

Lample, Paul, ch.1 n.21
Laszlo, Ervin, 2, 37
Latin America *see* North American Plans
Leadership, 7, 8
  Bahá'u'lláh's view of, 18–19
  Bahá'í concepts of, 126–28, 146
  changing role of, 145–46, 160–61, 162, 163–64
  consultation and, 128, 164
  decentralized, 123–24, 163–64
  during implementation, 116
  enhancing the role of, 123–24
  functions of, 123, 149
  goals and, 60

Leadership *(continued)*
  good or "enlightened," 18–19,
    64, 126, 163
  as a key concept, 164
  participatory approach to,
    124–26
  power of, 148, 163
  proper role of, 121, 149, 164
  qualities of, 122–23, 164
  social change and, 149
  "vision" and, 35
Locke, Alain, 38
Love, role in plans, 30

Marcic, Dorothy, ch.7 n.7
Martin, J. Douglas, ch.1 n.16
Maturation
  Americas, 129–139
  other national communities,
    139–46
Maxwell, Mary, *see* Rúḥíyyih
  Rabbani
Maxwell, May Bolles, ch.4 n.8,
  ch.5 n.33
Messages to America, 11, 105, 108
Monitoring *see* Evaluation
Motivation, 8
  by divine inspiration, 79
  by encouragement, 81–82, 158
  by examples of valor and
    courage, 80–81
  by giving praise, 84–87, 158
  vision and, 34, 55, 153

Nanus, Burt, 33
National Teaching Committee, 68,
  72, 133, 136–39
  plans, 136–39
Nehru, Jawaharlal, 6, 8
New towns, 6, 37
New Zealand, 112, 129, 139–47
  plans, 141–47

North American Bahá'ís
  mission, 49, 55
  spiritual destiny, 50
North American Plans
  Africa, 43, 86–87
  Americans' role, 132
  Asia, 43, 86–87
  benefits to Americans, 129
  consultation in, 128–29
  Europe, 43, 69, 73, 86, 88–89,
    104, 111, 115
  European campaigns, 66, 68,
    70, 73, 75
  Latin America, 48, 69, 80, 107,
    110, 111, 113, 114, 131
  objectives, 68–73
  participation in, 128
  summary of, 43–46
  Tablets of the Divine Plan
    and, see *Tablets of the Divine*
    Plan
Nyi Nyi, 95

Peattie, Lisa, 1, 5, 37
Pettit, Paul, 136, 137
Pinchot, Gifford, 124
Planning
  assessment, 119
  analysis, role of, 36
  building capacity for, 150
  and consultation, 20, 166–67,
    170, 171
  and cooperative dialogue, 20,
    166
  difficulties with, 4, 7
  economic, 6, 157
  evaluation, role of, 36
  functional, 2
  gathering information for, 150
  goals, choosing, 89–91
  implementation, role of, 37
  individual efforts, 163

Planning *(continued)*
    institutions, role of, 42-43
    large-scale, 2, 3
    leadership, 120
    objectives, choosing, 75, 88–89
    participation and self-determination, 158, 166
    personal, 2–3
    process, 34–42, 166–69, 174–76
    project, 2
    readiness, 169
    resources (material and spiritual), 25, 169
    spiritual principles, 31
    steps, 35, 41
    strategic, 35, 157, 174–76
    suggested strategies
        envisioning, 56–57
        goals to action, 89–91, 170–71
        monitoring, 120, 171, 172
        transactive, 175–76
    "universal process," 35
    vision of the future and, 34–39
    vision, role of, 42
Plans
    concentration, need for, 70
    evaluation or monitoring, 96, 161
    implementation, problems with, 61–62, 167
    implication of, 72
    love, role in, 30
    monitoring, 94, 117
        Myanmar [Burma], 94-95
    national, 5, 6
        Europe, 63
        India, 6-7

Plans *(continued)*
    Myanmar [Burma], 94–95
    United States, National Resources Planning Board, 5
    North American Baha'i community, 45, 51
    spiritual principles, 31
    tool for maturation, 130
    unity, role in, 30
    and responsibility, varying levels of, 76
    simple, 171–73
    and success, encouragement for, 73
    and success, standards for, 72, 73
    and success, strategies for, 72, 74
    very simple, 169–71

Racial prejudice
    role in plans, 76
Ransom-Kehler, Keith, 109–10, ch.5 n.33
Roberts, Peter, ch.1 n.9, ch.4 n.6
Rossi, Peter H., ch.5 n.4, 96, 97
Root, Martha, ch.5 n.33
Rouse, James, xiii
Rúḥíyyih Rabbani (*née* Mary Maxwell), 9, 43, 45, 70, 138, 142, 143, 144, 150, 151

Sala, Emeric, ch.6 n.16
The Secret of Divine Civilization, 15, 19, 31, 93, 126
Senge, Peter M., 37, 54
    and Spartacus, 37
Sherrill, Velma, 137–38

Shoghi Effendi
  and administrative development, 41, 131–32
  ancestry and background, 9, ch.2 n.1
  books about, 9
  and burdens, 85–86
  concept of vision, uniqueness, 54–55
  concept of vision, use of, 48–55, 56, 74
  death of, 136
  and decentralized governance, 129
  and developing new communities, 131–32, 133–34
  exposure to intellects, 38
  global plans by, three key, 46
  guidance from 'Abdu'l-Baha, 31
  guidance from Bahá' u'lláh, 12, 32, 48
  institutional vision, 39–40
  leadership, 17, 38–39, 42–43, 64–65, 74, 151
    and decentralization, 147
    and planning, 151
    in the Americas, 148
    providing critical commentary, 118
    and motivation, 78–90
  planning, relationship of
    action, 154–55, 157
    assessment, 108, 117
    calls to action, 81–84, 90, 104, 116, 156, 159
    conditions for, 65
    constructive criticism, 99, 117
    divine guidance, 80–81, 85, 91

Shoghi Effendi
  planning, relationship of *(continued)*
    goals, 154
    heroes and heroines, 80–81, 83, 90, 157, 159
    institutional capacity (building), 41, 152
    leadership, 150
    mission, 153, 170
    North American Baha'i Community, 46
    praise, 85–89, 91, 106–7, 110, 116–18, 157, 159–60
    responsibilities, clarifying, 76–77
    responsibilities, of Americans, 77–78
    responsibilities, of individuals, 77–79
    responsibilities, of institutions, 77, 79
    responsibilities, of travelers, 77–78, 81, 88, 110
    signs of success, 48–49
  "planning process," 40, 42-43, 61
  information (gathering and processing), 41, 65–74, 151–52
  objectives, 64–74, 171
  participation, 162
  standards, 159
  strategies, 65–74, 134, 159, 171
plans
  in the Americas, 129
  beginning, 103–7, 116
  significance of, 106–7
  end, 112–16

Shoghi Effendi
plans *(continued)*
  middle, 107–12, 116
  monitoring, 99–103, 160–63, 172
  strategies for, 100–3
  mechanism, 106–8
  praise, use of, 118–19
  multiyear phases, division into, 108
  priorities, 107
  structural progress, 108
  tool for maturation, 129–47
  racial prejudice and, 77
  spiritual development, individual, and, 77
  Universal House of Justice and, 64
  vision and, 49–57, 153–56, 171
  "visionary planner," 40, 49–57
  widow (Rúḥíyyih Rabbani), 9, 41, 44, 70, 70, 138, 142, 143, 144, 150, 151
Smith, Melanie, ch.1 n.21
Spartacus, 37
Strategy, defined, 61–62

Tablets of the Divine Plan, 12, 26-31, 32, 42, 44, 45, 67, 86, 104, 159, 169–70
Talen, Emily, ch.7 n.5
Thomas, John W., ch.4 n.7
Toffler, Alvin, 125–26
Travelers
  developing new communities, 134–35
  responsibility of, 78

Universal House of Justice, 10, 47–48, 127, 128, 155
  on plans, 162
  and Shoghi Effendi, 65
Urban planning, xiii, 5, 35, 62, 89, 154, 158, 160, 175
  implementation of plans, 161, 175
  and individual commitment, 158
  and "visioning," 154

Vision, 153–56
  inclusionary requirements, 38–39
  and leadership, 35
  limits to, 155
  motivation and, 35, 57, 80, 154
  role in plans, 34, 38, 42, 55–59, 61, 168, 169, 171
  and urban planning, 1 54

Unity, role in plans, 30

www.ingramcontent.com/pod-product-compliance
Lightning Source LLC
Chambersburg PA
CBHW051941290426
44110CB00015B/2058